AMERICAN FEVER

A Biography of Ole Ruud
Pioneer of the Washington Territory

by

Esther Ruud Stradling

authorHOUSE

1663 LIBERTY DRIVE, SUITE 200
BLOOMINGTON, INDIANA 47403
(800) 839-8640
www.authorhouse.com

First published by AuthorHouse 01/21/05

ISBN: 1-4184-3005-6 (sc)

Library of Congress Control Number: 2004093780

Printed in the United States of America
Bloomington, Indiana

This book is printed on acid-free paper.

Cover Photograph by Lois Ruud Stinson
Cover design by AuthorHouse.

To the present and future descendents of Ole and Augusta Ruud, I dedicate this work.

Og Bestefar, familien din vil alltid elske deg.

Ole Olsen Ruud 1879
Photo taken in Hamilton County, Iowa

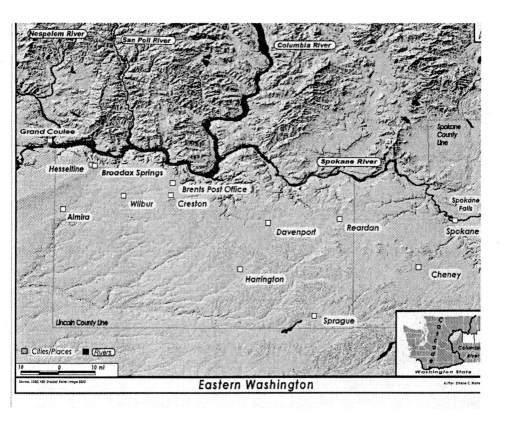

Eastern Washington as it appeared
when Ole Ruud began his journey
towards the Waterville Plateau in 1883

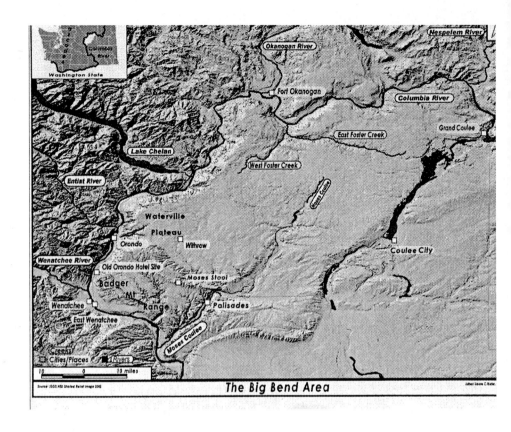

**The Big Bend area of Washington state
1885–1890**

Preface

This biography has been compiled and written not only in honor of Ole Ruud, a pioneer of the Washington Territory, but in honor of and with respect for all the adventurous pioneer men, women and children who tenaciously followed their ambitions to begin a new life in an unpopulated land.

Records of the 1900 census show that homesteaders steadily poured into the Big Bend. Locating themselves in the near-central point of the state of Washington, these stalwart pioneers plowed the semi-arid land and planted small crops of wheat and potatoes. Many added a few cattle, a horse or two, but all had the same goal—to begin a new life with aspirations for a secure future. Longstanding names continue to appear in the local post office listings in Waterville, as many offspring of these pioneers continue to cultivate the land originally settled by their forefathers. Each family has established its own unique legacies to be told by future generations.

Ole Ruud frequently wrote to his mother in Norway. Many of these letters were saved by her and returned to him by his brother following her death in 1913. Within the context of the early letters, he gives his observations of the Big Bend as he first viewed the dry land of present-day Douglas County. As he established himself on his chosen 160-acre homestead, adjacent to Badger Mountain, he continued to write letters describing the hardships and the economic status of the farmer. Elected the first surveyor of Douglas County, he wrote details of his job, and openly gave his views of local and national politics. He married at 45 years of age, and his family grew to five sons and three daughters. All of his offspring would inherit his common sense values.

In this manuscript I have *italicized* the words written by Ole Ruud to enhance and clarify his status within the text. Occasionally, I felt a need to further explain a statement in his letters, or intersperse aspects of history surrounding his world. I did my best to supply condensed information, and I fully realize that many of the historical happenings have been books in themselves. For example, I am more than aware that one cannot possibly explain the geological formation of the Pacific Northwest in one paragraph!

Incentives to write this book came upon me from several directions. My children, Rhonda, Dianne, Mark, Tom, and Randall Stradling, have sporadically heard bits and pieces about the life lived by Ole Ruud, and they have prompted me for many years to write his story. Ole's journey from Oslo, Norway to his grave in Waterville seemed deserving since it is so representative of thousands of pioneers who, like him, found their way into the West fueled by dreams, adrenaline and fortitude. Often working their muscles to the point of exhaustion, keeping purpose in perspective, and with little or no money, they began a new life.

The pioneer era has vanished forever. None of us who possess these courageous forefathers should allow their history to fade into oblivion. Those steadfast men and women toiled, struggled, occasionally collapsed, and often wept, but got back up, dusted themselves off, and began again. We are obligated to keep their memory alive.

A special thank you is given to Bjarne Breilid of Madison, Wisconsin, for his expertise and devoted interest in translating numerous letters written by Ole in his native Norwegian. Without Bjarne, this project might not have ever moved from an inspiring idea to a reality. Also, thanks to Gergana May of the Scandinavian Studies Department, University of Washington, for her assistance in translating several letters and documents. Additional thanks go to Simone Wolter and Stacey Warren of the Eastern Washington University Geography Department for working diligently to supply the maps for clarification of places and events, to Joanie Eppinga, whose proficient proofreading and editing gave me confidence in the correctness of my writing, and to Charles Mutschler, EWU Archivist, for his encouraging support.

I have very much appreciated my six siblings' sharing their knowledge and memories of our grandfather's life. Additional gratitude goes to my cousins for sharing many of the treasured letters, which added greatly to the story.

On the many long walks and talks with my father, Oliver Ruud, we discussed his parent's story over and over, and much of the information written here has come from these memorable conversations. Dad was a bit uncomfortable giving interviews, but if he had a shovel or hammer in his hand, along with a job to do, his memory and sentimentality seemed to flourish.

The journal written by Ole Ruud, his personal letters, stories told by Grandmother Augusta Ruud, Aunt Agnes Berg, and Oliver Ruud, as well as printed interviews and collected information, have been compiled so that all people who have a deep sense of pioneer history may share in Ole's story.

Introduction

In an illustrated book entitled *History of the Big Bend Country, Lincoln, Douglas, Adams, and Franklin Counties, State of Washington,* published by Western Historical Publishing Company, 1904, the following narrative appeared.

Ole Ruud is one of the most substantial men of Douglas County, and perhaps no other settler is as well known in his section of the country as he. Doubtless, too, no other man in Washington is as well acquainted with Douglas County as Mr. Ruud. Since 1884 he has been surveyor of the county and although he is a Republican in politics, and his name appears on that ticket, still he is the recipient of the confidence of all parties and has given a general and thorough satisfaction during his long term of service.

In May of 1883, in company with John Banneck, he came to Douglas County. On the 12th of that month he posted a notice on a claim he had selected, it being at the foot of Badger Mountain, and is two and three-fourths miles due south of Waterville. The only flowing water in that section is on Mr. Ruud's farm. He has added three-fourths of a section to this and now has an excellent estate, which is laid out with the best of wisdom and taste, and is a model Washington farm. Mr. Ruud had to endure the hardships incident to pioneer life and knows what it is to labor hard with scant supplies. In 1884, under the territorial government he was selected Surveyor and since then has been in that office. He had studied civil engineering and surveying in the old country. In addition to the occupation mentioned, Mr. Ruud also does stock breeding and has a fine herd of graded cattle.

At Waterville, on November 24, 1892, Mr. Ruud married Miss Christina Augusta Larson and to this union six children have been born. Mr. Ruud is a member of the Old Settlers Association of Douglas County. He and his wife, Augusta, belong to the Lutheran church. They are highly respected people and have labored faithfully for the advancement of the interests of Douglas County since coming here.

Table of Contents

Chapter I

Whether they delve in the buried coal,
or plough the upland soil,
Or man the seas, or measure the suns,
hail to the men who toil!
It was stress and strain, in wood and cave,
while the primal ages ran,
That broadened the brow, and built the brain,
and made a brute man;
And better the lot of the sunless mine,
the fisher's perilous sea,
Than the slothful ease of him who sleeps
in the shade of his bread-fruit tree;
For sloth is death and stress is life
in all God's realms that are,
And the joy of the limitless heavens is the
whirl of star with star!*

*1st verse from *The Glory of Toil*
            by Edna Dean Proctor

Aspirations and Goals

My daughters have requested from me the story of my background and also that of my wife, wrote Ole Ruud in his flowing penmanship in 1927. *This is indeed as it should be, and ought to be recorded in the family Bible of everyone exiting this house.*

We do not descend from a great or powerful family, only ordinary, average, hardworking, straightforward, genuine Norwegian farm families from the middle class. All of our relatives—in a straight line as well as in all its branches—have owned land and were born and grew up on farms in Norway, taking the names of the farms as their surnames.

Ole wrote that he was born to Ole Olsen of Rudsødegaarden and Johanne Frederiksdatter of Vik on December 24, 1847 on a farm called Nedre (Lower) Rudsødegaard, purchased by his great-grandfather, Ole Anderson Rørvigen, in 1751. His birth marked the third generation to be born on the small farm located near Hønefoss in the province of Ringerike, about twenty-eight English miles west of the city of Kristiania (Olso), capital of Norway.

The farm Vik was called such because it was located next to a 'vik' (bay) in the Tyrifjord (lake). At one time it was a fairly big farm, but it was divided into three parts. For a number of years it has also been the transportation center because the main road between Kristiania (Oslo), Hønefoss and Opplandet runs through the farm. The stage itself was located on Lower Vik but was later moved to upper Vik where my mother, Johanne, was born. It was only a ¾ hour walk between Vik and Nedre Rudsødegaarden, and Mother would often take us to visit, sometimes staying several days at a time.

Many of the farm names in Norway were attached to places after the outbreak of the Plague (Black Death) which, in the 1300s, had wiped out as much as two-thirds of Norway's population, reducing its inhabitants to 125,000. Because there were few people left to do the work, many fields and villages were abandoned, causing them to grow back into wilderness areas. Some of these lands then acquired other names, such as Ødegaard, meaning "deserted farm" or "wasteland." The gaard (farm) was the basic unit of the old Norwegian society. Until around 1890 the gaard names were not only family names—they were more often used as addresses. For survival, following the devastation of the plague, the weakened country joined with Denmark in 1380 and remained integrated under the same king until 1814.

When King Fredrik VI drew Denmark-Norway into the Napoleonic wars in 1807, many Norwegians disagreed with his alliance with France against Great Britain, since Britain had been a major trading partner. As a result of the alliance,

Britain ended the trade and also blockaded Norway's trade with other countries. Numerous Norwegians starved during this time of isolation. However, also cut off from Denmark, they began managing their own affairs.

Denmark was defeated in 1813. The dual monarchy was dissolved in 1814, not because of the dissatisfaction of the Norwegians, but as a result of the Treaty of Kiel when Crown Prince Carl Johan of Sweden was awarded Norway in return for his and Sweden's support of Britain in the final reckoning with Napoleon.

Although Norway, through its National Assembly, established a constitution in Oslo declaring independence on May 17, 1814, the country remained under the rule of King Carl Johan XIV of Sweden as King of Norway. It would not regain its total independence, acquiring its own king, until 1905, taking more than 500 years to recover from the scourge of the "Svartedauden" (The Black Death).

Before Rudsødegaarden was divided, it was, for several hundred years, used as a "seter" (mountain dairy farm) and summer pasture for horses, cattle sheep and goats. When it was divided, we got the southern and lower half, located next to the fjord (Tyrifjord), which wraps itself like a horse shoe around about half the farm. This place was later called the Lower Rudsødegaard.

The province of Ringerike is indeed a place of scenic beauty. From the eastern shores of the Tyrifjord, a traveler can find one of the most superb views in Norway from Kongens Utsikt (The King's View). Lying between the two lakes, Tyrifjord and Randsfjord, it displays a nature's wonderland of colors. The dark green of the pines in the background, the light green of the fields and meadows, white birch and farmsteads, all blend their colors in the blue mirror of the fjord.

In the kitchen in South Rudsødegaarden, under a woodstove, until 1960, there was a plaque made of sandstone from Ringerike with the inscription: "Completed by Ole Olsen Rudsødegaard 1846." The plaque lies today by the stairs in the farm kitchen. During Ole Ruud's childhood, the home also housed Maren Børgersdatter, a milkmaid, and Jørgen Jensen, age 13, a boy in temporary foster care who helped care for the animals. As was customary, the 2 horses, 6 cows, and 7 sheep were also included in the census records. Besides raising rye, barley, peas, and mixed grains, the family also raised 10 tons of potatoes, which they sold at the local market.

Grandmother, Kristiana Kristiansdatter, my father's mother, said that the Lower Rudsødegaard had been our family's property since time immemorial. She also said that the name of all the owners had been Ole. In other words, Ole Olsen. Therefore, this also had to be my name as the oldest son with the right of primogeniture to the farm as in England and other countries, except America.

The reason the name Ole is so popular in Norway, I believe, goes back to King Olaf Haraldsen the Hole, also called Saint Olaf, who introduced Christianity in Norway around the year 1030. He was killed in the battle at Stiklestad near Trondheim at that time. He built two churches in Ringerike: Bonsnaes and Sten's churches. The last one was in ruins, but is going to be restored. Saint Olaf left behind a famous history. No wonder that there are homes with as many as three men with the name Ola, namely father and two sons, going by the name of Big Ola, Little Ola, and Middle Ola!

Peder is also a common name, which must have originated with Saint Peder, who, according to the Catholics, had the key to Heaven, but he gave it to the Pope in Rome, who now has it.

Grandmother Kristiana said there had always been affluence on the farm. My grandfather's father, or my great-grandfather owned, in addition to this farm, the farm Rørvigen on the other side of the fjord to the east which they used as a seter, and they, therefore, had to row across the fjord morning and evening to milk the cows and the goats. This was a lot of work. He gave his son, my grandfather, Rudsødegaarden, and gave his daughter, Marie, Rusvigen, also called Rørvigen. Marie's oldest daughter, who had the same name as her mother, was about my age so we were, you know, somewhat related. Grandmother often used to tease me, saying I ought to go over to the young Marie Rørvigen and propose to her so that the farms could be joined again!

The names of Ole Ruud's grandfathers followed the traditional pattern. When Ole Andersen Rørvigen purchased Rudsødegaarden in 1751, he changed his last name to that of his farm. His son, born in 1755, named Ole Olsen Rudsødegaard, continued the tradition naming his own son, borne by his third wife Kristiana, in 1821, Ole Olsen Rudsødegaard. Even though Ole Ruud, born in 1847, was named Ole Olsen (son of Ole), of Rudsødegaarden, he permanently converted his name while attending college in 1867. When the family moved to Svarstad in Ringerike in 1879, each sibling continued signing the name Ruud.

Ole was baptized Ole Olsen of Rudsødegaarden on the 20th of February, 1848, and was confirmed in the Lutheran doctrine at Hole Kirke by Pastor Hans Lund on the 4th of October, 1863. His record states that he was vaccinated for smallpox (cowpox was the term used at that time), on July 19th, 1848.

Since their farm overlooked Tyrifjorden, a large lake in one of the most beautiful valleys in the area, the children of Ole and Johanne spent any leisure time fishing in the fjord, and all of them attended the common school. *The partaking of all of the sports that a large fresh water lake and the romantic mountain forests of Norway could afford has been of inestimable value to me,* he would later write in a journal. Helping with the normal duties on a Norwegian farm would create in young Ole a strong work ethic, which he would retain his entire life. *Life on the farm has one thing in common everywhere,* he wrote, *and that is plenty of hard work.*

In the fall, when I was just seven years old, my father took what was supposed to be an ordinary trip to town with our wagon and two horses in order to trade and make some purchases for the winter. He, along with several others, entered *and got a place to sleep in Merchant Hoxmark's Lodging House in Grensegaten, Kristiania, where he did his trading. They were tired and settled down to sleep. During the night the damper in the stovepipe, because of negligence, had closed. The stove was coal fired. In the morning six of them were dead from carbon monoxide, among them Father and Lars Aasen, our husmann (*a type of renter or tenant farmer who pays for the use of a smaller part of a farmer's land by working a certain number of days on the main farm). *Only one member of the group was revived. A man was hired to drive our horses and the wagon and our dead father home. He was brought to his half-brother's house in the neighborhood, Peder Olsen, and from there he was taken to his grave in the Hole cemetery.*

Ole's mother, Johanne Frederiksdatter, was no stranger to grief. Earlier, in January of that same year, she and her husband had buried a stillborn baby, Johan. The dark occurrence of Ole Olsen's death would place upon the young mother the sole responsibility of raising her four young sons—seven-year-old Ole, five-and-a-half-year-old Andreas, four-year-old Martin, and two-year-old Kristian. Pregnant with her sixth child, the thirty-three-year-old widow would give birth to a daughter, Olava, on January 6th of 1855.

During his youth Ole helped support his mother and siblings by hauling slate with a horse and sled in the winter and assisting with the farm chores as much as a young boy could physically manage, as well as attending to his studies, which were of the highest importance. Maintaining high marks, he would proudly wear his lue, a tasseled wool graduation cap with its round red-and-black checkered top woven onto a green-and-brown checkered band as he held his certificate reflecting his sincerity in his educational training.

Aarnaes Regular School
Age 13

5

Ole Olsen Rudsødegaard has, without fail, attended Aarnaes Regular School from his eighth year until he was confirmed in the fall of 1863. By nature he has been endowed with a good faculty for learning, and he has through unusual diligence and continual desire to improve himself acquired a very solid foundation of knowledge as he leaves school; if we, in addition, consider his quiet and modest behavior in connection with his yearning for, and appreciation of, the acquisition of knowledge, which at all times is in evidence, I feel justified in entertaining the solid expectations that he will meet with approval and satisfaction wherever he may be stationed in life. May God help him and be with him.

Aarnaes Regular School, April 18, 1865
Signed: Knut Knutsen, graduate student and teacher

After confirmation in the Lutheran Church at age sixteen, Ole appeared before the draft board to be registered for military service in accordance with the law of Norway. This law had been in effect since 1803. After serving a term with the Norwegian army, Ole attended, according to his own chronicle, *"the best agricultural college in the country,"* the Landbruks school in Aas, which had the rank of University. There he studied chemistry, botany, geography, geology, zoology, mineralogy and mathematics. Students also became learned in literature, and history, with discussions of application to the ideals of national values and the public spirit of Norway. The school encouraged the desire to read, study, and learn a wide range of subjects in order to develop the power to think, and to decide freely and independently. Social conscience was stressed as well, holding strict rules against all kinds of cruelty to animals—against all kinds of suffering—be it man or beast. After three and one-half years of study, Ole graduated in 1870.

F. A. Dahl, the director of the school, submitted a handwritten recommendation in 1867:

> Ole Olsen Ruud from Ringerike in the County of Buskerud has for about 1½ years been in residence here in the capacity of agricultural apprentice.
> During this period he has at all times with diligence and attentiveness taken part in any and all activities relating to agriculture, in which he has acquired a praiseworthy skill, and he has, in addition, in every respect displayed an honorable conduct for which we are awarding him free tuition here at our school for the course that starts on the first day of next October, of which the present note serves as evidence.
> Aas Higher Agricultural School in September, 1867
> Signed: F. A. Dahl

6

At the request of O. Ruud from Rudsødegaard in Ringerike, I hereby certify that he spent 1½ years as an apprentice and after that 2 years as a free-tuition student at this school, and that he during that entire time demonstrated a good and stable demeanor, and that nothing negative whatsoever can be said regarding his moral conduct. The certificate of the grades he received from this school will provide more information about the knowledge he has acquired.

Aas, January 27, 1870

Signed: F. A. Dahl

Agricultural College Graduate
Age 25

Rudsødegaarden was a small farm, of a size common in Norway. Due to the mountainous terrain and the lack of tillable farmland, properties generally ranged about 10 acres or less. The family loved the picturesque area often described by Ole *where the air was so fresh, the forests were romantic and the fresh water lakes were abundant with fish.* Even though Martin had gone off to work by the time Ole finished his college training, brothers Kristian and Andreas, and sister Olava were still at home. It was a struggle to make a sufficient living on the farm within the short growing season. Knowing that his future in Norway would never bring him a profitable life, Ole felt unsatisfied.

Adding to his frustrations during the 1870s, a political struggle between the old ruling class and the liberals was occurring within the Storting, (Norwegian Parliament)—the farmers and liberal urban citizenry versus the high office holders and the capitalists. After bitter arguments, two political parties would eventually be established in the 1880s—the Conservatives and the Liberals.

Ole worked for a period of time as a director and accountant in the dairy business and in the mercantile lumber business, but his restlessness did not leave him. In 1875, at the age of 28, he mortgaged the farm, Rudsødegaard, and purchased another farm, Svarstad, 3½ miles west, trying to appease himself, but he remained discontented. *The narrow surroundings and my roaming disposition brought upon me the "American Fever",* he would later write. Many people were emigrating at this time from their various native lands to America because of the vast financial opportunities and adventurous land-owning possibilities. He proceeded to study about America for the next four years and at the age of 32, in 1879, signed ownership of Svarstad over to his mother and booked passage, resolving to set his course. The Sales Contract was documented on April 15, 1879.

> The undersigned Ole O. Ruud, who intends to take a trip to America, acknowledges on this occasion to have sold and transferred to his mother, Johanne Frederiksdatter, his farm Svarstad, in Hole, tax roll no. 31, serial no. 99, which he acquired according to deed dated April 25, 1874, recorded March 20, 1875 with a tax assessment of 6 daler, revised to 6 daler 1 ort and 1 skilling, for an agreed-upon purchase price of 3,200 Spd.—three thousand two hundred Spesidaler*—to be settled thusly:
>
> 1. That she will assume the existing 3000 Spd. Mortgage resting on the property.
>
> 2. Prior to my departure she will remit the remainder of 200 Spd. to me— otherwise, I transfer the farm to my mother with the same privileges, additions, and obligations as listed in the above mentioned

deed under which I have owned and possessed the property. All personal property is included.

In case, after a longer or shorter period of time, I should return, I reserve the right, upon my return, to demand that the farm be returned to me at the same purchase price of 3,200 Spd., except for committing myself to paying for possible improvements made in the meantime. This right of mine shall be revoked in case my mother, before my return, should have transferred the present agreement to someone else.

Svarstad, April 15, 1879

As witnesses:	As seller:	As buyer:
Ole Svendbye	O. Ruud	Johanne Frederiksdatter
Christen Svendbye		

Johanne Frederiksdatter sold the South Rudsødegaard farm in January, 1879 for 16,000 Kroner to Kristian Johannessen Ruud (no relation), who was at that time living on the middle section of Rudsødegaard. She, along with Andreas, Kristian, and Olava, moved to Svarstad, where her twenty-seven-year-old son, Kristian, took over the duties of the farm. Years later, she would sell the ownership to Kristian; however, she would remain living there until her death in January of 1913.

*In general, around 1880,
One Riksdaler or Spesidaler was assumed to be worth about one dollar
One Spesidaler = 5 ort
One Ort—(approx. 20 cents)= 24 skillings
Four Kroner were equal to one Spesidaler

Sale of Rudsødegaarden –16,000 Kroner = approx. $4,000
Sale of Svarstad –3,200 Spesidaler= approx. $3,200

Rudsødegård etter maleri av Martha Ruud. Merk bestevardringer

Rudsødegaarden in the 1880s
Drawn by Martha Ruud, daughter of
Kristian Ruud (no relation)

Rudsødegaard as seen from Kongens Utsikt
in Ringerike. Farm is just left of center.

*   *   *

A common route for Norwegian emigration to America, in 1879, was out of Liverpool, England. The steamship line carrying the majority of emigrants was the British Wilson Line, although the Allan Line had a great deal of promotion going on in Norway through subagents. The average fare to New York for most lines was 105 Kroner (approx. $25). After crossing the choppy and often hazardous North Sea from Norway to England, the emigrant would then travel by railway to reach the port of Liverpool prior to boarding the ship bound for America.

England had, however, competition with Denmark and Germany, especially during the years of the mass exodus from 1879-1893 when an annual average of over 35,000 emigrants were leaving the Scandinavian countries for America. Subagents, especially those from Denmark promoting their lines, would promise the Norwegians a safe voyage along with familiar food, familiar language, and a guarantee of safe delivery of luggage. Traveling with those of one's own kind, they emphasized, would bring about a pleasant voyage with fewer conflicts with other passengers from diverse cultural backgrounds.

Crossing the Atlantic to New York in a medium-sized steam powered vessel took approximately 10-12 days. Whether the passengers rode in the cabin class section (some ships had fewer than 10 cabins), or with the hundreds in steerage, few had seaworthy stomachs. Some would spend the entire time in bed praying for survival, retching and heaving, simply too weak to lift their heads. But those who somehow tolerated the wavy seas could manage to find a card game, do some dancing, even engage in a few fist-fights as tensions between crowded passengers with varied languages could be high.

The Statue of Liberty was not presented to the United States by France until 1884, so Ole did not view this grand figure with her welcoming arms as do those who enter New York Harbor today. The detention and deportation center at Ellis Island did not begin until 1891. His entry point into New York in 1879 is assumed to have been through Castle Garden. Over 8 million people had entered the United States through Castle Garden from the time it opened as an immigrant landing depot in August of 1855, until it closed in April of 1890. As the lines of ships steadily arrived at the southwest tip of Manhattan, the thousands of immigrants of varied cultures and languages were shuffled into the different sections of Castle Garden and all were required to remain in the large circular building until they had been registered and their papers checked and cleared. As dreams and ambitions were high and financial securities generally low, every person needed to be on constant guard, for theft and greed at this point were commonplace.

What was the name of the ship that carried Ole Ruud to America? It was unfortunate that he never wrote it down, as the wooden structure of the original

Castle Garden was demolished in a raging fire in 1897, which destroyed all administrative records from 1855-1890.

Arriving in Hamilton County, Iowa in the late spring of 1879, and realizing that his English was inadequate, Ole spent the next three years in that state and in the state of Minnesota getting acquainted with the customs and language of his new country. Certain that his decision to live in America had been a correct one, he was adamant to proceed with his dreams for a new and more prosperous life. On February 10, 1880, he appeared before the District Court in Hamilton County to sign in the presence of A.A. Nicks, County Clerk, a document of intent to become a citizen of the United States renouncing all allegiance and fidelity to Oscar II of Sweden, who was King of Norway .

Finally, feeling more competent in terms of his communication skills, he sold the small coal mine he had purchased in the area of Council Bluffs, Iowa, where he had been selling coal for seventy-five cents a ton, and took the Union Pacific Railroad west, arriving in San Francisco, California in January of 1882.

What a change from the cold winter of Iowa to the rainy air and drizzling showers and green hills of California! Ole would write in his journal. *And fully as much of a change appeared to my eyes the looks of the people. From the pale and thin faces in some of the large Eastern cities to the full forms and rosy cheeks in California reminded me strongly that I once more was breathing the air of my native country.*

A second cousin, Johanne Walberg, lived in San Francisco. Ole had had some correspondence with her prior to leaving Norway and it was his plan to marry this lady and continue on his way with her to the Washington Territory, where they would settle. But she preferred life in the city and refused to leave her established home where she felt safe and secure. Ole wanted adventure and some affordable farming land, so after only one week's stay in Frisco, he took a steamer to Portland, Oregon. Spending only three days in Portland, he proceeded down the Columbia River to Astoria, Oregon and to Westport in the Washington Territory in search of employment.

After working as a fisherman and for a short time with an ox team in a logging camp operation, he was hired on as a chainman with a party of government surveyors to run township lines in the Nehalem Mountains south of Astoria. This was in early spring, when there was still snow in many places of higher altitudes. An added burden was the fact that all the workers had to carry all of their personal belongings in a pack on their backs. For Ole, this included his surveying instruments brought from Norway.

The chainman's job was to measure the ground that the team was surveying. This was accomplished by using a surveyor's chain, called Gunter's chain, each 66 feet long, made from links of solid steel. Each surveyor's chain consisted of one hundred links, with each link measuring 7.92 inches.[1]

It took twenty chains to equal one-fourth of a mile. The lead man would carry a fixed number of pins made of steel, each of which had a red strip of cloth tied through a ring for the purpose of easier sighting. If he used twenty cloth-marked pins and repeated the measuring process four times, he would have completed a measurement of one mile. (1 mile=5,280 feet. 66 feet x 20 chains x 4=5,280 feet.) It was less complicated for the team to think of measurements in terms of links and chains rather than feet or miles, and it was the responsibility of the lead man to keep the record as the team worked together to measure a segment of land.

One chainman would stick the pin attached to one end of the chain into the ground and call "stick!" When the chain had been extended to the point of desired measurement, a second chainman would stick his end into the ground and call "stuck!" This process was repeated until the assigned job was completed.

The difficult labor of cutting through the heavily forested mountains, clearing the way through the cold, slippery and steep terrain was a perilous job and a very discouraging one to Ole. He knew that this was not the life he'd come to America for and he began to feel defeated. He left that job after three months and returned to Portland very downhearted and not knowing what to do. He was thinking of leaving the country and returning to Norway, but decided to make a trip to Vancouver, in the Washington Territory, before he began his departure. Little did he know that his life would soon take a series of positive turns.

It was in Vancouver that I got in company with a man whom I told my wants and disappointments. He was a venerable man and told me he had once been worse off than I. Fifteen years ago, he said, he came to Oregon the first time, but went sick and disappointed back to his old home in the East. It was not before he came to Oregon the third time and was reduced to such poverty that he was forced to stay that success finally came his way—he was now in the milling business and considered himself worth about fifteen thousand dollars. "What I have done, you can do," he told me, "now take my advice. Go up to Medical Lake in Spokane County and you will find large vacant country that needs thousands of young men like you. From there and out west, you will find what you are looking for—where the bunchgrass grows tall and you can depend on the soil for growing good crops. And the best land is in the highest hills."

Feeling much more encouraged, Ole took passage to Walla Walla in the Washington territory, an area known not only for its rich lands, but for the Whitman massacre which had taken place 35 years earlier in November, 1847, just one month prior to his birth in Norway. With the intent of stopping at different points in eastern Washington to observe potential farmland and homesteading possibilities, he decided that if he was not satisfied he would take the Northern Pacific Railroad east to the Red River Valley, bordering North Dakota and Minnesota, where he knew Norwegian settlements existed.

Arriving in Walla Walla on the third of July 1882, he at once noticed the difference in the climate. *From the heavy moisture laden and depressing air of the lower Columbia to the dry and lighter breeze of the higher altitudes of eastern Washington was a great change and I felt like a new man. The heavy load on my body and mind was gone and from that time to this, I have forever praised the delightful climate of eastern Washington.*

The almost first thing I did was to examine the soil and the products of the country. Here were new wonders to me. How this seemingly, worthless light ashes could bring forth such a wide variety of oats, peas, beans, etc., was absolutely past my understanding. I thought I was a scholar in agriculture, having learned it by study, observation, and practice half around the earth, but here was something demanding new study.

A man from Yakima described to me the resources of that valley and explained how everything had to be irrigated, but that farming and fruit raising was yet in such a primitive state that little could be said about it. Ole was also told that the light ashy soil was partly volcanic ash mixed with soluble alkaline salts and that no kind of soil was better.

The whole Big Bend was then included in Spokane County and was a territory that no one seemed to know anything about. One man told me that all he had seen of Spokane County was a rock bed and that there was absolutely nothing there to go after. Another man told me that Medical Lake was only an Alkali pond and that there was frost every month of the year. Upon all my inquiry, no better information could be had. If I had went to Dr. Blelock or some other prominent citizen, which I was often thinking of doing, I would certainly have got better informed.

At thirty-five years of age, Ole found that he was the oldest man on his first job bucking sacked grain from one train to another where the roads of different gauges came together. While working his next job in Becker's lumberyard, he had many opportunities to meet people from the surrounding country and adjacent valleys. By October he would find himself in still another new place and would soon send a letter off to Norway.

Brents Post Office
Spokane County, Washington Territory
November 20, 1882

Mother and siblings!
It is now a really long time since I wrote and heard anything from home. In spite of the fact that I have been very busy, it ought not to be a valid excuse for not writing a few lines now and then; but you can't imagine what it is like when you get far out in the world and its turmoil. Our attention and thoughts get caught

14

up by something new constantly, causing us to forget the old, and if this was not the case, it would many a time get to be very depressing to roam around in this big wide world. At all times—almost, there is something new to hear and to see. New acquaintances are established and old ones are forgotten.

I'll have to relate briefly what has happened to me since I last wrote. I worked in Walla Walla in Becker's Lumberyard for three months at $2 a day without skipping a day. In Portland, I had gotten to know a Swedish boy by the name of Nelson who had come to the coast for the same purpose as I, namely to find land and become a farmer. He left Portland two months before me and traveled through the eastern part of Washington Territory and up to Idaho where he inspected several places and visited Norwegian and Swedish settlements. After this, he came back to Walla Walla where I unexpectedly ran into him just after he had returned. Through him, I got to know a Dane by the name of Hansen who had a wagon with 6 horses. He (Hansen) had recently arrived from Arizona and had decided to settle in that part of the Washington Territory called the Big Bend of the Columbia River.

The long 1,214-mile noble, arching Columbia River rises on the western slopes of the Rocky Mountains in British Columbia. After flowing northwestward for 180 miles, constantly being fed waters from the thaws of snow, ice fields and other rivers, mainly the Kootenay and Pend Oreille, it makes a sharp curve south into Washington State. In Washington, the water flow sweeps westward and southward, bending in an irregular curve resembling a jagged C. It is to the land within these bends and turns that the term Big Bend applies. Just below the point where the resource-filled Columbia is joined by the Snake River, the mighty river turns westward to form the boundary between the states of Oregon and Washington on its way to the Pacific Ocean.

As the ancient glacial floods moved over the Pacific Northwest once covered by massive lava flows, the topography was carved and sculpted. As the retreating glaciers subsided, fine particles of wind-blown loess were deposited thousands of years ago, evolving a land filled with organic soils—the more heavily deposited regions becoming part of the highest producing grain growing areas in the West, namely the Palouse.

Traveling toward the Big Bend of the Columbia River where the soil deposits have less density, one can observe broad basins, plateaus, rolling hills, scablands, high basalt cliffs hanging over deeply carved valleys, and occasional basalt boulders, known as haystack rocks, sitting prominently like sentinels amid the otherwise desolate fields.

Ole's letter to his mother continues: *The three of us decided to go on together. Nelson and I would ride along free on the condition that each of us would pay one third of the fodder for the horses. We outfitted ourselves and bought food supplies enough for three weeks.*

On the 2nd of October we left Walla Walla with all our things. Our first destination was Sprague, about 100 miles north of Walla Walla, which is a three-year-old city by the Northern Pacific Railroad. We arrived there after a trip of 5 days. On the trip we had to look for places where there was water for the horses, and those are not in abundance in eastern Oregon and the Washington Territory. Everywhere we had good, self-made roads. At night we allowed the horses to graze on dry bunchgrass after they had been given their portion of oats. For ourselves, we put up a tent and cooked our food outside.

Between Walla Walla and Sprague, we traveled through landscapes that varied much in appearance—through a strongly rolling prairie with excellent soil, but so full of mounds and hills that most of it was too steep to plow, no forest, but dry grass everywhere, no brooks or springs and generally difficult to find water, even if you dug deep down. If there was a flat valley, the land had been taken by people who had big herds of cattle and sheep. Other times we traveled through wild, rocky stretches with cliffs and boulders with only an insignificant amount of land that was arable and constantly hardly suitable for plowed fields, but excellent pasture for sheep and cattle. Other times, again, we came across stretches of flat land where we could see for 20 miles around us, places where one occasionally could see a nice looking farm, but the lack of water is bad and the top soil is shallow, full of rocks and, in general, of rather poor quality. At the place where we crossed the Snake River on a ferry, the landscape was especially wild, jagged, treeless, dry, windy, and mountainous.

We camped on the shore for the night. In the evening, an Indian came to see us for the purpose of trading horses (in Indian language "svap kajus"), but his real objective was to beg for food which he told us he needed for his "skva" and "papus" (wife and child).

As I said, after traveling for 5 days, we arrived in Sprague, still without having seen any land that we would want to acquire for the purpose of farming. We stopped in Sprague (pronounced Spraeg) for a couple of days and looked around in town. It has about 500 inhabitants, and we stocked up on a little more grub.

We figured that we were now near the boundary of the Big Bend, but after having been informed about the various parts of the land around, about most of the new settlements as well as the roads leading to various destinations, we realized that we were still about 50 miles from the place people generally call the Big Bend. Besides, we heard talk of areas as being very attractive to immigrants, such as Crab Creek and Cottonwood country, etc. The actual Big Bend country lies next to the Columbia River northwest of Sprague. According to the maps and the description, all the places I named are located in the "boining" of the Columbia River because the latter is of considerable size.

We then left Sprague, went through Crab Creek, and to Cottonwood; we saw lots of good farm land, but also much that was poor—even worthless, except *for pasture. Almost everywhere we came across settlers, all of whom have arrived during the last two or three years. The best land is taken first, of course, and where it is possible to find water and woods. After a couple of days' stay in Cottonwood (present-day Davenport), we traveled west about 30 miles, and we were now in the actual Big Bend country. Traveling these 30 miles, we saw nothing but land worthless for farming, only an occasional spot we could call plow land. For about 15 miles we went through a thin pine forest where we might see one big pine tree on a half acre of land*

There are probably between 50 and 100 settlers in the Big Bend, and the first settler we came to was Mr. Cooper. He arrived here three years ago this summer and was the first settler in the Big Bend. He has picked out for himself an excellent and beautiful farm right next to the edge of the forest. During the last two years, all the best land around him and closest to the forest has been taken, but I can still find reasonable good land from 1 to 5 miles from the forest.

In regards to finding water, it is the same here as everywhere else we have been—there is no abundance of it. However, by careful inspection and by digging down 10 to 25 feet in the lowest locations, you can usually be assured of finding a good well.

From Cooper's farm to the Columbia River it is 4 to 5 miles. The Columbia River runs through a cliff-like gully between 1000 and 1500 feet deep. On the other side of the river there is nothing but wooded mountains and long valleys. By the way, so far I have not been able to find anyone who can tell me much about the situation there where only Indians are living on their reservations. There is a strip of land along the Columbia River about 15 miles wide and 40 miles long, going west from Cooper's farm, which comes pretty close to being really outstanding farm land.

After having arrived at the Big Bend, we stopped at Cooper's place, and from there we made excursions in every direction, keeping within a six-mile radius, however. We found the land highly satisfactory, and decided to settle down. We thought this was the best we had seen here. Nelson had been to the Red River Valley in Dakota, in Nebraska, and in Kansas, but he liked this better than any other place he had seen. He didn't like Idaho anywhere near as much as this because it was much too hilly. It is not at all flat here either, but generally it is not difficult to find 160 acres which can be plowed in any direction whatsoever. Whatever is steeper, can be plowed horizontally. The land in Iowa is much flatter, but as we shall discover when we look more closely, there are benefits here not to be found in the east. However, there are some drawbacks not to be found in the eastern United States.

Now we had to deal with the next question, namely I and Nelson, had to acquire horses, wagon, fodder for the horses, food for ourselves for the winter, as well as housing and other necessary things. When Hansen started thinking about *his own situation, he discovered that his purse was pretty light, containing only $100, and this would not be enough to buy fodder for his 6 horses. He, therefore, had only two choices: either to sell two of his horses, or go to some other place and find work. I, and Nelson, considered buying a couple of horses and other things jointly and try to make do with that for the first year. We bargained for Hansen's horses; he wanted $200 for them including some old saddles that were almost worthless. The horses were also 8 or 9 years old, so we thought the price was high. I said we could offer him $150 for them, but Nelson did not want to go above $125. I didn't say anything and let Nelson offer $125. Hanson refused to accept that, and became offended and said he would go over to the military station about 15 miles to the northeast of Cooper's farm. I and Nelson put our things in storage at Cooper's and set off on foot back to Sprague in order, as soon as possible, to buy a complete outfit and be on our way again. Hansen left for the above mentioned place, and I have not seen him or heard anything about him since. Nelson and I walked the 50 miles to Sprague in 2 days.*

We did what we could to get the best and cheapest horses. It is, in fact, not difficult to buy horses in the fall of the year. We were pretty busy for about four days, but by that time we finally had our horses, wagon, good supplies, necessary tools, and things all loaded in the wagon, which we covered with a sailcloth tarpaulin. Everyone said we were as well supplied as anyone going out in order to settle. For the horses, with practically brand new harnesses, we had to pay $230, which probably was in keeping with $150 for Hansen's horses. Both horses, one of them 3½ and the other one 4½, are the same color and size as Brona, but perhaps a little taller. One of them is named Jack and the other one Thom. Since I have time now, I am, just for fun, going to write down our entire bill so that you can get an idea about the cost of various things here and what it takes for a settler here in America. However, most things are much more expensive here than out east except in some of the new places.

> *A team of horses and harnesses $400.00*
> *12 lbs. Coffee,$3.00,11 packages tea, $2.00, soap, $1.00, matches 50c*
> *Total=$6.50*
> *Bread knife, 50c, 5 lbs. Rice, $1.00*
> *Total=$1.50*
> *Nails, $2.00, 2 halters, $3.00, 2 pails, $1.25, one whip, $3.50*
> *Total=$9.75*
> *1 saw, $2.50, 4 windows, $6.00, 2 steel wedges, $3.00, 1 fork, $2.50*
> *Total=$14.00*
> *1 shovel, $1.25, 3 frying pans, $3.00, 1 hammer, $1.00*
> *Total=$5.25*
> *Having the horses shoed, $5.00, 1 lantern, $1.75, 1 saw for wood, $4.50*

Total=$11.25
3 axes, $4.25, 5 gallons of kerosene, $2.50, 1 case of apples, $1.25
Total=$8.00
This adds up to be $456.25. However, this is not everything; there is a long bill, which I am too bored to record, amounting to an additional $97.14 for a total of $553.39. This consists mostly of food supplies, cooking utensils, and various tools. Everything we had, along with some additional minor expenses for the trip, comes to $560.

Ole did not record the cost of his Bain wagon (presently on display at the Wenatchee Valley Museum and Cultural Center in Wenatchee, Washington), or his breaking plow (presently on display at the Douglas County Museum in Waterville, Washington). Journal records show that the total cost of all supplies purchased in Sprague including his wagon, a harrow sheet, a breaking plow, half a window for a cabin, plus supplies came to around $800, which was nearly all of his capital.

The Bain narrow-gauge wagon is a lightweight all-purpose wagon with a bed 4 feet wide and 10¾ feet long. With sideboards consisting of two pieces of wood measuring nineteen inches high over four twelve-spoked wheels with a diameter of fifty-one inches, it was capable of carrying moderately heavy loads. The elevated spring-held seat attached to the front of the wagon was placed adjacent to the brake handle, which was within arm's reach on the right side.

The breaking plow with its two wooden handles and slightly curved steel bottom is designed to turn one long gradual furrow at a time. This type of plow was used for turning prairie sod or other heavy soil. It was drawn by a single horse, whose harness was attached to the metal beam below the handles, and was held in position by the plowman, who walked along behind holding on to the handles of the plow as well as the reins of the horse.

Ole continues his November 20th letter to his mother: *In three days, we are back with Mr. Cooper at Brents Post Office two miles northwest of Creston in the Big Bend. I am starting to get acquainted with some of the settlers who have been here for two or three years and they seem to be sturdy people of the best class. We know approximately where we want to settle down, but we would still like to take a few days for a trip to look around in the area.*

This was the 1ˢᵗ of November, and the day after we had left Cooper's place, we ran into a snowstorm so that we had to turn back as quickly as we could. Nelson was completely terrified and saw no way out of it. All my talking to him was fruitless, he just became more and more depressed and wished he was back in New York where he lived before. It appeared that he had never had an inkling of the fact that winter was coming. I, myself, saw no danger since we could stay with Cooper. I believed that I had been worse off other times. Nothing helped. He had to get away.

He had paid for half of what we had bought, but he wanted to sell his entire part for $100. I then paid him $100, and he took his suitcase after having given me a few little things he did not want to bother to take with him on the journey back. He took the first opportunity to get a ride when someone left with a team and wagon, happy as a lark in spring. We had just had two inches of snow, which disappeared in a couple of days, and the weather was just as mild and pleasant as it had been before.

I was now alone and didn't feel like starting out building a house and settling down just when winter was approaching, but I was able to stay with Mr. Cooper, who is a kind, helpful, and respectable American. I was suffering at that time from an infection in my finger. Knowing that the nearest doctor was at Fort Spokane, 18 miles off, I made a small incision with my knife myself and removed a large piece of bone, after which it healed up.

I have built a simple stable for my horses and bought hay and oats for them—enough for the coming winter, I believe, but I have been promised more if I need it. If we don't get much snow, both horses and cattle can find half of what they need outside here. We got a little snow again now, but everyone lets the horses go outside every day, eating bunchgrass, which they claim is still good and nourishing, although it doesn't appear to be. I have noticed, however, that horses who are used to it, seem to like it. So far it hasn't been very cold, and according to what I have been told, winter here is like a very mild Norwegian winter. The climate here is, on the whole, far better than in the east. They tell me that the snow generally is gone around the beginning of March, and around the middle of that month, horses and cattle can, as a rule, take care of themselves. Summer is usually dry with a shower only now and then.

It is really astonishing to see how everything that is planted here grows without fertilizer and practically no rain. I have seen carrots here 1½ feet long and 4 inches across, and almost everything else from the garden in similar proportions. Wheat is as good looking as I have seen it any place else, yielding 20 to 50 bushels an acre—some say as much as 80! There isn't the abundance of land here as in the east, and what we have here is going to be spoken for soon, probably in one or two years for the influx of people is great and only about half of the Big Bend country can be said to be good farm land.

The reason why so many seek to come here is based on the fact that the main line of the Northern Pacific Railroad is expected to go through this area. The tracks have not been completed through Idaho yet, but what has been completed through here goes down to Portland. Another arm of the line has been staked out through the Big Bend and down to Puget Sound, which is the best harbor on the West coast. That is about 140 miles from here. It is claimed by everyone that in the course of about 10 years, the land here will go up in price to between 20 and 40 dollars an acre or similar to what it is in Walla Walla and I see nothing to keep that from happening since both the soil and the climate are at least as good here as there.

I must conclude for now since it is very late and the mail will be going early tomorrow morning. Mr. Cooper is the postmaster so the post office is right here. I have more I want to write about, so I'll try to write again in a few days. I haven't been ill a single hour since I wrote my last letter, and I can say that on the whole I feel as well as, if not better than, I have ever felt since I came to America. It is, of course, quiet and lonely here, but I'll have to accept that—I, similar to others.

A Merry Christmas to you and to others who are interested in hearing from me. Next spring I intend to homestead and take out a claim for tree planting on 320 acres which will cost me $30, but by then my purse will be getting rather thin so I shall probably have to go out and find work after I have taken care of what I have to do here such as building a simple house, plowing 5 to 10 acres, fencing it in and planting.

I hope you write soon. Kind greetings to all of you—as well as to everyone in the neighborhood.

While staying at Brents Post Office with Mr. Cooper, Ole became acquainted with Wild Goose Bill, Virginia Bill, and Clubfoot Bill. He described them as "three sqawmen of the frontier type." ("Sqawman" was a term used by some of the early settlers to describe a white man who was living with an Indian woman.) *I was told,* Ole later wrote in this journal, *that Virginia Bill, from time to time, used to get up a gathering of Indians of both sexes and Whites to a general enjoyable outing potlatch and pow wow called Cheenooke Dance which was considered by the sqawmen and cowboys to be very magnificent.*

Wild Goose Bill acquired his nickname from a story he jokingly told on himself. While on one of his packing trips to deliver goods to the miners, he came upon a flock of geese by a pond, so he started shooting at them. He was quickly approached by an indignant man who shouted that he was shooting down his flock of *domestic* geese! Wild Goose Bill's real name was William Condon; he was described by Ole as "*a sturdy pioneer and a tall, fine looking man.*" He would later be shot to death, at the age of sixty, in a dispute over a twenty-five year old Indian woman. In his dealings with Ole, however, he was very helpful in giving information describing the surrounding country.

While at Brents in the fall of 1882, a party of 5 or 6 surveyors came back from a trip into the Big Bend west of Grand Coulee, Ole wrote. *They reported the country empty of people, but as they expressed it, a country filled with oceans of good farming land.* The curious Ole decided to follow up on this newest information and on March 6th, 1883, started out on a new journey. This would take him with his new team of horses pulling his wagon full of supplies into the unsettled Big Bend. *I traveled west camping at Wild Goose Bill's place and then made a temporary*

21

camp at some springs in what was known as the Broad Ax Canyon. After setting up camp at Broad Ax Springs, which is located in a green valley about 20 miles northwest of Brents Post Office, Ole started exploring the country in all directions. He rode over the level plains to where the town of Hartline is presently established, but not far enough to find the old military road crossing the Grand Coulee where the small town of Coulee City is located. After returning to his camp at the springs, he chose a piece of land at the head of Broad Ax Canyon, well out towards the breaks of the Columbia River, set up a new campsite, and started working the soil in preparation for planting.

While working on the land one day in that later part of March, parties came to my camp to warn me that the Indians were on the warpath and that some settlers had already packed up and moved out and others were preparing to do so, Ole wrote in his journal. *I took no credence in the story as there was no real reason to anticipate Indian trouble. Absolutely safe we could not be, as it was in the time the northern part of the Colville Indian Reservation was to be opened for miners and old Chief Moses had made some threats to clean out the whites if certain demands of his people were not conceded to.*

It was in 1883 that the pioneers of Douglas County passed through the incipient stages of an Indian scare. The population of the entire territory now living in Douglas County would not much exceed one hundred. The Indians did not take kindly to the arrival of the few stockmen who came in 1883, and for a time it looked as though there would be serious trouble. A few became alarmed and, burying what treasure they had, moved to Sprague until the trouble should have blown over. Five hundred soldiers were sent to the threatened district and during the summer of 1883 they were stationed on Foster Creek, near the present site of Bridgeport. These troops held the hostile Indians in check and no outrages were committed. The suppression of the contemplated outbreak was assisted by the report of Chief Moses who returned from his trip to Washington, D.C. about this time. The Indians of this vicinity did not realize the strength of the whites in numbers, and believed that the white race consisted of the people with whom they came in contact, or of whom they had heard from the tribes in the vicinity. Chief Moses on his trip was compelled to realize the overwhelming numbers of the whites, and his report to his followers is said to have been sensational. His people were mobilized on the banks of the Columbia River. Seizing a handful of sand, he exhibited it to the braves and said: "Siwashes." Then waving his arm in the direction of the Cascade Mountains, he continued: "Boston men!" The hint was taken and the threatened outbreak was quelled before the Indians were made to feel the power of the whites, which were as mountains to a handful of sand in comparison with the red men.[2]

Moses was chief of the Sinkiuse, a tribe of Indians who roamed the area and lived on the Columbia Reservation, northwest of the Okanogan River, when the white man moved into the area. He had a reputation of being a very fine, quiet mannered, confident leader who generally tried to negotiate and keep peace with the early pioneers.

Although the tribe lived primarily along the Columbia, its members roamed a 5,000-square-mile area, mostly on the Columbia Plateau south and east of the Columbia River. The northern boundary of their lands (in present-day Washington state) ran along Badger Mountain just east of the Columbia and south of Waterville, and northeast to the Grand Coulee Dam, from which the territory extended southwest a few miles, following the eastern slopes of the Grand Coulee and then south to include Soap Lake, Ephrata, and Moses Lake. From Moses Lake the boundary ran south to approximately the forty-seventh parallel and from that line southwest to the Columbia at Beverly.[3]

On a volcanic outcrop high on the south side of Badger Mountain, up Titchenal Canyon, eight miles southeast from the land Ole Ruud would come to homestead, protrudes a scab rock area known as Moses Stool. From this 3,619 ft. elevation Chief Moses sunned himself atop his perch during the root-gathering season as his women and children dug into the dry soil around him. Warming his aging bones, he observed the sagebrush slopes filled with the purple-blossomed camas, bright yellow sunflowers, and bunchgrass covered plains—the land of his people. On a clear day, Moses could view a panorama over 30 miles, no doubt harboring a special sentimentality as he gazed towards the Wenatchee Plateau— the place of his birth. The diverse topographical formations display themselves in all directions. To the northeast lies the glacial terminal moraine and Okanogan Highlands; to the east, the ridge of Moses Coulee, the birthplace of his father; to the west, the snow-capped Glacier Peak in the majestic Cascade Mountains radiates into the deep blue skies. The Palisades to the southwest display a jagged topography resulting from thousands of years of thawing snow and creek runoff, also known for its dangerous flash floods. Three to four miles southwest from his outlook, Moses' summer camp lay secluded in a wide green meadow. The valley could at times be filled with hundreds of men, women and children from his tribe as they hunted or gathered roots and berries in the hills during the day, sleeping in the grove at night amid the abundant sheltering quaking aspen.

Moses had assumed tribal leadership in 1858 after his older brother Quiltenenock had been killed by white miners below the mouth of the Wenatchee River. Named Loolowkin at birth, he had received his biblical name, Moses, as a boy from Rev. Henry Spalding in a school run by the American Board of Commissioners for Foreign Missions at present-day Lapwai, Idaho. Today a coulee, a lake, and the city of Moses Lake, Washington bear his name.[4]

The Columbia, or Moses Reservation, was established for him and his followers by executive order on April 19, 1879. It had been extended to the south on May 6, 1880, so that it stretched from Lake Chelan north to the Canadian border and from the crest of the Cascade Mountains to the Okanogan River. The fifteen mile strip across the reservation's northern end was withdrawn at the insistence of miners by an executive order of February 23, 1883. Then the diminished reservation was relinquished by an agreement with Moses on July 7, 1883. The land was restored to the public domain on May 1, 1886 and was never occupied by Moses and his band; however, the Chief collected rent from its white cattlemen. He and his people were removed to the Colville Reservation in north central Washington, across the Okanogan River east of the Columbia Reservation.[5]

Disagreements, killings, massacres, and general distrust between the Indians of the Northwest and the Whites had been going on since the 1850s, when miners had started moving into the land with an aggressive and relentless approach. It had been just five years prior to Ole's arrival at Brents in 1882, that a well-known historical event had taken place in the Wallowa Valley of the present Eastern Oregon. In the spring of 1877, the Nez Perce Chief Joseph had been ordered to remove his people from the valley to the Lapwai Reservation. Rather than sign the agreement to turn his land over to the Whites and be confined on the reservation, Joseph began his retreat to move his entire tribe out of the country. His plan was to join Chief Sitting Bull in Canada, thereby protecting his people from the persecutions and oppressions of the White men.

Again, most of the disagreements were over land use and ownership. The miners, searching for gold, had moved in on land promised to Chief Joseph and his people by the government in 1873. This promise created such anger among the Whites that they relentlessly took land any way they could—shooting or hanging Indians at their whim until President Grant revoked his order, which further oppressed the Indians.

A great deal has been written about Chief Joseph, who is historically known as a superior leader. Outmaneuvering the U.S. Calvary several times, he journeyed about 1800 miles through the generally treacherous terrain in 110 days. Although he could have escaped himself, he surrendered within a day's ride into Canada, refusing to leave his women, children, and wounded men. After being kept for a period of years in the Indian Territory in present-day Oklahoma, he was transferred to the Colville Indian Reservation in north central Washington in 1885, where he lived as a neighbor to Chief Moses. He died in 1904 and is buried near his friend, Moses, in the Nespelem cemetery.

At the location of Ole's camp at the head of Broad Ax Canyon, a few days prior to his being warned of the possibility of trouble with the unfriendly band of Indians, a company of soldiers came out from Camp Spokane. One of them asked Ole if he had seen any Indians about. *I told to the soldier that only a few days earlier a lone Indian had come into my camp late at night, on foot and unarmed, and asked to get something to eat and a blanket to sleep in under the wagon. That I had granted his requests and gave him blankets to sleep in one end of the wagon while I slept in the other seemed to satisfy him. The soldier said I need not to be afraid and that they would see to it that there should be no trouble. I was, at that time, the only white man in the whole township.*

Later on, in the first days of April, John A. Banneck came by horseback to my camp. He said he came from Cheney and was out to find a location, which he did, close in my neighborhood. Ole told him that during his stay at Brents he had heard about other country even farther west called Badger Mountain, and suggested they make a trip out to see the unsettled area. Banneck agreed.

Two other land hunters, Charles and Lever Fiering, joined their party. They followed an abandoned military road located north of Jameson Lake. This road, which followed along Foster Creek, led them towards Old Fort Okanogan located at the confluence of the Columbia and Okanogan River, or to Lake Chelan. Both of these military posts had been abandoned by the soldiers two or three years earlier, according to Ole's journal.

Progressing over the abandoned road, they passed through the Upper Moses Coulee. However, they found it so steep that they had to double-team the wagons. They followed the long road running adjacent to the winding Foster Creek until it turned off to Lake Chelan. *Looking southwest,* Ole wrote, *we could then see the timbered top of Badger Mountain about 20 miles to the southwest so we set our course in that direction, picking our way as best we could.*

To travel southwest, it is surmised that Banneck, the Fierings, and Ole left the Foster Creek military road and made their way overland. Without a road or trail, they slowly traveled westward, passing by what is now the town of Withrow, Washington. By traveling in that direction, the party would have a full view of the green timbered land on Badger Mountain, the snow-capped Cascades in the distant west, and the bunchgrass plains later to be known as the Waterville Plateau.

On the 12th of May 1883, when he was 35½, Ole arrived with his party at a small dip in the terrain. *At a kvickenasp* (quaking aspen) *grove near the foot of the mountain, later to be called Fitches Grove, we made a temporary camp.* This grove, located where the families of Bob Hedges and Eno Daling later farmed, remains today, displaying a unique patch of aspen surrounded by the dusty wheat fields.

We spent four days surveying and looking over the country which we found was unsurveyed. We found a few notices of location bearing the date of April 8th, 1883 and noted the names of Platt M. Corbaley, Al Pierpoint, Mrs. Mary Jefferson and others. No people or improvements were found, but we respected the notices and looked for other locations, although we knew that only actual residence could hold down a claim on unsurveyed land. We liked this country so much better that we decided to abandon our former locations. On the 16th of May, 1883, I stuck up my notice and plowed a small patch of land in Sec. 4, T.24 N., R.22 E., W.M. This,

I believe was the first time sod was turned in the vicinity of Badger Mountain and the present town of Waterville.

It was only a short distance (about one mile) from Fitches Grove, in a southwesterly direction, that Ole would stake out his squatter's claim at the foot of Badger Mountain. At this appealing location displaying an abundance of full-bloomed sunflowers, he felt at peace. He climbed to the top of the hill adjacent to his claim, deeply inhaling the fresh air at that 3400 ft. altitude. The flowing creek from the canyon filled with willow and aspen trees, an encompassing view of the grassy plains to the east and north, a continuance of the panorama including the majestic snowcapped Cascade Mountains to the west, filled him with the satisfaction he had yearned for since arriving in America. He was struck by the surrounding land and recalled the beauty of his former home in Norway, where similar snowcapped peaks also added splendor to the already picturesque scene. He would call his land "Breidablikk" (wide view) and speak of it in that Norwegian term for the next forty-five years.

He put up a tent near the creek, his sleeping quarters for the next seven months, set up his small iron cooking stove alongside, and began measuring his land. Plowing the first furrow in what would later become Douglas County, he knew he had found his home. But while he was plowing one day, a party of sixteen Sinkiuse Indians came riding bareback from the mountains into his property claim. It was the season for the digging of the indigenous camas root. The Indians roamed through the mountainous area regularly each spring, spending about three weeks or more at their familiar summer camp, gathering the bulb for a source of food. The young riders, with the reins of the bridle in one hand and a rifle in the other, formed a circle around him, all barrels pointing in his direction. Being a quiet and peaceful man and realizing that it would be of no use to run, Ole communicated with the men as best he could, using Chinook jargon. He invited them into his camp and offered them food. They sat around him, eating, smoking and jargoning for a period of time before mounting their horses for their return ride to their camp up the canyon. Oliver, Ole's eldest son, would later say that from that day on the Indians were his friends.

Each tribe of the Interior Indians spoke their own dialect of the Salishan language. Most of the early miners and settlers learned to communicate with the various tribes by using the combination of a limited amount of words and gestures, as it was a necessity for social interaction or interpretation of any kind of trading, land boundaries, or treaties.

Oliver, who referred to jargon as "Pidgin talk," would later tell his own stories about speaking with Antoine, an old Indian man, who would visit the farm often when he was a child. He said Antoine always seemed to know when a hot meal was on the table and he was welcomed. He would demonstrate to Oliver and his brothers many of his skills—the most memorable being "how to make a straight arrow out of a crooked twig." Holding a bowed willow in his hands, Antoine would very slightly bend the shaft, always keeping it warm in his palms. Gingerly applying pressure on the twig, he would stretch and manipulate the fibers, finally achieving his straight object ready to be attached to a carved piece of flint. "We traded a pony to him for a shotgun one day and he stayed around to make us a bow using a dogwood split in half," Oliver remembered. "He then wrapped string around it in both directions, and held it over a fire to smoke the exposed wood. Afterwards, he removed the string, showing us the design captured by the unexposed lines. My brothers and I thought Antoine was magical."

On June 26, 1883, 2½ months after leaving his claim near Broad Ax Canyon, Ole sent another letter to Norway.

Spokane County, Washington Territory
Mother and Siblings:

I suppose you have received my letter a long time ago in which I told you that I would move still farther west. I took possession of my new place the 16ᵗʰ of May, went back to Brents Post office to pick up the rest of my things and returned to Badger Mountain around the 6ᵗʰ of June. I sold the few crops I had planted on my earlier land for $50.00 and I gave the land back to Uncle Sam.

There is now already a small settlement here, and settlers and people looking for land are arriving every week. The new city I mentioned, whose proposed name was Nashland, has been renamed Bragen. They are now putting up a log building, which is intended to serve as a store, and will be the first house in town. They are using round logs to construct it and the 4-6 inch wide openings between the logs are packed with clay. I have made about $8.00 working for them.

We have been busy getting some hay together for next winter. The grass is now full-grown and the summer drought has set in. I planted around an acre of wheat and also some potatoes on the 20ᵗʰ of May, and it looks much better than expected. I wasn't sure the wheat would sprout since I planted it much too late. The correct time for planting spring wheat here is the month of March. We haven't had any rain since the middle of May. However, some years it rains off and on all summer. Around the end of September or by the 12ᵗʰ of October we are sure to have rain again, and prior to that time the winter wheat ought to have been planted.

We are now going to start putting up buildings. I believe there will be a Norwegian settlement here. Many have already been here and looked the land over, and they want to come back as soon as they can. Many of them had families.

Some Americans have moved in who want to raise horses and cattle. One is expected who has a flock of horses—250 of them. It is impossible to get enough hay for the winter for so many. However, horses manage to take care of themselves anyway. They kick the snow away until they find tufts of grass. It is only 2 or 3

27

months during the winter when it may be necessary to feed the animals inside. There are many who leave them outside all winter, saying that if they don't want to live, they can die. And often that is what actually happens.

The part of the Big Bend where I now live is about 15 miles from the outlet of the Wenatchee River, or between this one and the Entiatqua River. A few days ago, I was down by the Columbia near the outlet of the last named river. It is a narrow valley about 800 feet deep with very high mountains on the other side. A few Chinese are digging gold down there. The climate down in the valley is quite tropical so I was glad to come up and out of it again.

The Chinese were among the earliest to come to the Columbia River country, the majority coming from California following the trails of Indians, fur dealers, and other miners. Up and down the river and its numerous tributaries the Chinese miners wandered, panned and rocked out an enormous volume of deposits from the various sand and gravel bars and creeks. However, most of them left, except for a few stragglers, following an Indian war against them.

In 1875 when the Indians reached a point on the Columbia a few miles below where Chelan Falls now stands, they discovered a number of Chinamen at work on the benches three hundred feet above. Surrounding them on three sides, they began an uneven fight. The Chinamen were unprotected and unable to escape, easy prey for their antagonists. How many were massacred was never known, but it was an awful fight that sent terror into the hearts of the other Chinamen along the river.[6]

Ole's letter continues, *I wrote in my previous letter about how you were to send money, but in case that one should have been lost, I will explain again. Buy a Bill of Exchange from New York, Chicago or San Francisco, or, if you can, from Lad and Tiltons Bank in Portland, Oregon. This bank is considered to be good and I have had Bills of Exchange on it before. Send the Bill of Exchange to O. Ruud, Brents Post Office, Spokane County, Washington Territory, North America. I am taking a trip to Brents around the 20th of September. What time we'll be getting a post office here, I don't know. Until that time it will continue to be difficult for us to receive any mail.*

All the rest is going well for me with good health and hope that I hear the same from you. The finger whose tip I lost is now healed.

When Ole planted a pail of potatoes on the 20th of May, he cut them small, only one eye to each piece. He also sowed a small patch of barley along with his wheat. *The yield of the potatoes in the fall was six sacks well filled,* he would later write in his journal. *Many people came around during the summer to see my crop, and they all expressed their satisfaction that the country at least would produce potatoes and barley. Next year I will add patches of rye and beans.*

During the summer, Walter Mann of the firm Adams and Mann, in the company of a stranger, came around to see my crop. They were particularly fond of the potatoes and wanted some to eat. This, I, at first, refused because they were not yet full grown and I wanted to save the whole crop for seed next year and that they would be very expensive if they got any. This counted for nothing. Potatoes they must have. I took a pail and dug under the hills until I got it full and told them the price was one dollar, which they paid, and said it was cheap enough. This, I think, was the first produce bought or sold in this section of the country.

Potatoes became one of the major crops in Douglas County, a state of affairs that continued until the majority of farmers began raising wheat. Productivity of wheat expanded once the completion of the short (4.5 mile) Waterville Railway Company was established in 1910, connecting it to the Great Northern railroad line already built as far as Douglas. By 1928, the Waterville Union Grain Company was shipping out about 300,000 bushels of wheat per year.[7]

Spending much of his time cutting down trees, notching and hewing each log with his axe, Ole took seven months to build a shelter for his horses and complete a cabin for himself. He split shakes, heavy with pitch, to provide a waterproofed roof. On Christmas Eve, his 36th birthday, he moved from his tent into his new home at the base of the mountain just as a snowstorm blanketed the land. Within the seven months since he had staked out his 160-acre claim, many other settlers homesteaded nearby. Most chose claims near the foot of the timbered Badger Mountain because they felt secure in the gathering of sufficient fuel for winter and, because of the numerous springs, felt confidence in digging for an adequate well.

About three miles to the west, a twenty-five-year-old, Platt Corbaley, had put his stake in the ground in April 1883, preceding Ole by one month. He left his unworked claim to return later with his twenty-one-year-old wife Nellie, baby daughter Ida Mae, and mother-in-law, Mrs. Mary Jefferson. The following May his father, Reverend Richard Corbaley, and his brother Alvaro came north from California, making six people living in tight quarters. Since manpower and logs were plentiful, plans commenced for a larger house. Cabin builders often wrote their families, thankful to declare a roof over their heads, but few described the dawn-to-dark labor. Alvaro wrote in his diary on February 10, 1885, "Arose at 5:50 a.m. After breakfast Platt and I went to work upon the kitchen of the new house. We laid the foundation of the kitchen last December. We had to shovel the snow away this morning before we could begin work. We then put down the remainder of the sleepers and hewed and laid five logs. The kitchen is to be of logs hewed and the dimensions are 12 x 16 feet, the main building will be built of lumber in dimensions of 16 x 24 feet. We laid up and hewed two rounds before dinner which was at 12:30. We notch the logs, put them to their places and then scored and hewed them. We cut about thirty more logs in the afternoon and hauled down seven at one load in the evening. Louis Titchenal was there on the mountain, and he had hauled the largest load of logs that has been hauled this year to the mill.

The load consisted of two logs and they scaled 1046 feet! The next day we went to work again. Father and I cut some of the ends of the logs off with the crosscut saw and Platt and I marked and sawed the rafters and put them up. We also boarded up one gable end." On February 14th he continued, "We laid up, scored and hewed four rounds today, making nine rounds above the foundation. We roll the logs up upon skids, then notch them, and score and hew them afterwards. We also split up some wood and the shake cuts into bolts before eating our dinner of boiled venison, potatoes, gravy, pickled beans and tea. Then we went to the woods for more logs and cut about thirty. We had brought down 14 logs in two trips before dinner and went for another load in the afternoon. The road was very bad as it has been thawing all day and we stuck in the snow twice and had to unload each time. We had the load bound with a chain and rope but we lost two logs before we got home." The February 19th entry reads, "Finished putting on the shingles, put down the floor, boarded up the north gable and Father finished sawing down the corners. We also sawed out the logs for a door, rived shakes before dinner and more in the p.m." On February 20th, he wrote, "Up at 4:30 a.m. Sawed out and cased two windows. There will be two more windows and two doors, but we will now have, at present, a north door in the front side of the house. Platt made a door and I mixed some mud for chinking and began muddling the cracks in the house, which I finished in the evening. Nellie tacked a cloth over one of the windows as there are no window sashes here for sale." Finally, on February 23rd, Alvaro wrote, "Built a fire at 5:30 this morning. After breakfast we carried the stove from the front room up to the new house and made a hole through the roof for the stovepipe and set the stove up. Platt moved his bed, truck, etc. in as well and he and Nellie are sleeping there tonight."[8]

Douglas County, May 31, 1884
Mother and Siblings!

    Two weeks ago I received Olava's letter of February 4 this year. I see various bits of news in it, and it is very amusing to find out what is going on in the old country. It was too bad that Kristian ended up with a loss in his trade, but nothing is ever so bad it isn't good for something, according to the proverb. I have never believed that anything could be done with the Eger farm in regards to forest or land trade.

    Anders Stadum ought to take along one of his girls and move out to Dakota or some other place where he could get cheap land. No one ought to come as far as to here unless he is well provided with money. The work opportunities for men here are now very poor because of the halt in the work on the railroad. It is true that they are still working on a railroad from Ensworth through the Yakima country to Puget Sound, but with relatively few men. Capable girls, however, who can get along fairly well in English, can make good money in small towns along the railroad line. In Lewiston and Moscow, in Idaho, as well as in Walla Walla, there is plenty of work for girls, and the pay is twice as high as in the East. Frankly, I have to say that it is not easy for a poor girl in Norway. If she has to work for others, the pay is miserable, and the prospects for getting married are equally dismal. Here, on the other hand, a girl can expect a good future, to say nothing about the fact that she enjoys the same respect as women in general. I would not recommend to anyone recently arrived to come directly out here to the coast, but to stop first in the East and learn the language.

Olava is asking what kind of neighbors I have. They are of all kinds, and it is best to stay clear of them as much as possible. There are only a few I stick with and have any dealings with. In general, everyone must fend for himself. It is the American way to be nice to you, but behind your back they may play all kinds of tricks against you.

The colonel I told you about, Mr. Nash, didn't move here, but gave up his land. However, he built a sawmill and has been back here a couple of times this spring. The first time he brought along a whole company of money men from Spokane Falls for the purpose of establishing a city here, which he will name after himself, and they signed a contract with me regarding access to water from the brook that runs through my land. When I asked for some compensation for it, they expressed the opinion that I ought to be satisfied with the fact that if they establish a city right next to my land, its value would increase tenfold. This is all that was done at that time. It is now almost two months ago, and I have heard nothing more, but they said they would be back in June. It is also rumored that they have abandoned their plan, while others claim that they want to start the city in another location. So, I don't know what is going to happen. The town that was started here last summer, 6 miles from my land, is growing slowly, but that would be the case with the start of any city until a railroad has been built. It appears that anyone who is able to think a little about the future, envisions a big city some place around here.

Nash, who had arrived in the Big Bend in the spring of 1884, was engaged in freighting goods from Spokane Falls to the Badger Mountain country. Since his sawmill on the mountain was supplying the area with a vast amount of lumber, he decided, in the autumn of 1884, to build a store near Platt Corbaley's place. He held hopes in other directions as well, for the town six miles from Ole's homestead, Okanogan, was slow-growing due to lack of well-water, giving Nash reason to compete with the dry, dusty town for the county seat.

Ole's letter continues, *For a couple of weeks now we have had a lot of Indians around here. They come mainly to dig for camas roots on the hills along Badger Mountain, but they have been no trouble whatsoever. Our worst enemy and chicken thief is the coyote, especially in the winter as their rations can be scarce when there is a deep snow. They are so plentiful that I can look up almost anytime and see one or more on the hill. Disregarding the distance, I can send them a bullet, often making a good hit. It is quite a sport to see how they take to their heels! Coyotes are as smart as dogs and know pretty well what the whistle of a bullet means. Game is plentiful, especially deer and even bear can be captured in the mountain and adjacent plain. While out on a hunting trip this past February, one of the neighbors killed 5 deer and several sage hens all in one day, 11 deer within a week.*

It is now already dry and warm so that those newly arrived and many of the settlers are greatly disappointed, and some of them started out again, claiming that nothing can grow here. I am not worried about that, and what I have planted, altogether about 5 acres, looks good. It turns out that the land I plowed last year, has the highest yield. Taken together, I have now plowed about 10 acres. That is not a lot, of course, but there are few who have done any more. It is now already too dry to plow with two horses. But there have been many discouraged settlers and some say it will be impossible to make a good living here so have gone farther west down to the river, others back to the east where they came from. I, myself, feel that I will stay as the land, as I said earlier, responds well to plowing and I think can be worked to give excellent yields eventually.

"The spring of 1884 found the first settlers very short of provisions and the Indians brought potatoes and wheat around to sell," William Stanley Lewis said in a speech he gave at Crab Creek, Washington in 1917. "The hungry settlers paid them six cents per pound for potatoes and the same for wheat. The teams had to go to Spokane after supplies and the store, which had been set up by J.B. Nash, O.H. Kimball and Peter Bracken, ran out of supplies before they got back. The little settlement still had a little flour left and managed to kill a grouse or two, so they did not suffer. A good crop of wheat was grown that summer and threshed enough for seed—tramped out with horses and cleaned by a fanning mill built of wood except the sieve, which was made out of a five-gallon oilcan. The Titchenals made a rope drive from the fan and it did a good job of cleaning. When they were through with their own job, they loaned it to a neighbor and he loaned it to the next one, then on to the next one until it disappeared and was never returned. The next year they had to make a new one. Sam C. Robins, the elected sheriff and early homesteader, brought the first threshing machine into the county from Ellensburg in 1887 and it was a second-hand one."[9]

* * *

In the fall of 1884, when Douglas and Lincoln Counties were divided off from Spokane County, Ole, as a candidate on the People's Party ticket, and well qualified for a detailed job, was elected to the office of Douglas County Surveyor. Some surveying had been done in the present Douglas County by Joseph M. Snow and party during the years of 1880-82 when there was as yet no settlement. While doing his work, as well as observing the terrain and soils, Snow decided that there were many excellent agricultural regions open and that he would settle himself in the north central area of the county near Waterville, where he became an active member of the community, was elected to the office of Territorial councilman, served as Probate judge, and later, in 1889, was elected Joint Senator.

A petition was written by Richard Corbaley to be presented to the Land Commissioner for the acceptance of surveying the land around Badger Mountain, and requesting that the land be put upon the market in the near future. On February 16, 1885, Corbaley posted a "road notice" at the post office in Okanogan City to be signed by the settlers. Ole's first road survey resulted from this petition, extending from Okanogan City, the first county seat north of Douglas and east of Waterville, to the top of Badger Mountain. The surveying commenced on April 6th and was completed on the 8th—two days' work. The need for new roads increased steadily as more settlers rapidly moved into the Big Bend. By 1885 the Douglas County Territorial Census in Washington Territory had grown to 362. It claimed 254 males and 108 females. Of the 362 residents of the county, 346 were white and 16 were Chinese. Marriages equaled the number of women (per Douglas County, Washington Territory, 1885 Territorial Census, including present-day Grant County. Submitted by Ed Godfrey, March 22, 1997. U.S. Gen Web Archive).

After being elected to the job of Douglas County Surveyor, Ole spent the next 18 years in the office laying out many of the county's earliest roads and plotting the town sites of Ephrata, Coulee City, Wilson Creek and Douglas plus others that no longer exist. He was defeated in his bid for re-election against a Republican, P.T. Sargeant, in 1894, losing by two votes, but won his office back in the 1896 election.

His volumes of leatherbound notebooks with the smudged penciled entries were later donated by his son, Oliver, and are held at the Douglas County Engineer's office. Frank Englehorn, the engineer who received these records commented that the man who made them was meticulous and extremely accurate in his calculations, especially for his time. The notes detail the measurements between "turns in the road" and some give reference to "a rock," "a mound with a stone," "a pine tree," "a spring," and rarely, some "settler's house." A right-angle turn, not far from Okanogan City, was "near Kimball's store," one note said. In 1974, some surveyors were checking his calculation for a corner, where his notes said he buried a whiskey bottle in 1903. After digging at the spot Ole had marked in his notebooks, they found the bottle intact.[10]

Later, Ole wrote about his job. *In the capacity of County Surveyor, I have traversed Douglas County in all directions. In the early days, owing to the lack of wagon roads, I traveled mostly by horseback, bringing my instruments* (presently on display at the Douglas County museum in Waterville, Washington), *chain, etc.*

33

in a pack behind the saddle. When traversing, I would often go 30 to 40 miles a day. All surveying was done fast and cheap for my time was worth fully as much at home. I believe that during my time of office, I have located over two thousand miles of county roads and traveled more than six thousand miles in Douglas County. No work of greater magnitude, at least in my experiences of frontier life, ever came to my observation. With the exception of a few cases, this has been a settlement of hardy, well meaning and industrious pioneers, the oldest of which is now fast disappearing.

After the Badger post office was established in Platt M. Corbaley's home in 1884, receiving letters became easier. Mail delivered to the settlers was brought to Okanogan from Brents in Lincoln County, from Spokane Falls in Spokane County, or from Ellensburg by stagecoach when weather permitted, but delivery was often delayed up to two weeks or more, east and west, during the winter months. Alvaro Corbaley described in his diary the cold 4-hour trip, traveling by horseback, where he would pick up the sacks of mail from the Okanogan post office, bring them to Badger where settlers from the mountain could pick up letters, packages, or the much anticipated newspapers—the *Spokane Falls Chronicle*, the *Plymouth Democrat*, and the *Flag Enterprise*. The Badger post office would be moved to Nash's store that year, remaining there until the townsite of Nashland was ordered vacated by the county commissioners in 1890, disappointing many of the Badger Mountain settlers, who had wrongly foreseen the growth of a large city.

The first county seat was temporarily established in Old Okanogan City by J.W. Adams, a forty-year-old real estate promoter from Kansas, who together with a surveyor, twenty-seven year-old Walter Mann, laid out a township six miles east of the present town of Waterville, 2½ miles northeast of the site of the town of Douglas. At first, there was only a tent occupied by Mann, who wintered there in 1883, holding down the location. Along with another fellow, H.A. Meyers, the men organized themselves under the name of Adams, Mann & Company, Real Estate Agents. Circulars were mailed around the country describing the delightful resources, one claiming every quarter-section of land had at least one good spring and that there was living water all over the country. Shacks were soon being built, followed by a hotel, a post office, and a 24 x 36 ft. goods store also serving as a courthouse. But the occupants of Okanogan City were soon disillusioned. Before the town site was platted, Adams and Mann had neglected to actually *find* the vital substance they claimed was plentiful—water. A few diggings 60 to 90 feet deep in the dry earth proved futile. Even after bringing in a well-drilling machine and digging to a depth of nearly 300 ft., still no water was found. The settlers gave up, some leaving the country, others relocating as they came to the realization that they would have to continue to haul water if they stayed. The promised town would soon disintegrate. Adams, the professional townsite boomer, would leave the country in the fall of 1886. Mann remained for several years before moving on to the coast.

In the spring of that year, about 3 miles to the south, toward Badger Mountain, A.T. Greene, later to be known as the "Father of Waterville," dug a well, finding a good supply of water at about 28 or 30 feet. He staked out a government townsite of 40 acres of his ranch and gave the town its name. Many lots were staked and several business houses were built in the fall of that same year. Following the platting of the town, the new residents hauled a barrel of water from Waterville to Okanogan for truthful evidence, presenting it to the board of trustees' meeting. Waterville was voted the county seat and the transfer took place in May of 1887, although several citizens living in Okanogan City were reluctant to give up the official records. Removing them from the goods store, which also served as a courthouse, required Sheriff Sam Robins to make a wagon trip to Okanogan and demand that they be turned over.

When the county records, along with a stove, a homemade table, the commissioner's journal, and a few books, were brought to Waterville, a courthouse had yet to be established. Judge J.M. Snow convinced a friend to quickly assemble a building for county business. The roughly constructed quarters revealed daylight between the boards in many places. A dry goods box was used as a desk for the auditor, the commissioners sat at a table made by placing boards on sawhorses, and in place of chairs, the commissioners sat on the ends of the "horses." This building, the second erected in the town, was also the post office, and Judge Snow used the rear portion as an office.[11]

The location had been discussed in every cabin that year. Most settlers hoped the vote would place the county seat position nearest their settlement, giving potential for large city growth. On March 8th, 1886 Ole sent a letter to his mother. *Badger Mountain, Douglas County, Mother and Siblings: I received Olava's letter of January 3, a short time ago and I would have answered sooner but have been too busy with my work along with attending some official meetings here. There is much quibbling going on in the area about where the county seat will be located. As it looks now, Okanogan may be out as a source of water is lacking. Perhaps this will be Nashland, but a vote will soon decide. It appears that our settlement will make a speedier progress this summer than ever before. Immigrants are already arriving from the East. A steam ferryboat was built this winter down by the Columbia River. And there is talk of a steamboat coming soon and working its way up the river.*

I am very glad that you have had such good luck with the colts; but if I were in Norway with one of the best American racehorses, the best Norwegian horse would be left a good distance behind. America now has the fastest horses in the world. Harness racing sometimes takes place on the ice with a sled, but usually it takes place in the fall on a roadbed prepared for that purpose with a light two-

wheeled sulky. Huge amounts of money are lost and won during those competitions. A man in California won 13,000 dollars in one week on a racehorse.

Another race of horses is the so-called "Runners", quite different from the previously mentioned "trotters". The runners are ridden in a race by a light man or so-called Jack (Jockey). One of the best runners by the name of Tubrook ran the mile in 1 minute 39¾ seconds. Of work horses there are many here weighing 2000 to 2500 pounds. In Walla Walla there are also several who breed fast horses, and eventually we will have them here in this settlement also. It is only men with capital and experience who can make money raising racehorses.

I recently read a long report about the mineral-bearing regions of the Cascade Mountains and other places in the Washington Territory. It is referred to as being excellent and rich beyond all imagination. There is no doubt, either, that the gold and silver deposits in those mountains are worth millions. Hundreds of mines have already been established and have yielded thousands of dollars. There is a lot of turmoil up by the Okanogan River because of some recently discovered gold deposits, and hundreds of gold seekers have already streamed in. A party from the settlement here is now preparing for a gold digging excursion. Eventually, I may also try my luck. But in no way can I set aside my work here at home for the very unreliable gold digging.

This winter has been very mild and we haven't had any snow in 6 weeks. I was very comfortable in my cabin during the coldest winter months as I had plenty of firewood so it was quite pleasant. A few days ago I went to Wenatchee and got several hundred little trees of various kinds along with a lot of grapevine saplings, which I now have started to plant. In a few days I'll start planting wheat.

I am supposed to go out and plot some new roads on the 25ᵗʰ of March until the 12ᵗʰ of April, and one on the 24ᵗʰ of April. I am very busy. Otherwise everything is just fine. It would be good if you could send the money soon since I intend to buy cattle this summer. Hereby greetings to all.

Bain wagon purchased in 1883, in Sprague, WA.
Presently on display at the Wenatchee Valley Museum and Cultural Center

The first cabin built by Ole Ruud – 1883
Described by Oliver Ruud – Painted by Clara Rock
Birthplace of the first four babies

With the railroads being built closer to the area, the population of the Big Bend steadily grew. Among others, the local preacher expressed his views, hoping to encourage others to settle in this land of fresh air and vast opportunities.

The Big Bend Country*

Your sons will not be drunkards in all this goodly land,
No whisky here or lager beer, the mother's heart to rend.
The ladies here all vote, you know,
and vote for temperance, too.
They're all for prohibition – for morals good and true.

One thousand population is all Big Bend can boast.
Good schools, and Sunday preaching at very little cost.
No doctors, yet, or druggists, nor printing in the Bend,
Though all will find a welcome and an open friendly hand.

Across the great Columbia, along its western shore
The mines are rich in silver, in lead and copper ore.
Along the Salmon River some sixty miles away
The silver mines are very rich, I hear people say.
I do not speak from knowledge, not having been that way
For I am here to preach the gospel on every Sabbath Day.

What more ye sons of labor than these can ye desire?
Good health, good soil, good neighbors,
good fuel for your fire.
Choose timbered land or prairie or both combined are best.
Don't tarry in the cities! Go West, young man, Go West!

James Edwin Fitch, Home Missionary

P.S. If you should ask more questions, please send along some stamps;
For all things here are somewhat dear, Save pitch pine knots for lamps.

* (Date written unknown- J.E. Fitch, age 70, originally from New York, appears on the June, 1900 population census-Waterville Precinct)

Antoine with wife and daughter
Note the cornhusk bag, used for root collecting, hanging from the digging
stick

* * *

The nearest railroad points were Spokane, Cheney, and Sprague, a distance
of about 150 miles where we used to go once in the year to buy supplies, Ole wrote.
When we got a road built to the Columbia River, we had much of our trading done
in Ellensburg, a round trip of about 150 miles. It was not until the time that the
Great Northern Railroad was built that communication got any better and the mail
sent from back home in Norway arrived within a reasonable length of time.

Prior to the establishment of the Badger post office, annual trips were
taken to Brents Post Office to collect mail, then on to Spokane to buy supplies. It
would be about three weeks before Ole returned to his land. He would leave with
his wagon full of produce to sell, the majority his own, occasionally some of his
neighbors'. It often proved impossible for his team to pull the heavy load when
ascending the canyon road in Moses Coulee. By removing a partial amount of
the sacked potatoes, barley, beans or wheat from the wagon, the horses would be
enabled to pull the remaining load up the steep, rutty grade. Ole would then secure
the team, giving them a deserved rest, and walk back down the hill to carry each
heavy sack, one by one, until his wagon was reloaded and he could be on his way.
Strength and determination were vital requirements of pioneer life. At 185 pounds,
brawny and resolute, 5' 9" Ole did not complain.

Detailed records in his ledger give an excellent indication of the financial status and the general economy of the area in 1886 and early 1887. He filed his records and correspondences in the safety of his desk. This private area was not permitted to be disturbed when he married, by either his wife or any of the children. Samples of his dealings posted in his daybook of late 1886 and early 1887 are as follows:

November 1886:

		Income	*Paid Out*
Nov 24	*Paid for lumber to Anderson*		*1.24*
	Sold—12 ½ lbs. lard	*1.75*	
Nov 26	*To D. W. Martin – meat*	*.50*	
	Hog's head & cabbage	*.50*	
Dec 5	*Sent to Gurley and Appleton for Books*		*3.92*
	One ink stand		*.15*
	Stamps & envelopes		*.05*
Dec 10	*Sold to Cloninger*		
	40 lbs. lard	*5.60*	
	Sold Meat	*13.00*	
	Bought from Cloninger		
	12 inch plow		*18.00*
Dec 11	*Bought Paper*		*.25*
Dec 30	*Sold to Cap Miles*		
	6 ½ lbs. lard @ 14c		
	7 ½ lbs. meat @ 12c		
	Cabbage	*(settled by credit)*	

January 1887:

Jan 5	*Sold to Miles*		
	16 lbs. side meat @ 11c		
	27 ½ lbs. meat @ 11c		*6.76*
	18 lbs. meat@ 11c		

Jan 9	Sold to Koufman	
	11 lbs shoulder @ 10c	1.10
	30 lbs meat @ 11c	3.30
Jan 9	Bought from Koufman	
	2 sacks flour	3.50
Jan 10	Bought in Okanogan	
	10 lbs. sugar	1.00
	To Ogle for a sausage mill	3.00
Jan 14,1887	Paid Taxes	6.00
	Paid to Cole for the compass	10.00
	For Blacksmithing	.50
Jan 20	Bought postal stamps	.20
	Sent for pocket field notes –stamps	1.00
Jan 31	Sold to Anderson	
	29 lbs. meat @ 12c	3.48
	Meat to Kummer	2.64
	To Cap Miles	
	5 lbs. lard	.60

<u>*Spring of 1887:*</u>

May 4	For recording of a brand	.50
	Paid freight for fruit trees	2.30
May 20 Received of E. C. Fisher for surveying		5.00
May 26 Received of J. Boner for surveying		2.50
	Received of L. Detwiler for surveying	5.00
May 28 To T. Williams for medicine		10.00

<u>*Fall of 1887:*</u>

Oct 16   Bought in Orondo in Block 100 lots

41

101 ($15), 103 ($5), 107 ($5). In Block F, lot 102 ($15)		*40.00*
Oct 16	*Sold to Dr. Smith in <u>payment</u> for the lots:*	
	10 bushel corn @ .50	*5.00*
	20 bushel potatoes @ .50	*10.00*
	20 bushel barley @ .75	*15.00*
	to give surveying	*5.00*
	to give tracings of Orondo	<u>*5.00*</u>
		Total- 40.00
Nov 19	*Sold to E. Walberg*	
	14 lbs. beans	*.70*
	48 lbs. cabbage .	*45*
Nov 21	*Sold to Chr. Aanerud*	
	4 ½ bushel potatoes @ .50	*2.25*
	65 lbs. cabbage @ .01 ½ c	*.97*
Nov 30	*Bought for myself:*	
	Suspenders	*.60*
	One hat	*.60*
	Shirts	*1.50*
	Stockings	*.50*
	Shoes	*2.00*
	Milk pail	*.60*
	Sugar	*1.00*
	Rope	*.70*
	One halter	*1.50*
	Tobacco	*.10*
	Wages to Anderson (has worked 8 days @ $1.25)	*10.00*
	Sold to J. Willms	
	448 lbs. barley @ 2 ¼ c	*10.00*
	22 bushel rye –25 lbs @ $1	*22.25*

Paid for Blacksmithing and 2 clavesis	*1.10*

In September 1888, Ole, now 41 years old, applied for United States citizenship.

IN THE SUPERIOR COURT OF THE STATE OF WASHINGTON, AND IN AND FOR THE COUNTY OF DOUGLAS:

In the matter of the application of O. Ruud,
A native of Norway, to become a citizen of the United States:

On this twelfth day of September, A.D. 1888, the said O. RUUD appeared in open court with his witnesses E. A. Cornell and James Melvin and made application to become a citizen of the United States. And the court being fully satisfied from the evidence of said witnesses, as well as other evidence produced in court, that said applicant hath fully complied with the laws of the United States relative thereto. That he had resided in this Territory for one year last past, and in the United States at least five years; That during said time he hath behaved as a man of good moral character, is attached to the principles of the Constitution of the United States and is well disposed to the good order and happiness of the same, and having in open Court taken the oath as required by law, therefore, it is ordered and adjudged by the court that he, the said O. RUUD be and he is hereby admitted to be a citizen of the United States.

Signed: L.B. Nash, Judge

The certificate of naturalization states:

TERRITORY OF WASHINGTON
County of Douglas

I, R.S. Steiner, Clerk of the District Court of the Territory of Washington and for the Fourth Judicial District thereof, holding terms at Waterville, Douglas County, said territory, do hereby certify that the above is a true, full and perfect transcript
From the record of said Court of the admission of said O. RUUD as a citizen of the United States, as the same now appears on record in my office.

In Testimony Whereof, I have hereunto set my hand and affixed the seal of said Court, this 17th day of October, A.D. 1888.

R.S. Steiner, Clerk

Top Row L to R: Howard Honor, Bill Mitchell, Walter Mann, Arch Barrowman, Al Pierpoint, Sanford Hundly. Middle Row: Billie Walters, Hector Paterson, Major Nash, Tom Powers, Billie Wilson. Bottom Row: George Kneuver, Morris Buzzard, John Banneck, Rash Wilcox, John Stevens

**Badger Post Office – Built 1884
Courtesy of Douglas County Museum**

First Waterville City Hall
County Seat established-May 1887

Ole Ruud's homestead certificate.

Ole Ruud's homestead certificate

**Copy of field notes of survey No. 1 road beginning at the town of Okanogan and terminating in Badger Mountain. Work commenced April 6, 1885.
Notes 1-10**

No. angle	Course	Distance chs. lks.	Remarks
11	S 54° 30 W	80. 00	On line between Township 24 and 25. a rock mark. O bears S 60° E dist. 2 chs. 71 lks. a permanent rock mark. T bears N 67 E. dist 3ch. Set 3 mile post
12	S 77° 45 W	7. 55	Leering to mile post N 32° 30' E. dist 1 ch. 56 lks. a permanent rock mark. a bears N 4° 30' E. dist 79
13	S 68° W	60. 00	a mound with a rock in mark S bears N 23° 15' W a mound with a rock in mark R bears S 36° E. dist. 3
14	S 56° W.	80	At the cor. of sect. 36 and 35 on line between T 24 a a mound with a rock in mark C bears S 28° 10 a mound with a rock in mark D bears N 28° 15' Set 4 mile post 50 lks from center of road.
		9. 40	
15	S 74° 15 W	44. 93	a stone mark. + bears N 50 W. dist 74 lks. a mound with a rock in mark L bears S 50°
16	S 22 E.	80	At the cor. of sec. 2 and 3. Set a rock mark T bears N 72° 30' W. dist 6 a mound with a stone in mark H bears S 72° 30' E Set 5 mile post
		2. 88.	To ¼ rock post between sec. 2 and 3
17	S 68 W	80	Through center of sec. 3 Set 6 mile post. from whence a line tree bears S 33 W. a fine
		285	To ¼ sec. post between sec. 3 and 4 a pine tree bears S 29 W.
18	S 22° E	13. 78	a pine tree bear S 55° 15' E.
19	S 75° 15 W	45 81	a post mark T bears N 31° 30 E. dist. 56 lks. cor. of Kembals house bears S 50° E dist. 86 l a big rock mark. 4 bears S 6° W. dist 42 lks.
20	S 69° 35 W	53. 00	a rock mark. 7 bears S 66° E. dist 1 ch. 18 lks. a rock mark K bears S 35° E dist. 53 lks.
21	S 25° 15 W	56. 68.	a rock mark O bears S 66° E dist 75 lks. Crossed the creek and following the same as so
22	S 62° W	61. 63	
23	S 46° E	65. 88.	Set 7 mile post. dist from creek 30 lks.
24	S 40 W	80	

Notes 11-24

No. of Angles	Course	Distance Chs. lks.	Remarks
		4.00	
25	S 17° W	25.50	Distance to creek on up side 20 lks.
26	S 4° E	33.00	
27	S 11° 30 W	35.50	A pine tree marked R 1½ feet diam. bears N 84° W dist 1 ch. 20 lks.
28	S 48° 30 W	45.50	An alder 4 in diam. mark R bears S 50° E dist 70 lks
29	S 32° 30 W	80.00	Set 8 mile post. from which a bunch of swallows. bears S 6° E dist 1 ch. 50 lks. A mound with a 3 edged stone 8 in long bears N 42° W dist 1 ch. 50 lks.
30	S 20° W	30 16	A pine tree 1 foot diam. bears N 89° E dist 34 lks.
31	S 5° E		A pine tree 3 feet diam. bears S 6° 30' E. dist 1 ch. 27 lks
		39. 50	To Miles spring
		48. 00	A pine tree 2½ feet diam. bears N 54° 30' W. dist 1 ch.
32	184° 45 W	65. 14.	A pine tree 3 feet diam. bears N 54° 15' E. dist 1 ch. 37 l
33	S 38° 45 W	48. 00	A pine tree 2½ feet diam. bears S 28° E dist. 43 lks.
			A pine tree 2 feet diam. bears N 21° 75' E dist. 87 l
34	S 5° 15' E	79. 71.	A pine tree 1 foot bears S 25° W dist 1 ch.
			A pine tree 1 foot diam. bears N 69 W. dist 1 ch. 78 lks
35	S 44° 30 W		A pine tree 4 feet diam. bears N 47 W. dist 40 lks.
			A pine tree 1 foot diam. bears S 38° 30' W. dist
		80. 00	Set 9 mile post.
~~37 S 68 W~~		8. 50	A pine tree 2 feet diam. bears N 30° 30' W. dist 9
37	S 68° W		A pine tree 2 feet diam. bears S 66° 45" W. dist 2 ch
			On the line between secs. 7 and 18. to cor.
			secs. 7, 18, 12 and 13. Township 24 N. on line betw
			Range 21 and 22.
			Set post mark R on termination of road
			Work furnished April 8th 1885 O. Pen County Sur

Notes 25-37

* * *

The terrain west and southwest from the top of Badger Mountain drops dramatically, approximately 3772 ft., into the picturesque 672 ft. elevation of the Columbia River Valley. Quite different is the climate within the semicircle of the river, as well as the change of soils from volcanic ash to light and sandy. If traveling from Eastern Washington, pioneers could encounter irritating dust storms, which discouraged some of them from settling down in the open range; their grit-filled eyes were directed toward the river land. Getting there required taking a wagon or riding horseback down the 10 mile perilous switchback narrow grade of Corbaley Canyon, and Ole, or any traveler, found it imperative to be on guard for rattlesnakes, as the venomous serpents were numerous, large, coiled and ready to put fright in passengers, or startle the horses as they shied abruptly away from the unnerving sound of the rattler.

Settlers were generally filing in to the Columbia River Valley from a southerly direction via the Ellensburg Mountains, another potentially hazardous journey. Climbing through Colockum Pass, whether by wagon, horseback, or pack mules, they could find themselves halted abruptly by an unexpected snowstorm, requiring them to seek hasty shelter for an undetermined duration.

The Colockum Creek Valley is referred to as the "Colockum Pass"; the name is appropriate and true insofar as the valley leads up to the base of the section of the Cascades where the illusion ends, for the would-be traveler finds himself facing an ascent of nearly 5000 feet over a difficult road. The climb from the Kittitas side made possible this spur of the Cascades, and enabled the Valley of the Colockum to be the highway for heavy freight and emigrant traffic to the Big Bend country, ruby mines, Okanogan and Methow Valleys, which travel reached a high tide in 1887. This road, near the mouth of the Colockum, forks: one route crosses the Columbia River and continues on up Moses Coulee into the Big Bend, while the other leads up the river on its west bank to the Wenatchee Valley and other sections of the north country.[12]

Many were coming in search of gold, prospecting along the river's banks. But here, they also found a paradise abundant with accessible, tall timber; canyons fragrant with the blossoms of syringa and wild roses, holding musical creeks adaptable for irrigating orchard groves; rich, valley soil found to readily grow oats and corn for stock feed. The mountains, plentiful with deer, goats, bear, and elk, gave them satiating meat and skins for tanning. The salmon-filled river required only men with sharp spears to further fill their bellies. Because of the low elevation and shelter of the mountains, the climate maintained a lengthy growing season dealing heavy, sultry summer temperatures described by Ole as "quite uncomfortable and very tropical."

One of the early valley pioneers was Sam C. Miller who, in 1871, ventured into the river valley with the definite purpose of establishing a trading post with the Indians. His entrance was timely, as two other men holding ownership of a trading post at the confluence of the Wenatchee and Columbia Rivers were anxious to give up the post and leave the country, as they had been threatened with arrest by federal authorities for selling whiskey to the Indians. Miller, known for his humorous tales of early experiences, told of the 1872 earthquake, which had torn vast quantities of rock from the perpendicular cliffs of the west side of the river, north of Entiat, hurling them with such massive thrust as to completely dam the river for many hours. Miller declared that to go to the Columbia for water, as had been the custom, and find it completely dry was a most paralyzing experience, and that he would have given every gray hair in his head to have been out of the country.[13]

The population of this fertile area would grow steadily, as the early residents and community leaders were cognizant of the wide potential in both business and fruit farming. Early landowners, who had brought in fruit trees on packhorses from Walla Walla, received high yields in both quality and quantity. With the advent of the Great Northern railroad in 1892, shipping of the succulent apricots, peaches, grapes, and apples would greatly enhance the economy and eventually bring world-famous industry to the Wenatchee Valley as the rich sandy soil gave of its plentiful harvest. The late 1880s showed the Wenatchee settlement population, with its rows of roughly built buildings and tents along the riverbank, comparable with Waterville, but this perfect location, known for its long growing season, irrigation canals, and shipment facilities, would grow to be the city in the area boasting a population of 16,000 by 1970, increasing to around 28,000 by the year 2000.

Waterville, April 19, 1889
Mother and Siblings,

I received Olava's letter of January 30, a long time ago, but a lot of activities and other circumstances made me neglect to answer. It is strange to find out that so many old acquaintances have passed away.

Tomorrow I'm supposed to do a surveying job along the Entiatqua River, which flows down from the mountains and joins the Columbia 1½ miles above Orondo. After this trip and a trip I made two years ago, I will have surveyed almost all the land for 15 miles along this river above the Columbia. I promised an Indian that I would come and survey his land in about a month. I could get quite a bit of surveying work if I cared for it and wanted to buy the necessary instruments. I need a surveyor's level. The cheapest one I could use costs $40.00. However, I am getting tired of being away from home so much.

On Ole's assignment to survey the first road from Entiat to Quartz Creek, he was assisted by four axmen. These burley workers hacked out the trees and brush, which obscured the sight of the proposed road. While attending a community meeting in 1918, Ole described this trip. On that same survey assignment he had climbed to the top of a high mountain far up the Entiat, put a message in a bottle, which he buried under a pile of rocks, and told those attending the community meeting to be on the lookout for it in their mountain climbing adventures.

His letter continues, *I see that you have started up again with bee culture; I am sure it will be profitable if they get the proper care. I know about that from old experience. Here the bees would no doubt do well, and I have often thought of getting a few hives, but I would have to go to a place 100 miles away to get them.*

You want to know how many domestic animals I have. I have 14 head of cattle including heifers, calves, and full-grown animals. Two months ago I sold a two-year old steer for $70.00. This spring I also bought a mare that will be 3 years old soon for $85.00 cash. This was an exceedingly good buy since it is big and well-built and about half-blooded Clydesdale race. It is much bigger than any of my other horses. I now have four—two males and two females including the riding pony. I have broken both mares and used them for plowing this spring.

Spring came early this year, so I started plowing in the middle of March. I have planted about 50 acres of wheat, oats, and barley—already sprouting, and about 3½ acres of potatoes. I am now selling potatoes at 75 cents a bushel, but in Waterville the price is supposed to have gone up to $1.10, so I can raise my price some. Barley I am selling almost daily at 2¼ cents a pound or $1.80 a bushel. Oats I have been selling at 2¾ cents a pound or $1.99 a bushel. I still have about 500 bushels left to sell. If I didn't have any expenses, I would make money, but it costs a lot since everything I have to buy is also very expensive.

I have had 2 men working for me for some time, paying them $1.00 a day. One man is working almost year round. But I have also improved my farm considerable; among other things I have planted 60 fruit trees this spring. They are already beginning to sprout. As far as new land is concerned, I have plowed 20 acres this spring, and I expect to plow more if we get more rain. Next week I am going to start planting beans, cabbage, and other vegetables. We have a little machine we use for planting beans. It is a profitable crop, and I have sold all I could grow at 5 cents a pound.

They have now started work on the railroad, which is supposed to go through here and to Seattle, but I still don't know if it is going to Waterville so I am being careful when it comes to buying lots. I did, however, buy two a while ago, paying $120.00. If it doesn't come to Waterville, it will come to Orondo, and there I am more interested. Orondo hasn't grown much, but if the railroad comes through there, which is not unlikely, there will be progress and business. There are proposals for several railroad lines through this area with surveying already done in several places, but everything is going on in secret, making it difficult to find out anything. The reason for this is that the companies are battling each other constantly in regards to the best location and the best route. A lot of people are coming here from the east all the time and the land is increasing in value. I could sell any time now and get $2,000--$2,500. I have no debt, but have credit in the amount of $300.00 and some cash.

Last winter was the mildest we have had since I came here. The health problems of last summer disappeared when winter came. Things happen around here, but nothing you would be familiar with, so it is not worth mentioning.

I do not hear from old acquaintances any more so I can't tell you anything about anyone. I assume I am now totally forgotten. The conditions in this country, its policies, and its ordinary affairs make up the daily news items here, and I have become so absorbed in this that things of old fade away, although not to such an extent that I no longer frequently think of Norway, my family and my acquaintances, and I do expect to see them once more.

We now have a steamboat making two trips a week on the Columbia River, stopping in Orondo. Most of its business consists of bringing food supplies and passengers to the mines by the Okanogan River. They brag a lot about the wealth of these mines. When I was up by the Entiatqua River the other day, I found an ore vein, which I believe has silver in it, if I am not mistaken. I sent a piece to Portland to have it analyzed. It is well established that gold and silver are present in the Cascade Mountains, but because they are so craggy and inaccessible, only a little has been checked out. One man alone could not accomplish it in a lifetime.

I am, as before, fortunate to be in excellent health, although many in the area have been extremely ill. I hope this will find all of you in good health as well. Write soon and let me know all that is new with you—such as if there are many who are leaving for America, etc. (I have heard nothing from brother Martin.) With friendly greetings to you, and to all relatives and old acquaintances.

Forty-one-year-old Ole was very lucky to be in excellent health, for a siege of illness had swept through the area of the Big Bend, taking many lives, both young and old. Some people called it "malaria of a virulent kind"; others spoke of it as "the mountain fever," and some said it was like "typhoid." The new doctor in town, a recent graduate of medical school in Michigan, had arrived in the Washington Territory in 1888, located in Waterville, and soon found himself nearly overwhelmed with work.

Young Dr. Colin Gilchrist used to give humorous accounts of what he termed his nerve in breaking into professional life. He declared that while the country was young and poor, it was so far ahead of him in wealth that he felt doubtful about ever catching up with the procession; that the meager furnishings of his sleeping room, obtained on the installment plan, while sanitary, were far from sumptuous, as proof of which he spoke of a bunch of shingles used for a pillow. Since Waterville was surrounded by an extensive country, Dr. Gilchrist found himself in a wide-ranging practice. Between fever cases, broken bones, and the imperative summons of the stork, he had little time for sleep. Owing to crop failures and kindred hardships, some of the families were brought to the verge of destitution, and it sometimes devolved upon him to furnish the means of relief. He spoke of one family so reduced by illness as to be unable to take proper care of itself. The baby of the house was burning with fever, and the doctor broke the ice on the water barrel and, with the freezing contents, gave the baby a sponge bath, which, though it may be considered desperate and heroic treatment, proved beneficial. One can believe that an automobile would have greatly reduced the hardships of such a country practice, for it was the long horseback or buggy rides that consumed much time and robbed a doctor of sleep.

Dr. Gilchrist said that he sometimes was so worn out for as to be compelled to get out of the saddle and walk to avoid falling off the horse. At one time he was so exhausted with illness and weariness that he fell by the wayside and for some time lay on the frozen ground. From this exposure he was threatened with pneumonia, and thought perhaps his time had come, but constitutional vigor brought him through, with but little loss of time in his practice.[14]

Dr. Gilchrist was such a devoted physician, he even asked his bride to delay their wedding for an hour while he took care of his duties and made a house call. Waterville maintained his services for about ten years when he moved his practice to Wenatchee, where he erected a home on the corner of Miller and Washington streets, and later, in 1908, built and maintained a hospital for several years. His serving and useful life would be cut short in 1924 when he succumbed to pneumonia after having undergone an appendectomy. The communities of Waterville and Wenatchee suffered a great loss upon his death.

* * *

The first state elections the next fall of '89 would decide on a state constitution and the location of the state capital, select senators, and elect county clerks and a superior judge. Douglas County cast 619 votes and would increase by another 400 by 1892. The county was rapidly being settled, as its voters were increasing at a steady rate of about 100 per year. Democratic and Republican county conventions were held every two years, nominating competitive members of the community anxious to have a voice in the politics of the area. A.T. Greene, Rev. Richard Corbaley, E.D. Nash, R.W. Starr, Richard S. Steiner, Joseph M. Snow, J.W. Stephens, Matthew B. Malloy, A.T. Greene, John Banneck, Ole Ruud, and many other upstanding citizens were holding or running for county office, some of whom would win or lose by a very slim margin. Banneck, who had traveled with Ole on the first trip from Broad Ax Springs into the Big Bend, and who owned a neighboring farm, was disappointedly unsuccessful in his bid for County Commissioner in 1888. Banneck soon sold his land, moving on to Seattle.

Local government in Waterville seemed to be in harmony with the settlers in the area. The population had grown to 442, the community was in control of the churches, schools, social events, and there were few problems with lawbreakers. What they did not have any control of were weather patterns, and many farmers found themselves unprepared for unexpected harsh winters, even summertime annoyances.

Poor yields resulted from the harvest of 1889 due to the area's being overrun with squirrels, which occasionally destroyed whole fields, in both Lincoln and Douglas Counties. It was such a problem that finally Douglas county provided strychnine free of charge to the ranchers who wished to poison the pests. Adding to this, heavy rains came, followed by an excessive hot spell that burned the grain, ruining the head. This loss affected the businesses of the county as well. But the winter to follow would be catastrophic, one to be remembered and talked about for generations.

That winter there was an early snowfall amounting to three to four feet, which stayed on the ground until late spring, taking both Lincoln and Douglas Counties by surprise. After arriving in the Big Bend Ole had found the winters quite mild, at least for the first few years. But this atypical winter caught many farmers off guard as their stock perished, fruit trees were lost, and mail delivery was blocked from east and west. The surrounding area had considerable losses, mainly in terms of domestic animals. Most of the settlers who owned horses and cows lacked hay due to the ruined crops of the last harvest. Surely they were hoping for a mild winter, or at least an early Chinook to expose areas of grazing. But it didn't happen and suffering ensued. Notes written by an elderly local historian, Nell Dicksen, daughter of Sheriff Sam E. Robins, described the Coulee City area, about 20 miles east of Waterville: "It was especially hit with heavy loss that winter because some settlers left their animals to fend for themselves. Some lost their entire herd of cattle," she wrote. "When spring finally arrived, carcasses were seen sprawled over the pastures in massive numbers." Pioneers talked of the "heaps" of carcasses five and six deep. As the animals died, other starving ones climbed on top to escape the deepening snow. They ate the hair off the dead ones, so that the corpses were almost bare. With four feet of snow on the ground for 180 days, lasting until the first of May, 90% of the animals perished.

On Rudsødegaarden, the barn was constructed adjacent to the house as protective shelter and fodder were imperative in animal care. Ole was adamant in keeping his stock as well fed and secure in America as he had in Norway, where heavy snowfall was commonplace. He worked throughout each summer and fall preparing for the winters, steadily gathering wood to warm the cabin, and storing hay and grain to adequately support the cattle and horses in the deepest of winters. Just two cows in his herd died, but many of the 60 fruit trees he had planted were lost. By 1892, his convictions of responsibility to the animals proved rewarding as he had profited financially, mainly from the sales of his cattle and butchered meat.

Around that time he was feeling more affluent. He was corresponding with a business acquaintance, discussing real estate investments west of the Cascade Mountains on the coast of Washington State. On the 19th of March of that same spring, he received a letter from Lars Johnsen, a land investor, who, like many others, obviously did not comprehend the potential or foresee the future of the Seattle and coastal areas.

"Good friend O. Ruud:

Speculating in real estate any more is too late, I believe. The land around here sells at $100.00 per acre, and most of it was taken 8-10 years ago. Lots in Everett are now so expensive that I believe it is too late. I am quite sure the prices there are the same as in Anacortes and Fairhaven, which were big towns but now deserted. [Fairhaven is now known as Old Bellingham, or the Fairhaven District in Bellingham. It went bust after losing a rail terminus to Seattle in 1892.]

A town like that 'booms' just so long and then it is over. It is a good guess that Everett will boom for about a half a year, so if you have ownership of property in such a town, it is important to sell at the right time. If one could get hold of something cheap in the beginning, when a town like that is about to boom, one could make good money by selling at the right time. But once a town has reached its high point, there is probably nothing to gain.

Everett is located on a tongue of land. The sound is on one side and the Snohomish River on the other side so that the town itself is about a mile wide and the entire tongue has been plotted in lots, but the major part of the town is on the river side so I imagine the cheapest lots are on the seaside, but it is very shallow there so that when it is ebb tide, a big boat cannot come in unless the pier is very long. Similarly, down by the estuary of the river a big boat cannot come in when the water is ebbing. If I decide to stop in Everett, I'll try to find something to buy or make you acquainted with the real estate business there. If you write to me, you ought to send letters to Burlington; then they will send them to me wherever I go. And so, I'll conclude with a friendly greeting from me, Lars Johnsen, Burlington, Skagit Co. Washington."

Chapter II

Still reigns the ancient order—to sow, and reap, and spin;
But oh, the spur of the doing! And oh, the goals to win,
Where each, from the least to the greatest,
    must bravely bear his part—
Make straight the furrows, or shape the laws, or dare the crowded
mart!
And he who lays firm the foundations, though strong right arm may
tire,
Is worthy as he who curves the arch and dreams
    the airy spire;
For both have reared the minster that shrines
    the sacred fire.*

*2nd verse from *The Glory of Toil*
by Edna Dean Proctor

A Firm Foundation

Whether or not Ole invested in any land on the Washington coast is not known. He was, at that time, focusing on his financial and personal future. Now that his cabin was built, his land ownership established, his citizenship secured, and his capital increasing, Ole decided it was time to find a wife who could give him sons and daughters, as the continuance of his lineage was vital to him. He placed an ad in the "Lonely Hearts" section of a Scandinavian paper in Chicago, Illinois, searching for an appropriate bride. This was not an uncommon practice in the male dominated West. Many of these ads would carry definite specifications, such as ethnicity and age. Ole, at the age of 45, had been in America for thirteen years.

Extensive research was unavailing for his specific ad. However, it was no doubt short and to the point, similar to others being placed in Eastern papers in 1892 by single or widowed men needing a woman's companionship. It could have easily read:

A Norwegian gentleman, without children, age 45, with farm and livestock/equipment worth $5,000, wishes to correspond with a Scandinavian lady or widow without children, between 25 and 35 years old, in good health, with respectable reputation and sufficient fortune. Send picture and letter to O. Ruud, Waterville, Douglas County, Washington.

Several hopeful females who wanted to move out west answered his ad. But the name and picture that caught his attention were those of Christina Augusta Larsdatter Larson, a 5'2" twenty-eight-year-old who had immigrated to the United States from Sweden with her older brother, Sven Adolph, on April 15th, 1883, nine years earlier. In the immigration procedures an error was made in the spelling of Augusta's last name and it was written Lawson, so she signed it that way for legal reasons, but her father was Lars Magnes Jensen, which gave his sons the last name of Larson (son of Lars) and his daughters received the name Larsdatter (daughter of Lars). In coming to America many immigrants, as Augusta did, Americanized their last names.

Augusta's original plan was to accompany the twenty-one-year-old Sven across the ocean, visit her half-sister Karolina Anderson and half-brother Rheinholt Larson in Lakewood, New York, and perhaps travel on to Illinois by train to visit another half-brother, Carl Johan, before returning to her home in Lind Brufal, Kalmar County, Sweden. Sven contacted typhoid fever within the first year in Brooklyn and subsequently died. Augusta had been so violently seasick on the ship coming across the Atlantic that she adamantly refused to submit herself to suffering from such weakness again. Besides, she didn't want to leave Sven buried all by himself in a strange and lonely country, so she decided to stay. Augusta remained in Lakewood with Lina for a few years, worked for a time as a domestic in Jamestown, and eventually moved on to Chicago.

On the farm Brofald in the parish of Frodinge of Kalmar County, Sweden, Augusta was born to Lars Magnus Jensen and Inga Sara Eriksdatter on September 9, 1864. The family, which would grow to include three daughters and two sons, was barely able to make ends meet on their minimal income. Being devout Lutherans, the men would gather in a group next to the field after broadcasting the grain each spring to ask God's blessing for a fruitful crop. Each of them removed his hat and bowed his head for quiet prayer. One uncle always brought his tall silk hat because he knew such an occasion deserved the highest solemnity and the deepest respect. But God did not always answer their prayers and the family struggled to keep sufficient bread on the table.

The girls did domestic work for neighbors, and Inga taught her daughters dressmaking skills. As a child of seven or eight years, Augusta had become so adept with a needle that her mother assigned her all the mending for the family. Her mother pinned the patch in place and Augusta hand sewed it on. Later, her mother taught her the more detailed ways of making patterns, hats and dresses. When she was just twelve years old, her parents talked about sending her to Wimmerby, a sewing school, for six months, but Augusta didn't want to be away from her home for such a long time and also felt it would be too much of a financial burden on the family. After completing her education in the common school, she continued working as a seamstress, making clothes for her siblings, Sven, Ida, Hilda, and Johan Gottfried. But always, tucked away in the corner of her dreams, was a hope that one day a chance to visit her half-sisters in America would come her way.

The Scandinavian steamship lines had subagents in America, as well as across the Atlantic, promoting visitor travel. Advertisements showed up in newspapers as well as on posters. Prepaid tickets from a previously emigrated relative or acquaintance could be purchased and sent to family or friends who had little means of their own. The emigration from Sweden, Norway and Denmark grew substantially during the 1880s as many received this gift of opportunity.

Augusta took advantage of her skills as a seamstress when she was living with Lina by working in a dressmaking shop. Upon moving to Illinois, she found employment as a domestic, which was considered a respectable job for an immigrant girl, especially if her employer was of the upper class. She was working in that capacity, while living in Evanston in 1892, when she read the "Lonely Hearts" column from the state of Washington in the Pacific Northwest. Not wanting to continue her life as a servant girl, she answered the ad in hopes of bettering her future.

On October 17, 1892, in a registered letter, Ole sent Augusta enough money to pay her fare west to the Big Bend country. She took the train from

Chicago to Spokane and on to Coulee City, Washington, where the railroad line ended. Augusta continued her journey riding in the horse-drawn stagecoach on a ten-hour trip through the steep coulee and over the grassy plains to Waterville. The story was passed down that Augusta spent "a proper period of time" working in a restaurant and as a maid for the Ben Spears family for six months before she and Ole decided a union between them would be satisfactory. However, the wedding took place in the local Lutheran church on November 24th, just five weeks after the train fare was sent to Chicago.

Building from a firm base consisting of purpose and duty, the couple was well aware of the requirements of their individual roles and took on their tasks without question. Ole, who had been born on December 24, 1847, and Augusta, who had been born on September 9, 1864, had a difference in their age of 16 years, 9 months, and 16 days.

Nine months later, on August 12th, 1893, Augusta gave birth in the rustic cabin to Agnes Inga Johanne. In seventeen months, on January 15, 1895, another daughter, Signe Kristiana Jane, would be born, followed eighteen months later by still another daughter, Synneva Augusta Olava, on September 20, 1896. Carl Oliver was born on April 4, 1899. He was followed by Albert Martin on November 29, 1900, Gustav Adolph on September 17, 1902, Lewis Andreas on May 10, 1905, and Otto Fredrick on October 30, 1907. With the assistance of a neighbor midwife, Augusta would give birth to eight healthy Scandinavian babies over fourteen years.

The couple was grateful for the hardiness of their offspring. They vowed to raise all of their children with a sense of spirituality and devotion to the teachings of the Lutheran Church. Oliver, the eldest son, would later reflect upon his father's religious beliefs. "He believed that through the Trinity, all people were given the gifts of love, hope, and kindness. He did not believe, however, that God's people should walk in the fear of the Lord or dwell on any aspects of religion which would frighten his young family. To honor God, one simply needed to have faith in His Word, and live a life of high morality and honesty." The comfort of this philosophy would be absorbed by each of the children and passed on to future generations.

Following the tendency of the majority of immigrants, the language of the native country was slowly left behind. Once the children started school, English was practiced continually and spoken almost solely in the home. However, one routine was always adhered to at the end of each day as the family gathered around the dinner table. Prior to the evening meal, Ole would recite the same prayer of thanks he had learned at his table in Norway.

I Jesu Navn Går Vi Til Bords
In Jesus' name to the table we go

Å Spise Og Drikke På Ditt Ord
To eat and drink according to his word.

Deg Gud Til Ære, Oss Til Gavn
To God the honor, us the gain,

Så Får Vi Mat I Jesu Navn.
So we have food in Jesus' name.

As the blond, blue-eyed children matured, they were given responsibilities to assist and protect each other. Chores were assigned to each child within his or her capabilities and gender, the younger ones churning butter by the age of three. Each of the girls was taught by Augusta to cook, sew, spin, wash, clean, and take care of their men. Although their marks in school were better than average, the girls learned that becoming efficient in the roles directed to them as women would not only ease their mother's burdens with the work in and around the house, but would be essential if they were ever going to grow up and become wives themselves. It was their duty with unwavering commitment and they knew it; yet it seemed to them that there was an unending task of watching over the little brothers and keeping their diapers washed and clean. By the age of nine or ten, Agnes knew that another new baby would probably be coming along soon and Augusta would later relate to her daughters that, as the scriptures dictated, the bed was also a duty for all married women, and reluctant or not, it was a duty with which they must comply if they wanted to keep their men uncomplaining.

As the seasonal vegetables matured, the girls harvested the produce, keeping the root cellar filled with potatoes, cabbage, turnips, carrots, and onions in preparation for each coming winter. Working alongside Augusta, they hot-packed the perishable vegetables, applesauce, plums, and cherries into quart jars, all grown in the garden area southwest of the house. The sealing of the jars with the boiling-hot rubberized ring was essential, for nearly everyone had heard horror stories of the consequences of eating spoiled food. Augusta hesitated one evening as she prepared to heat a jar of canned vegetables in the saucepan. The food looked almost the same as the other jars, perhaps a bit darker. It had no odor of spoilage, but she knew the seal had released without the usual tug on the lip of the ring. She remembered the rim of the jar having a rough edge where a chip of glass was missing, possibly preventing a solid seal. Always frugal, she debated whether to feed it to the dog or continue to heat it for the children. As she scraped it into the dish on the back step, the dog lapped at it hungrily. The next morning he was dead.

Laundry was a tiring, thankless chore, "women's work," with which men rarely helped, but Augusta accepted this and did her duty. Three miles west of her cabin the Corbaley family relied on Nellie, one of the few wives with a young man in the house, who occasionally volunteered his services at the tubs. In his diary, twenty-three-year-old Alvaro wrote, "Since we are having a snowstorm from the east, at 10 a.m. I went to work at the washtub. Nellie, Platt's wife, had about half the white clothes rubbed through the 1st water when I took her place. I finished rubbing out the white clothes, and after they were boiled took them through the rinse and bluing waters. Then I rubbed the flannels and calicoes through the 1st waters, turned the flannels and took them through the second suds and rinsed the calicoes. I have had considerable experience in washing clothes since coming up here as I did most of the washing last summer. If anybody wishes to acquire this magnificent and profitable art, please address me for further particulars, or call next washday and I will let you do the whole washing for one lesson as cheap as though you did but half of it! Finished the washing at 2 p.m."[15]

Daily, at the Ruud cabin, the girls carried water-filled buckets pumped from the nearby well to keep the washbasin full, carried water to keep the drinking pitcher filled, and carried water once a week to heat over the wood burning stove for Monday washday. They did their scrubbing with homemade lye soap, followed by scrubbings in two rinse tubs, before hand-wringing the dripping laundry, draping it over an outside rope line. Summer or winter, it was hung on the same clothesline to sun or freeze-dry. The wooden rack hanging from the ceiling near the cooking stove in the kitchen held items more immediately needed, and regardless of the season, the girls, unobserved, tucked any laundered under-clothing, or strips of rags used during their menstrual cycles, inside the pillowcases, hidden from the eyes of the men, keeping intimate details of womanhood in obscurity.

By boiling a combination of lard and lye in a deep pot until it bubbled, the pioneer women had a proportionate recipe for making their soap. It was stirred cautiously with a long paddle-shaped stick until it came to a full rolling boil. Augusta kept the small children away as she had learned from personal experience that the boiling liquid could explode, giving blistering, miserable burns. The soap was carefully poured into a wooden box with a depth of about three inches, then left to cool until the block firmed up and could be cut into bars. When washday was upon them, the women would shave the soap bar into the hot water to eliminate clumping before adding the heavily soiled laundry. Then began the tedious washboard scrubbing. Up and down with sweaty brows, up and down with chafed hands, up and down with perhaps occasional bewailing, as the drudgery seemed never-ending; but it wasn't negotiable. They did their jobs simply because they had to be done.

It was not that the girls didn't have any playtime. On many sunny spring or summer days they would walk upon the mountain gathering serviceberries for making pie or jam, picking wildflowers for the dining room table or just walking for the pleasure of being on the mountain with their father. But in the role of being girls, each learned early from their mother how to sew an apron, a petticoat, or a pair of bloomers from the flower-printed calico cloth of emptied flour sacks. Finer dress material could be purchased from the Wenatchee Mercantile Company for 9 cents a yard, muslin for 8 cents, and flannel for 10 cents. Once adept with scissors and a needle, they moved on to more complex projects, becoming skilled at adjusting their basic bodice pattern to fit one another. Once the darts and waist lengths were fitted, the creation of any style of sleeve, neckline, or skirt would be easily designed and assembled on the treadle machine. Tenaciously, they tore any material scraps into two-inch strips, sewing them end-to-end. By adding a carpet cord, they braided the strips, and hand-sewed them together, usually in a circle, making a durable rug. Once a year, generally in the springtime, these carpets were taken outdoors, draped over the fence and beaten as well as swept with a broom to rid them of the dust accumulated during the fall and winter.

The girls worked alongside their mother mashing peeled boiled potatoes, mixing them with butter, cream, flour and a sprinkle of salt, making lefse, a favorite family treat. They would knead the mixture until it was the perfect texture ready to be rolled thin with the rolling pin. Then it was lightly browned in the frying pan. Coating it with a generous amount of butter, they knew this favorite Scandinavian food would be quickly devoured and their men would be pleased. Agnes had confidence that her lefse could make tongues melt and added the recipe to the collection of favorites entered in the annual Potato Fair held in town.

Life for the girls and Augusta was like that of most pioneer women. William S. Lewis, corresponding secretary of the Eastern Washington State Historical Society and treasurer of the Spokane County Pioneer Society, described it well in an address at Lincoln and Adams counties' pioneer associations' picnic at Crab Creek on June 17, 1919.

"It has been remarked that the pioneer women endured greater trials than the pioneer men, for they not only had to put up with all the hardships that the men put up with, but they also had to put up with the pioneer man.

"Life was often a desperate struggle for a bare existence. In this, the man had the easier part in that he was engaged in the active struggle while the woman kept the home fires burning and passed her days in the lonesome monotony of household drudgery. Every woman then did her housework as a matter of necessity. If necessity demanded, as it often did, she could also do her husband's or her brother's work. These women were true helpmates and companions of their husbands. They had no so-called modern conveniences. Even water was often a luxury—laboriously hauled from a great distance and carefully conserved. The nearest neighbor was often miles distant.

"None of these pioneer women had an opportunity to indulge in high-heeled shoes—often they had no shoes—or in fancy corsets and French lingerie. A few plain garments constituted their whole wardrobe. They rarely had the assistance of a 'sewing woman,' or of a sewing machine, and few of them ever had a ready-made dress, or as much as one hundred dollars in cash at any one time.

"They grew tanned, lined of face, faded and weatherworn—wrinkled and bent with hardships and service to their families. They mostly lost all the superficial beauty of face and feature, and grace of movement, and had no means, time or opportunity to devote attention to dress and the little luxuries and refinements of personal care and toilet, which women crave. None of them ever had a hairdresser, or a facial massage. They became hard and calloused-handed, but they had clear eyes and warm hearts.

"They raised babies that were often rocked to sleep in a dry-goods box or in homemade cradles hollowed out of a log. These pioneer women raised good babies—babies which, when they grew to manhood, have taken the lead in our country in all lines—business, professions, war, and in politics.

"This type of early pioneer womanhood—sturdy, capable, self-reliant and unselfish, is entitled to all the honor and reverence we can bestow upon them and their memory.

"But if her lot was hard, the children never knew it. She taught them that indolence and inefficiency were a disgrace, and if they ever expected to have anything or be anybody they must work for it, as nobody ever succeeded who wasted his time. The idea of looking to the government for support, or to luck for prosperity, had not originated then. Children knew better than to spend their time frivolously, and come down to a dependent old age. Women and men in those pioneer times were of strong fiber and stout hearts. They were not afraid of the appearance of economy, or of simple living. It took hard-muscled men and women of great faith and sincerity to break paths through the wilderness that was the old west."[16]

Ole kept the robust boys busy, teaching them his learned skills in agriculture, his techniques in butchering and smoking meats, and his acute sense of history and earnest beliefs in a fair democratic government. They learned to predict the weather by the "feel" of the air, tell time by observing the placement of the sun, sew sacks of wheat or barley with swift dexterity (winning in any contest in town), excel in bareback horsemanship, repair a harness or wagon, and sense when the soil was right for planting by digging down six inches to test the moisture with their hands. Above all else, Ole taught his sons that if one has honesty himself and for others, rich or poor, that individual will reap the harvest of this good earth. He wanted his boys to grow to be good men and to always give thanks to God for the privilege of life itself.

Although working alongside their parents was the central focus, time was spared for making a few toys. Ole made each of the boys a pair of stilts from long sticks of unused lumber, which proved difficult in plodding over the rocks and uneven ruts in the road. Together, in the springtime, they followed the creek up the canyon, and cut sap-filled green willow branches to carve fluted whistles. "Whistle making was easy if you had a sharp jackknife," Oliver remembered. "Just need to cut the branch in a few places; the length, then the angled top where your mouth will go, next the circular line to mark the base, then make a notch through the bark at the top for the air to pass, and cut a few eyes on the stem if you want to change the tone. Then start tapping it ever so lightly against a hard surface to loosen the bark from the branch stick. It will slip right off. Then chisel out one side of the stem, rewet it with a little of your own saliva, slip the green-barked jacket back on, and blow a nice little tune. The smaller the willow branch, the higher the tone." In the house, the girls created rag dolls from darned socks (worn through multiple mendings), made simple toys to entertain the younger children by threading large buttons with string, twisting it around until it wound tightly, then pulling in an accordion fashion until the button whirred and sang, giving it a feeling of elasticity.

As each child matured, Ole's quiet, methodical and peaceful manner, along with his strength and dedication to hard work, would be reflected in the child's development. In later years, Oliver would recall his father's way of discipline at the dinner table for any unruly behavior. "He would simply stop eating his own meal," Oliver would remember. "He then would gently start tapping the end of his fork against his own dinner plate and we all knew it was quiet time. Each of us held our father in high regard and he, unfailingly, treated us with equal respect. Never once can I remember his striking a child or even raising his voice. When my father asked us to do a job or change a behavior, it was done."

Augusta Larson before her marriage to Ole Ruud

REGISTRY RECEIPT.

Post Office at *Bridgeport Wash*

Registered Letter Parcel No. *14* Rec'd *Oct 17*, 189*2*

of *O Rund*

addressed to *Miss Augusta Larson*
Chicago Ill

Boyd Teter, P. M.

Registry Receipt of letter to Augusta Larson containing fare to Waterville, Washington. 1892

Before America
Standing: Sven, Augusta, Hilda
Front Row: Lars Jensen, Gottfried, Inga, Ida

Augusta Larson Ruud
Wedding day
November 24, 1892

Ole Ruud
Wedding day
November 24, 1892

Courtesy of Douglas County Museum

**Main street in Waterville, Washington
1892**

**1899
Left to Right: Ole, hired man, Agnes, Signe, Synneva,
Augusta holding Oliver
Stakes indicate newly planted trees**

* * *

The same year he married Augusta, Ole decided to fence his land using barbed wire. Lacking adequate cash, he made a trip into town to visit the local banker and arranged to borrow $100 to buy the supplies. The next year began the Panic of '93. When Ole was unable to sell his crop to pay off his loan, the banker started foreclosure on the farm. By cutting firewood from the mountain and selling it to the townspeople, Ole acquired enough money and saved his farm, but from that time on, he mistrusted all bankers.

Times were tough. All of the settlers who came to farm on the plains spanning out from Badger Mountain were struggling financially and helping each other out as their time and energy would allow. Ole, who welcomed any opportunity to read newspapers that carried agricultural information from other parts of the country, decided to share his view of hard times with the editor of the *Corner Stone* newspaper in Lansing, Michigan. Only an extract of his 1894 letter was published:

Times are so hard and money so scarce here in this good wheat country, "the Big Bend of the Columbia" that property can hardly be sold for money. A band of horses was sold the other day at sheriff's sale for one dollar a head, and if times don't change, more sheriff's sales will be made at the same rate. Our local wheat buyers advertise that they give 30 cents a bushel for No. 1 wheat delivered at the steamboat landing. When we subtract from this the sacking; five cents, threshing; six cents, and harvesting; six cents, we farmers will only have thirteen cents left for seed, plowing, harrowing, sowing, hauling to market and all the heavy lifting. Interest on money, which everyone must pay as all are in debt, is two to three percent a month. Taxes are 35 mills to a dollar.

It takes two bushel of wheat to pay the interest on $1.00; twenty bushels or two-thirds of a ton to buy a pair of poor shoes, two bushels for a meal at a hotel. (one gunny sack filled with wheat equals approximately 2 bushels.) *Our local gristmill gives from sixteen to twenty-four pounds of flour for a bushel of wheat in exchange, and asks twelve dollars a ton for bran when they will give only nine to ten dollars per ton for the best wheat. Farms and other real estate are passing over to the money loaners. I expect to hear of many foreclosures before the year of 1894 is out.[17] O. Ruud*

Joseph Q. Tuttle, publisher of the Big Bend Empire county paper, received a copy of the *Corner Stone* newspaper. Functioning as an outspoken editor who exercised his privilege of freedom of the press with a sarcastic pen, Tuttle did not seem to care if the local farmers, fellow businessmen, or politicians agreed with him. He somehow remained as the publisher of the paper for approximately twenty-five years, even though he could nearly crucify a member of the community with an editorial. In one article, Tuttle, with both disagreement and dislike of a candidate, decided to take on R.W. Starr, an ambitious and hopeful politician from the local community who was running for office. Before he zapped him, Tuttle quoted an article from the *Spokane Chronicle*. "R.W. Starr, the democratic war-horse of Waterville and candidate for Attorney General, arrived in Spokane last evening. Mr. Starr says the Democracy is in the best of condition and predicts a clean sweep at the next election. Mr. Starr leads the democratic procession in Douglas County and was looking over the slate, checking up for future fights. He left late last night for Sprague to attend to legal matters."[18]

Tuttle couldn't resist printing his comments. "If the *Chronicle* will send a representative out here we will convince them in 30 minutes with Prominent Democrats that Starr is only a broken down Texas mule. He only "assumes", when visiting, to be a War Horse. Gentlemen, you are mistaken. Mr. Starr only imagines that he is a leader when away from home. John J. Graves and Andrew Jackson Davis are the only two Democrats in Douglas Country that are halter broke enough to be led by Starr."[19]

The fact that Tuttle had in his hand a copy of the letter Ole had written to the *Corner Stone* newspaper must have brought him concern, and with good reason, as the letter brought a quick response from Mr. Tuttle. He was outraged and printed the results of his sharp tongue in his next editorial. "When we hear a man decrying his own country and proclaiming its drawbacks, it may generally be set down that he lacks energy or foresight. That he argues from a standpoint of his own inefficiency to succeed. But when a man has prospered beyond a point that he knew in the east, (just because he feels the pinch of hard times that is now affecting the whole world,) deliberately writes for publication in Eastern papers, articles calculated to place the country in which he has made his accumulation before the people in a bad light, we think he is open to the charge of ingratitude and malevolence.

"As to the writer of the above article; he removed from the home of his childhood across the waters, and came to this land of the free to take advantage of our liberal laws, to acquire for himself a competence which it was impossible for him to do in his native land; and some years ago he came to this western country without capital. He secured for himself a homestead of 160 acres of land some four miles from Waterville, which he now values at $5,000. He has also acquired valuable property in the town of Waterville and not yet being satisfied with his possessions, has taken a half section of land on the Columbia River bottom under the Desert Land Act.

"The good people of the county made him county surveyor, and he did so well out of the office in those early days of the country that he was able to hold the products of this farm until he found some poor neighbor who was obliged to buy, then he, Ruud, would sell at an exorbitant price. He was not weeping for the poor farmer at that time. His milk of human kindness had so nearly dried up that he was glad to sell hay for $30 per ton and oats for three cents per pound, or ninety-six cents per bushel. Ye Gods! What a subject to cry extortion!

"But times have changed. Mr. Ruud is not County Surveyor anymore. (He lost his bid for reelection that year, but regained it in 1896.es.*)* He has to work for a living and this hopeful county has produced so bountifully that his neighbors now have plenty of hay and grain for stock, and plenty for themselves to eat, which fact he appears to look at with dismay, for to be sure, it cuts off his market for hay at $30 per ton and oats for 96 cents per bushel.

"And now this ex-official and prosperous farmer attempts to injure the county that has given him his prosperity, by publishing to the world an article that is false in many and misleading in all particulars.

"Our local money loaners have not foreclosed a single mortgage in the last twelve months. Land is not 'passing over to the hands of money loaners.' Diligent search has failed to find a band of horses that sold at the figure he claims.

"People out here have stood by each other with the determination to weather the hard times, and are coming through with flying colors. Mr. Ruud's article is nothing more or less than a libel on this county, which is one of the most prosperous and promising sections in the west. He is only one among many who have prospered by settling in Douglas County."[20]

Perhaps Tuttle had a point assuming it would discourage new settlers or businessmen, contemplating life in the Big Bend, to read of the hardship of the farmers. And it was a fact that Ole had staked out his claim for 160 acres with little capital remaining after buying supplies, and had gained in worth since his arrival ten years previously by adding cattle, a few horses, and additional property to his ownership. But the panic of '93 affected the whole nation, resulting in the collapse of the stock market and the failure of many banks and businesses, causing the farmers to sell crops at low market prices. Possibly, when Tuttle wrote of the "many who have prospered by settling in Douglas County," he was referring to the active lumber business on Badger Mountain.

During the late 1880s, five sawmills within a five-mile radius were doing profitable, competitive business, quickly depleting the dense timber. Major Nash and J.W. Stephens had the first mill set up as early as 1883, hired a crew, and used up to five separate teams of horses. Early settlers who worked on the mountain often supplied their own teams and sleds as they cut, loaded, and hauled logs to the mill. They ground their axes, further sharpening them with a whetstone, filed the saws, and used a sledgehammer and a wedge for splitting logs. They shod the horses and kept iron rudders on the sleds, for they could find themselves working in 1½ feet of snow at temperatures of twenty below zero. The loggers were given free board at the camp, and many took lumber as their pay, enabling them to build a small house, which explains why many more shacks were seen than log cabins. It was hazardous labor from daylight to dark, often resulting in injury to the horses and the breakdown of the sleds, not to mention personal injury such as frostbite, a gash from an ax, or broken bones from a misdirected fallen tree. Competition was intense, resulting in flaring tempers as the brawny loggers aggressively notched claim to any tree fit for lumber, hurrying to cut down as many as possible before the Chinooks came and thawed the snow to slush, bogging down the sleds and muddying up the trails.

Twenty-three-year-old Alvaro Corbaley, who worked with his father and his brother Platt, wrote in his diary of January, 1885, "It is now mid-winter and the snow is about 17 inches deep upon the level. I arose at 4:50 this morning, built fires, and Platt and I did chores before breakfast after which, we hitched up to the log sled, and taking the saw and ax with us, started up to the mountain to cut and haul in logs. I was up to where I had been making rails to get the ax, sledge, and wedges. Wilson and Hetley are making quite a stir because the boys are cutting logs upon land which they have notices on and are trying to hold as homesteads, while at the same time, they are cutting and hauling logs to their mill from the same land. They threatened to have some of the boys arrested if they did not quit, but nobody pays any attention to them. I cut a tree which fell across our logging road. When I went to work on it again after dinner I found Tibbets, who is cutting for Hetley and Wilson, cutting notches in all the good saw trees. The tree, which I cut, was one they had notched. In the evening he came by where I was at work. He asked me if I didn't see that the tree I had cut was notched? I said yes, and that it looked as though he was trying to corral all the good trees fit for lumber by cutting notches into them and he said that an officer would be along in a few days to stop all those who were cutting logs upon the land claimed by Wilson, and that I might just as well take the logs which were cut as to cut the trees which he had notched, and if I was going to cut the trees anyhow, then it would be no use for him to notch any more trees. I told him I would pay no attention to his notches. The very next day Wilson and Hetley began cutting logs in the same gulch from which we have been logging. I went up the gulch a short distance above where I had been working that morning and began chopping upon one of the trees, which Tibbets had notched the day before. He was but a short distance behind me when I commenced chopping and he came up to the tree saying that very tree belonged to him. I kept on chopping telling him that we would see about it. He caved around a little and said that he would wait till Hetley came along, which he did in a few minutes. Tibbets told him that I was chopping one of the trees, which he had notched the day before. Hetley got mad and asked me what I meant. I asked him what he meant and told him that I had started to cut the tree down and Tibbets had come up and claimed it. Just then, Norman Titchenal called out to me to stay with it. Hetley told Tibbets to come on and told me that we would let the government settle it. I said that that would suit me exactly, and they went up the gulch a short distance where there were two large trees about 20 feet apart, both of which Tibbets had notched the day before, and started to cut one of them. In a short time Norman Titchenal came up the gulch looking for a tree to cut. He passed me and went to the tree near which Hetley and Tibbets were working and was getting ready to chop it down when Hetley told him that if he struck his ax into the tree he would split his head open with *his* ax! Titchenal told him that he had a very good ax himself and started to cut down the tree. Hetley swore around for a while and called Norman all kinds of names, as did also Tibbets. After a while Hetley said that he would go down the gulch and get Wilson. After a while Wilson came up, stood around and then talked to Norman for a while. He said he would make it warm for him if he cut any more notched trees, but Norman gave him but little satisfaction. Wilson even complained to Platt about how badly he was treated by us. They (Hetley and Wilson) are disliked very much here and if they don't go slower may get themselves in trouble. We hauled 7556 feet of logs last week, and the Titchenal boys have hauled over 100,000 ft of logs."[21]

While the heavily timbered land, thick with Ponderosa Pine, was being depleted of its resources in Douglas County, the population and need for houses and businesses grew steadily. Ole and C.A. Harris owned the mill in Sec. 17, T.24 N., R.22 E., W.M., and sold lumber to build the first schoolhouse and the first court house in Waterville. It was during that time that Ole became involved in other construction. From the mill on Badger Mountain located at 3800 ft. elevation, he hauled lumber by wagon down the steep and treacherous grade of the Corbaley Canyon Road to the 740 ft. elevation location where a hired builder was starting construction on the first hotel in Orondo.

The actual site of the original structure was 475 feet from the east bank of the Columbia River and is now covered by the Rocky Reach Dam pool. The building was put up on a site at the present Pioneer Road about one mile north of Orondo and would be in operation for about thirty years. After a destructive fire took its toll, the building was torn down in 1923. The salvageable lumber was used for other building purposes in the area.

There was a real need for a stopping place at the little riverside settlement. Stages met all boats and several trips a day were made between Orondo and Waterville. It was the gateway to the county seat and the Big Bend wheat country. The Pioneer sternwheeler *City of Ellensburg* stopped there and later the *Columbia and Okanogan Steamboat Co.* vessels made it a regular point of call. John H.D. Smith, a retired Orondo postmaster and lifelong resident of the area, said that the hotel was put up on two lots forming a space 50 ft. by 87 ft. The building itself, he believed, was about 24 ft. by 40 ft. The hotel later got additions, a kitchen on the east and a post office room on the south. Smith said the first school at Orondo was taught in the hotel by Miss Cora Brown and pupils Mary, Kate and Roy Spinner, and Bill, Sam and Dave Vaughn attended. The hotel was also the site of community dances. Smith, whose father, J.B. Smith, laid out the town site, recalls being at one of these in the early 1900s. The family lived only about 200 feet from the hotel.[22]

The original materials bill indicates that the total price for 15,460 board feet of Badger Mountain lumber, which also included the door and window frames plus shingles for the whole roof, was $318.97.

The framing material included:

19 pair of windows @ $2.00		$38.00
13 doors @ $1.70		$22.10
13 pair of hinges @ .25c		$3.25
13 locks @ .50c	$6.50	
3 kegs of nails @ $4.00		$12.00
Total material cost for the building		$400.82

The cost of labor was not indicated; however, Ole was paying his hired men on the farm $1.25 per day, according to his record book.

Ole sold out his share of the sawmill to C.A. Harris at a precise time. By 1891, the government officials were expressing serious concern, trying to suppress the cutting of timber on government land. In September an official arrived in town specifically to issue an arrest on Mr. Harris. The Big Bend Empire wrote of the prosecution of "Harris, the Badger Mountain Sawmill Man: The Ellensburg stage arriving Tuesday evening brought among its passengers a Mr. C.E. Bayard of Seattle. Wednesday he made an appearance at C.A. Harris's sawmill on Badger Mountain and made known the object of his visit to Waterville. He was a special land agent of the United States government and had a direct commission from Washington, D.C. to investigate and act upon complaints against Mr. Harris made to the Interior Department. The mill was not ordered closed down. United States Commissioner, Pendergast, fixed Mr. Harris bond at $500, which was promptly furnished with H.N. Wilcox, as security. Mr. R. S. Steiner, and Mr. Wilcox, both of whom had accompanied the agent up the mountain, unwittingly, not knowing his designs on Mr. Harris, were subpoenaed as witnesses and ordered to appear at the same time and place as the defendant. Mr. Bayard took his departure the next day. He is reported as having said that in his report to the government he should appraise them that Nash and Stephens were in the same boat with Harris and equally liable to prosecution. The news quickly spread. Much alarm was manifested at the prospect of the lumber supply being cut short, fears that both mills would be obliged to stop their saws. Many expressed concern that such a calamity could force closure of the land office, entirely stop immigration, paralyzing trade."[23]

Nearly every business and professional man in town attended the meeting at the Matthews & Lockes office. Several speeches were made and resolutions adopted. "It has been learned that prosecutions are about to be instituted against all mill owners operating saw mills on government land in this county......that the cutting of timber and the manufacturing of it into lumber is absolutely necessary for the continued development of Douglas county, that all of this lumber is used for domestic purposes and is applied by settlers in making needed improvements upon their lands........there is no means of transportation from such places where other lumber is manufactured, except at excessive cost to the settler for hauling the same for a distance of sixty to eighty miles and be compelled to pay almost double the price of lumber in this county.......that Badger Mountain lumber is of inferior quality and would have no market value were there any transportation facilities from lumber markets........that it is believed that the complaints entered against the said sawmill men were actuated by selfish motives, that if the Interior Department were informed of the true state of affairs and the needs of the settlers, these, or any prosecutions would never have been instituted......therefore, it is unanimous at this meeting to use all honorable means to secure the dismissal of the prosecutions."[24]

It would be one year before the civil case was dismissed by a U.S. attorney in Spokane, Washington. He also wrote that unless the public good demanded a criminal prosecution, no further action would be taken, summarizing that the trespasses were not for the purpose of shipping timber to other areas for profit, but used to serve the needs of maintaining a pioneer neighborhood. Dallam and Lawrence, Receiver and Register, from the land office in Waterville replied: "We will say that the depredations have been discontinued on Badger Mountain for more than a year. As a matter of fact, as indicated in your letter, these were excused by local necessities.....A dismissal of the criminal cases would be an act of justice and appreciated by the whole community. Please notify us when the cases are dismissed, that parties may be saved the necessity of an expensive trip to attend court."[25]

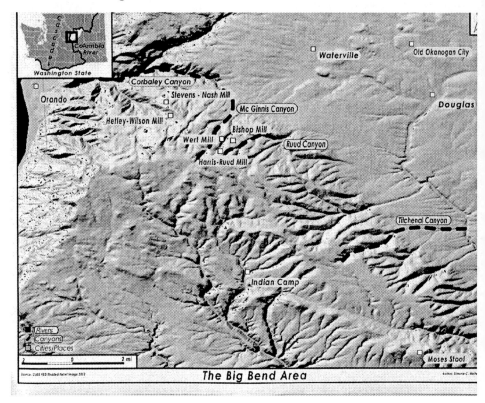

The Big Bend Area

**Badger Mt. in the late 1880s when 5 sawmills
were active within a five-mile radius**

* * *

The Big Bend was widely known as good stock country with open, plentiful grazing land, wide basins, and rolling hills. The majority of the farmers cringed at the mention of sheep, but sheep were driven in from the Crab Creek area in 1886 nevertheless, and they came in a band of thousands, estimated to be 4,000-5,000. The stockmen did not receive the intrusion kindly. They claimed to be able to smell the stinking approach of the blasted, bleating woollies. What irritated them, even more than the odor, was the overgrazing done on the rangeland by the wandering herds. The men decided to take the problem into their own hands. First, a few sheep were found shot dead, but the incidents were ignored by the sheepmen who found the corpses in early dawn. Then a few more were shot in hopes that the sheepmen would back off from grazing their band on the Badger Mountain range. Again, this did not discourage the sheepmen, so a meeting was held in the store at Nashland to decide what to do next. A committee was appointed to address the sheepmen directly; it asked them to immediately remove the band. One can only guess whether diplomacy or caustic sarcasm was used in the face-to-face encounter, but one can safely assume it lacked friendliness. However reluctant they might have been, the sheepmen soon obliged the evictors and drove the flocks from the country. Almost at the same time, the stockmen noticed fires burning along the foothills and at different points on the mountain! Disaster would have ensued had it not been for the quick acts of the settlers, who feverishly fought the blazes until they were all contained, for thousands of tall timbers could have been lost and many properties destroyed. A resolution by the board of county commissioners was written, offering a reward of $300 to anyone apprehending the person or persons responsible for starting the fires. No cash reward was ever collected. Herds of sheep have never since been put to range upon Badger Mountain, perhaps a reward in itself to the stockmen.

It was a relief to Ole and the other settlers to be rid of the sheep, as the cattlemen bragged that any respectable cow wouldn't think of grazing after a ewe had left her stench as she chewed the grass away to mere stubs. Free of the sheep, Ole concentrated on building his stock. *The value of my cattle comes to $420.00, and includes Cows—4, Heifers—5, Steers—8, Bulls—1, Yearlings—4, Two years—6, and Three years—7. Lost during the winter of 1889-1890 was one red old cow bought from a German and one 3 year-old heifer with calf.* By describing each animal in the stock account section of his record book, he kept track of his small herd, which numbered 35 in 1890 and would grow to around 90 by 1914.

Heifer—2 years old. Brand- O. R. left thigh
Under bite in right ear. Color—dark red,
No star—a little white under belly—white bag.
Value $25.

Steer—4 years old. Brand O. R. on left thigh
Under bite in right ear. Color—light red, no white horns—right horn a little drooping.
Value $30.

Heifer—2 years old (bought from R. Hayden in spring '89)
Brand—Hayden's brand and O. R. on left thigh or hip
Color—red, a big white star, a white spot on place of
Dulap, a little white under belly.
Value $20.

When the financial panic set in, steers were selling at two cents a pound and wheat at 18 cents a bushel. During these times, Ole and many of his neighbors tanned leather and made their own shoes. Exactly what process they used is not known; however, in a book from his library, *The Art Of Leather Manufacture* published in London, a revised fourth edition by Alexander Watt, a few pages were highlighted with markings from his pencil.

One of these worn pages instructs the tanner to "immerse the skins into a liquor of salt or alum in the proportion of two ounces to the gallon and combine the whole by stirring well. The skins are handled until they are saturated and the fiber fully swollen. The saline substances may be dissolved in water alone, without any tanning material, and the skins saturated with this liquor, and after complete saturation, they are passed into the tanning bath. The strength of the bath is to be increased from 2 to 4 degrees every day and the skins stirred and handled until they are tanned. The time required for tanning by this process;

Sheep skin---2 or 3 days	Calf skin---8 days
Heavy leather---30 to 40 days	Sole leather---40 to 50 days."

Or when using the Bell's process, "The hides being unhaired and prepared as usual, are to be immersed in tanning liquor from two to four days. The tanning liquor is composed of: Wood ashes—1 bushel and Water—50 gallons. After settling, draw off 40 gallons; to this is added 40 lbs. of terra japonica (vegetable bark), and the whole boiled until the latter is dissolved. When cold, the solution is ready for use. The inventor says that by the combination of the alkaline lye and tannin, he is enabled to prevent the tanning liquors from becoming sour or decomposed, and he is enabled to strengthen them without accumulating more than is necessary, and the skins will tan in a shorter time and with less labour than by other processes."[26]

Information about what method Ole and his neighbors used and when the tanning was actually done was not handed down, but the long process, according to his reference book, is best done in the spring when the bark has four times as much "astringent matter" (tannic acid) as in winter. The most desired barks used on the continent were hemlock, sumac, oak, birch, chestnut, or willow bark.[27]

Making shoes for his wife, his children and himself took weeks, if not months. The scraping of the presoaked skins to remove the hair, the tedious scraping to remove the inner membranes had to be completed before the drying and stretching process was begun. Once he was satisfied with the preliminary procedures, and the drying and stretching were adequate, Ole placed a sheet of leather over a carved wooden model of each foot to cut out the shoe. The final assembling was saved for evenings when outdoor chores were finished or for those stormy days when he postponed work until the skies cleared. The sometimes ill-fitting shoes took weeks of wearing before they brought a feeling of comfort, but the children wore them gladly. At least there were no holes in the soles and sides of the new ones and their knitted socks would remain dry.

By warming a mixture of lard, petroleum and paraffin and rubbing it well into the leather, Ole waterproofed the children's shoes as well as his own worn, resoled boots. During these hard times he went barefoot when plowing the fields, saving his dilapidated work boots for other times when shoes were absolutely necessary. To help out, Augusta made him moccasins out of old overalls. But Ole was not alone in his struggle trying to make ends meet during those tough times. A neighbor, Schillar Robins, observed how the denim moccasins protected Ole, so he requested a pair for his own sore and callused feet. Embarrassed, humbled, and disgusted with his own poverty-stricken situation on his farm, Schillar adamantly instructed Augusta "to make 'em good and make 'em fit."

As they had done each spring since Ole's arrival, a group of Indians came by about the same time each year to their familiar campsite beside the creek at the base of the south side of the mountain or to the summer camp farther up the canyon. They would set up their teepees, gather wood for their cooking fire, and settle in to spend a few weeks gathering the camas root to dry, smoke, or grind down to mix with other food. During one of the days, a couple of Indian women were lingering by the cabin, sitting with their backs against the log wall. Ole asked them, if they had the time, to make a pair of deerskin moccasins for his girls, Agnes and Signe. Within a few days they sauntered to the cabin door presenting their gift of two pair of soft slippers. Shyness, not trepidation, kept the girls from approaching the Indian women to express their gratitude. "But we felt so proud of Papa as we watched him talk with his sign language and softly spoken jargon," Agnes would recall. "Peeking from behind our cabin door and quietly to each other, we whispered 'balokumtux' (very good) as we were indeed deeply grateful for the smooth tan moccasins soothing our callused feet."

Even during these hard times when money was scarce, the population continued to grow. Bills that could not be paid by cash were resolved by barter, or a few days of free labor. G.M. Cumbo, who came to the Big Bend from Ellensburg, settling a couple of miles west of Ole in 1888, took a separate path. Instead of sowing grains or raising cattle, Cumbo would, on a mere forty acres, build a small house and large barn. He then began to cultivate his land, rotating crops of radishes, lettuce, cucumbers, parsnips, potatoes, cabbages, carrots, and corn, storing it in numerous root cellars paralleling each other in the side of the hill. The truck gardener took pride in his place he claimed was free of weeds, "because they cannot get a start if they are taken care of in time," ran an efficient business, and had money in the bank. He would be quoted as saying, "I have always tried to keep all of my land working for me all the time and I have succeeded. What one crop takes out I try to put back by the planting of another that requires different elements, and at the same time furnishes food for the soil, which can be used by a still later crop." In 1913 he would grow between fifteen and eighteen tons of potatoes on seven and a half acres. From two pounds of carrot seed, he grew seven tons of carrots, selling them for winter stock feed, and four thousand cabbages, as sauerkraut had a ready market and stored easily in crocks. Cumbo sold one hundred gallons of currants and loganberries, ground horseradish, selling it in quarts, and grew 20-pound watermelons. Sixteen acres were in wheat hay and a small patch grew alfalfa. Having only two milk cows, four horses, four pigs, and a few chickens, he kept his growing brood well fed and working in the fields, as by 1914, he would have fathered twelve children.

*   *   *

The Alaskan gold rush of 1898 held thousands in a state of excitement, mostly men, but many women as well. These seekers were invading the northern land in droves, many ill-equipped in terms of both materials and experience. As a result, some lost their lives. Hopeful miners with the "gold rush fever" came from the north, south, east, and west with dreams of striking it rich. Some of the men left their families, hoping to return exhibiting pockets brimming with the gold nuggets. Ole felt himself being pulled in both directions, expressing his mixed feelings on January 23rd as he wrote to his family in Norway.

We received Mother's letter today and thank her so much. It is delightful to see that Mother still is able to write this well. She warns me against the trip to Alaska. I, myself, also believe it is best to postpone it, at least until I have served out my office time as county surveyor. I am well acquainted with the dangers associated with such a trip. But it can be carried out without special difficulties by two or three men who are suited for such an undertaking, and are well equipped with food and clothing. It is almost like going on an expedition to the North Pole.

I read in a paper that eight boats were seen drifting down the Yukon in between the floating ice, all of them loaded with food supplies, etc., but without a man in any of them. It was assumed that the party had camped on the shore, fastened their boats to the edge of the ice which had broken off while the men slept in their tents during the night. Fragments of boats can be seen floating down the river past Dawson City. Lots of things probably happen that are never discovered. I can state without reservation that 9/10 of those mishaps are just simply due to carelessness and incompetence on the water. Americans, in general, are very reckless and poor sailors.

It is not true that the roads are marked by skeletons of those who have lost their lives—although skeletons may have been found. But along the road across the mountain from Dyca to Lake Bennett it is said to be marked by dead horses. A good many of the travelers bring one or more horses along to transport their belongings across the mountain, and once they are over, they shoot their horse if they can't sell it.

There are also other places to go besides the Yukon River and Klondike, which, according to the latest reports, are just as rich in gold and much more easily accessible. Two of those most often mentioned are Copper River and the *rivers that flow into Kotzebue Sound. Look at the map above the mouth of the Yukon River and St. Michael. I should prefer Kotzebue if I decide to go. According to reports by the natives, there is lots of gold in all those rivers. Two men came out of that area last fall because they ran out of food, and they had $15,000 after six months work. In San Francisco a huge party is now preparing to sail for Kotzebue on the 10th of April. It is claimed that in one or two years, there will be other places just as famous as Klondike, in spite of the fact that at least 20 million dollars in gold will come from there this spring and summer. It is difficult to tell how much Alaska will produce in a few years. Last fall I ran into a man in Orondo who was a native of New Zealand. He told me that he had been in Siberia Strait west of the Bering Strait where he had found very rich gold deposits. But the Russian government prohibited gold digging and they chased them away!*

The papers are full of reports about wealthy gold diggers returning from Alaska. Last summer I became acquainted with a Norwegian minister by the name of Harstad. He is the editor of the Pacific Herald, and he is also teaching at the Pacific Lutheran University, a higher Norwegian American school in Tacoma. He has written to me a couple of times and wants me to go along on a gold digging trip to Alaska. Among other things, he said the following: "It may come as a surprise to you that I am seeking the despicable gold, but I just can't help it. I am responsible for a large sum of money for this school, and if I find some, I can do something good with gold. If I find nothing, it is still nothing less than what I am getting here." Pastor Harstad has eight children, the youngest one only a few months old. He was supposed to leave on the 10th of this month. I wrote back to him telling him that I was going to forget about it this year, but if I was going to go, I would rather go to Kotzebue Sound. The influx to Yukon is now so great that all the combined means of transportation are insufficient. In order to be well equipped for such a trip, it would take $500 to $600, although many set out with a lot less.

In the midst of all this gold fever comes the astonishing piece of news that gold can be made from silver. I heard this story last fall, namely that a professor in New York made gold from Mexican silver dollars and sold them to the United States Mint, and that all tests and analyses this gold had been subjected to could not prove that it was not real gold! I, along with others, took it with a grain of salt or just another political fraud, and I still lean in that direction. But now the papers report that this same professor and others are giving lectures about the great discovery, claiming that this discovery is for real and not "humbug". They say that gold and silver are one and the same element and that it is a lack of sufficient heat during the moment of formation which is causing it to become silver and not gold, or, in other words, this element can be white or yellow in color. Be that as it may—we should soon be able to find the real truth, I should think.

(Today is the 20ᵗʰ of February and I must try to get this letter finished.) These last two weeks I have been hauling firewood so that we'll have enough for a year. We are beginning to see indications of spring. The snow has dwindled to less than a foot with a hard crust. Last night we got enough new snow for easy tracking. The wolves were sounding alarm all night up in the hills. I have been plodding around looking for them all day today without being able to catch up with them. There had been four of them all together, and two had been almost down to the buildings. I had set out poison for them, but they had eaten just a little, and then they had gone over to a neighbor and eaten off a dead horse that was lying next to a haystack.

By 1899, with his family increasing, Ole gave up his dreams of going to Alaska, although he would maintain some penny stocks in some of the small mines within the Pacific Northwest. He had a small income from his family in Norway, worked at his surveying, and kept his cattle business profitable, but his central focus would stay in the farming of his land in the Big Bend and the well-being of his maturing family.

With seeds he had received from his mother in Norway he planted an ash tree on the northeast corner beside a thriving black walnut. Realizing the cabin was becoming overcrowded, he started construction on a larger house. He worked as many hours as possible building the four-room structure, and later added a long upstairs bedroom entered only from an outside ladder attached to the northwest side of the house. Under the southwest corner he placed a glass jar containing coins, pictures, and a narrative of the family to that date. As he put the jar under soil and in cement, he said to his workers, W*ho knows? Maybe one day, someone might be interested in what we have been doing.* The house was completed in the fall of 1899 and would become the birthplace of the next four babies. On November 30, 1900, a letter went out to Norway.

Mother and Siblings:

I received Olava's letter of October 18ᵗʰ not long ago and learned from it that things are going fine with the exception that Mother has been seriously ill.

Yes, it is bad that my family and I cannot take a trip home while she lives, as she would have surely enjoyed seeing the children. They are very happy and healthy and none of them have been sick yet or shown signs of any weakness. They are all talented children, especially Signe, who is known in school for her talents. Signe has inherited the gift of art and, like myself, likes to draw and paint.

I should also tell you that yesterday, the 29ᵗʰ was the American "Thanksgiving Day" and it so happened that on that day our family grew by one more boy. Everything is going well. We haven't decided on a name, but it will probably be Albert or something similar.

We have advanced a little the past year. I bought some livestock in the fall so we now have nineteen animals in all and I still have $100 to buy something or other. Maybe I will buy more sheep.

This year the harvest was very good, but I had the misfortune this fall that I didn't get it threshed. There were three threshing machines in our neighborhood this fall, but all of them sped away in order to arrive first at another location, leaving me and two of my neighbors, who also did not get their harvest threshed. This type of behavior is generally considered a shameful, mean spirited trick, but it happens now and then when those who own the threshing machine try to hurt the other ones. It wouldn't bother me so much if it weren't for the fact that I have so many swine to feed through the winter—namely 40 of them. Those I now have to feed un-threshed barley and wheat, which is very cumbersome, and then I can't make good use of the straw. I had expected to get about 1000 bushels of barley this fall as well as a few hundred bushels of wheat and oats. I lost a colt this fall (when he got tangled up in the barbwire fence) and cut himself, several places right to the bone, so I had to kill him. I now have 9 horses including the colts.

How is it going with the property exchange at Svarstad? Don't forget to tell me about it next time. I understand that Kristian already is able to cut straight timber in the Svarstad forest. Well, I had also figured that the forest would pay for Svarstad, but I suppose it can't do that yet. I advise Kristian not to sell the forest away from the farm. Rather, he should buy more. Preferable forest. Forests will always remain an inexhaustible gold mine in Norway. Prices, in the coming years, will not go down, but up.

If I lived in Norway now, I would concentrate on cattle for the market more than we used to do. I would raise all the calves, castrate all the bull calves, put them on pasture in the Krog Forest for two summers, and then feed them the second winter, or let them out on pasture also the third summer and sell them when they were 2-2½ years old as it pays best to sell at that age. This would be for calves born in the fall. Our calves here are born mostly in the spring

The recently built four-room house had been advantageous to Augusta, giving her increased room for the cooking and washing for her continually growing brood. Ole kept the smokehouse filled with salted pork, the root cellar filled with potatoes, onions and carrots, and within the granary, sacks filled with rye and wheat stood ready to be ground into flour. There was always ample food on the table and no serious illness had yet weakened any of the children. Albert was twenty-two months old when yet another new baby was born. Ole sent a letter of announcement to Norway on January 17, 1903.

It is now a long time since I wrote; I ought not to have waited so long. Three months ago, on September 17th, our family was increased by a boy whom we named Gustav Adolf, so that now there are 3 boys and 3 girls. I believe that is just about sufficient. All the children, as well as the rest of us, are in excellent health. Agnes and Signe stopped attending school a few weeks ago, but when school starts up again in the spring, Synneva is also going to start. She is already able to read a little.

Uncle Edvart Berg came back this fall from Minneapolis. He now seems to be fairly well satisfied since he didn't find Minnesota as agreeable as he had expected. Several Norwegians are expected from that area in the spring. Those people must then purchase land here, and land has gone up in price considerably this past year. Based on previous land sales in my neighborhood, what I own in one piece of land, namely 424 acres, ought to be worth about $5,000.00. But I do not intend to sell at that price, especially since I am making some progress each passing year. We now have 35 head of cattle, including the calves, and 9 horses, 6 sheep, and 8 swine. We have recently butchered 4 swine and sold them for $67.00.

Last fall I was re-elected as County Surveyor, so now I'll have that position for another 2 years. These last years it has brought in $500.00 annually, but then I don't get much else done. As soon as the snow is off the ground, I have to go out again. Now during the winter, I'm working with drawing etc., relating to my job. Otherwise, I take it easy since Uncle Edvart Berg is taking care of the cattle and providing us with firewood. Cousin Hilma is with us also, but her sister Anna left for another place in the neighborhood a couple of weeks ago.

This last year hasn't been quite as good as usual, so I have had to buy fodder for horses and cattle for about $60.00. Cattle thieves were really running rampant last summer. I lost 2 head and others in the neighborhood a few miles around have no doubt lost 100 head of cattle from their pasture. Some of those may have died of one cause or another, and others may still turn up, but doubtless, many of them were stolen. This pack of thieves are so well organized in a gang and so well trained in their business that they are not easy to defeat. If one of them is caught, the others are willing to swear to all kinds of lies to get him freed. Only one out of a hundred ends up in prison. All the thieves I know are not immigrants, but are native-born Americans.

I'll write again before the busy season starts. Have you heard anything about what Martin intends to do—if he first wants to take a trip to Norway and later come out here to the coast? A Winter season greeting from all of us.

In England, Ole's brother Martin was floundering, unsure of his future. Serving thirty-four years as the third engineer on trade ships, he had traveled all over the world, but he was feeling ill and tired of his life on the seas; he wanted a change. He vacillated on which direction to go—back home to Norway or to the Pacific Northwest. While in Liverpool, he received a letter from his mother, Johanne.

"My dear son, Martin: We have been worried about you as we read from your last letter that you are still feeling poorly. If you were home and got good care and good food with milk, it would serve you best in every respect. We could provide you with good warm clothes all over, clothes we have put aside for you and I believe you would be satisfied here if you could come home as soon as possible. Be careful! Do not suffer damage to your health! Don't wear yourself out going for long walks! I see from your letter that you would like to go to Ole, but it would probably be best if you come home first. Here, it is not so expensive, and we can send you money so as to fix you up for the trip. Ole has a lot to do, writing and sketching maps of towns, land areas and new roads he has to plan and measure and make maps of. He makes good money and is doing well and has a respectable position. And he is completely sober which benefits him and his family. Do you have good warm clothes for use during the winter? The best remedy for illness is to stay warm, using wool clothing, wool bedding and wool stockings for your feet. Take care of your health above all else; then all will be well! And we hope you stick to sobriety and lead an orderly life both in front of God *and* human beings. Then we'll be content here and in all eternity. When do you think we'll meet again here in this world? You must remember that I am old and can expect to take leave of this world very quickly. My eyes are poor, and I am rather feeble, but am able to be up every day. Write soon and tell us how you are. With loving greetings from your Mother."

Martin was just thirteen years old when he and his mother, Johanne, had a quarrel. He had been slacking in his studies so his mother told him to either give more attentiveness to his schooling or leave and find a job. They continued to argue, so she found a large piece of cloth and laid it on the floor instructing him to put everything he had in a pile upon it. After he finished, she picked it up, tied it in a knot, and told him to leave. He went down the road, sat down, and cried. A man, who happened to be a sea captain, came along, took him in, and used him as his cabin boy for several years. Gaining experience doing odd jobs for the captain, Martin learned various skills helping out where he was needed. Later on, he spent eight months training at the Albion Foundry in London, where he became proficient working with the melting and shaping of heavy metals. He finished this training at the age of twenty-two and soon began his long career on the seas.

Martin, now 54 years old, did not go home as his mother wished, but arrived in New York on the Norwegian ship *Holy Olof* in 1904 to start a new life and work with his brother in the Pacific Northwest. On his way to Washington State he stopped in Chicago, became inebriated, and was robbed, so when he finally made it to Douglas County he was totally broke. The only thing the 5'6", 160-lb. bachelor had in his brown leather billfold was a thick accumulation of discharge papers from services on the sea, ranging from six weeks to a year's duration, all with a similar message.

Mr. Martin Ruud (the bearer of this) has served as third Engineer on board the S. S. Myrtle Branch for a period of nearly six months in Mediterranean trade (March 19 to September 9, 1885). We can, with confidence, testify to his ability as a mechanic, his thorough trustworthiness in charge of machinery, his indefatigable industry and general good conduct and sobriety.

Signed: Arthur Ritson, Master
I. N. Gilby, Engineer

Millwall Dock—London, September 10, 1885

As his brother had done in 1888, Martin would apply for citizenship. In 1908, in Douglas County, he signed his Declaration of Intention renouncing forever all allegiance and fidelity to any foreign prince, potentate, state, or sovereignty, particularly to Håkkon VII, King of Norway.

Martin would prove to be beneficial to Ole with the various labors of repairing equipment for the wagons or horses, constructing sheds for wood and produce, and building barns for the animals. Together they built a small room at the south end of the rectangular workshop. This roughly floored room, which would be Martin's sleeping quarters, contained one small window, a shelf for his clothing, a narrow cot, and a pot-bellied stove for warmth in the winter months. Only a few feet away from his bed, on the dirt floor, was the anvil secured on a large flat stump beside the forge and bellows. This necessary equipment was frequently used by the men to heat, pound, repair, or shape any broken metal parts of the wagons and harnesses, or to adjust the fit of the shoes for the saddle horses. Using the heavy steel hammer and the long tongs to hold the extremely hot pieces of metal, the men worked together on the maintenance of the implements.

Until he left the farm, Martin worked with Ole on the final addition to the house. The finished structure would be solid, and large enough for neighborhood dances or special parties for the children. A local Norwegian contractor, Mr. Burgeson, worked with the men starting in 1903, but the project would not be completed until 1913. The stately two-story home, built at the foot of the mountain near the spring-water creek, would contain twelve rooms with four walk-in closets overlooking the view of the land Ole had earlier described—*where the beautiful plains of agricultural land, the luxuriant bunchgrass pastures, the plentiful timber and sparkling streams of Badger Mountain are exceedingly attractive. I have never regretted coming here.*

Before the house was completed, Ole became ill. This necessitated his undergoing surgery in Seattle for a double mastoid procedure. Unable to work at his outside chores during his recuperation, he took some time to write his chronicle up to that date of 1906 on sheets of his surveyor's paper and placed them in his personal trunk. Following his recovery, he continued to farm for eighteen more years.

*   *   *

With Ole and the fathers of the Miles, Martin, and Bonwell children serving as board members, the first school in the Badger Mountain area opened in December of 1885. Named for its teacher, Richard S. Steiner, a local resident and County Auditor, the school, located in Ole's cabin, would be short-lived, as closure occurred the following February. Steiner, a graduate of a Michigan university law school, was first elected as Douglas County Auditor in 1883, later served as Clerk of the district court and as bank president; he practiced law in Waterville before being elected Superior Court Judge of Chelan, Douglas, Okanogan, and Ferry Counties in 1904. The young students he taught from five families during the short duration would attend a school on the north side of the mountain the next term, when Ole and D.W. Martin served as directors.

The Douglas County School District, organized in the spring of 1900, contained five schools capable of educating children through the eighth grade. The Mountain View, Waterville, Fairview, Pearl, and Pioneer schoolhouses had in attendance an average of eighteen students of various ages, all walking or riding a horse to the building.

One family with children attending school usually provided board and room for about a third of the teacher's $50-$56 per month salary. If a horse and buggy were not provided, the teacher rode a horse to her schoolhouse. Upon arriving, she began her daily duties. First, she would tend to the horse, either putting it in the barn or tying it to the hitching post. With dried pine, split by the older boys whose job it was to keep the wood box filled, she started a roaring fire in the pot-bellied stove and saw that the bucket of drinking water was filled before she could concentrate on the lessons of the day. Not only did the teachers supply their own teaching materials, but many also brought vegetables from their home, along with a piece of meat, to start a pot of stew cooking for those children having inadequate lunches. So educating her students was only a fraction of her duties as she found herself being a cook, nurse, mother, disciplinarian, and janitor, as even the outhouse was her responsibility, for she routinely poured lime into the pit every few days in an attempt to contain its odor.

If a student was able to pass the teacher's examination, he or she was qualified to teach after graduating from the eighth grade. Some would hold the certificate after passing the exam but continue their high school education. The majority of one-room schoolteachers were girls who were discouraged from dating, fired if suspected of smoking tobacco or drinking liquor, and required to dress properly, which meant wearing long skirts touching the ankles and blouses covering their arms. All were required to be self-reliant, dependable girls, able to handle all ages of children, since some of the pupils were as old as or older, and occasionally larger, than their teacher. They were expected to teach basic values along with subjects of knowledge. Many used the Holy Bible as a guide for teaching mores of society, using the commandments as examples of proper and accepted life—respect and honesty being of high priority both in and out of the classroom.

Following the completion of the eighth grade, students could attend Union High School, the first school building built in the town in 1900 at a cost of $3,000. At the beginning, this school would employ two teachers. Later on, in 1913, with a population of about a thousand inhabitants in the town and surrounding community, an imposing two-story brick building would be constructed to serve as the central school for several outlying districts. General education was taught, as were many branches of practical work. As agriculture was the principle occupation of the residents of the community, this area of study was given a very prominent place in the curriculum of the school. Many residents of the community termed it "The Agricultural School," as a large acreage of land was used by the students for experimental work supervised by a graduate of the State Agricultural College.

Seven of the children of Ole and Augusta would attend the Mountain View school, which was located about two miles northeast of their home. All of the children, with the exception of Signe and Oliver, would go on to complete their high school education at the Waterville High School. Two of the brothers, Lewis and Otto, would continue on at universities. Lewis entered the School of Engineering at the U. of California. Otto began studying Forestry at the U. of Washington. He would later switch to Business Administration.

Maintaining healthy minds and bodies had been the family's fortune. Up to this time, no one had suffered from broken bones or any serious illness. Except for occasional bouts of quinsy, which Augusta treated with warm saltwater gargles, the children were robust, their eagerness visible. But on December 12, 1908, tragedy struck. The sorrowful event was the acute illness and subsequent death of Signe. That mournful winter day would mark her parents and each of her siblings with a scar of grief lasting the duration of their lives.

The person with the most medical knowledge in the immediate area was Dr. Adams, the local veterinarian, who was known to drink at least a pint of whiskey each day. As feared, he was found intoxicated, but nevertheless was brought to the home where Signe lay in pain. Attempts were made to sober the only possible source of help by giving him many cups of strong coffee. Feeling exasperated and desperate, Ole saddled his horse and rode 1½ miles across the fields to the Ricedorff house, the closest neighbor having a telephone, and summoned Dr. McCoy, a physician who was 25 miles away in Wenatchee. Dr. McCoy came by horseback on that cold crisp day, making his way along the Columbia River, up the steep wagon road through Corbaley Canyon to the home—a half-day's ride. When he entered the house, the other children were sent upstairs, but they did not go to their rooms as directed. Instead, they sat on the stairway, listening to their sister's screams as she was carried to the table, overcome by her fears. Signe was three days short of being 13 years, 11 months old at the time of her death.

Three days after the funeral, the grieving father wrote on the back of Signe's certificate of baptism:

Signe Kristiana Jane Ruud was born on January 15, 1895. Baptized July 7, 1895. Vaccinated August 29, 1899. Died on the third day after an operation for appendicitis by Dr. McCoy of Wenatchee on December 12, 1908 in the house of her parents.

Signe played the organ Sunday, took sick Monday morning with vomiting, headache and pain in her side. Said she was glad she did not go to school that day—that she could not have stood it. On Tuesday morning I realized it must be appendicitis and went down to Ricedorffs and called for Dr. Adams who came by the time I got home. He could do nothing. I decided to call for Dr. McCoy of Wenatchee.

At this point, Ole laid his pen down. He would not resume his narration of that day for several years. But when he did pick up his pen, his memory quickly revived details, tormenting and vivid, as if her death had just occurred.

Operation was done by Dr. McCoy of Wenatchee. Dr. Adams of Waterville giving Ether. I, her father, stood by under the operation, which was performed in our house. This was a mistake. We should have taken Signe to Seattle. The operation was also made faulty and took over 1½ hours. The Doctor put in a rubber tube split open on one side and stuffed full of something, but very tight. The tube did not drain the wound a particle and peritonitis set in.

On the night of Saturday, December 12th, 1908 she became uneasy and said she felt like something running around in her abdomen. She called for the doctor, also Uncle Martin, and sisters and brothers. Became delirious for a short time and cried that she was "going, going" and said, "hold me, hold me", so I took her around her shoulders and said, "No, you are right here with Papa, don't be afraid." She became quiet. I was constantly at the side of her bed. When we saw that death was sure, I asked Dr. Adams to pull the tube out of the wound because I suspected that it did not drain properly. When the Doctor pulled it out, she cried that it hurt. My suspicion was correct. When the tube was pulled, stuck to the outside was thick yellow matter, but nothing but some thin water inside. It oozed out of the wound, that thick yellow matter, enough to fill an egg twice. And it stunk so bad that those in the house, except me and the doctor, left the room.

Signe was conscious to the last minute and was spoken to and closely observed to the last by her father and mother. Was delirious a moment, then became quiet. Called mother to her and throwing her arms around her neck and said, "Oh Mama, don't let me die." Her mother quieted her by saying "My child, my child, nobody die" and saying the Lord's Prayer for her. She repeated it after, word for word. Then she called for Papa. Folding her arms around my neck she only said "Oh, Papa, Papa." I told her not to be afraid of anything and that she would get a better home hereafter. She became quiet realizing she must go. She then called Oliver and Agnes—then Albert, but Dr. Adams took Albert away by the arm. She also called for Lewis and Synneva. Otto was the baby and too small to realize it. Little Signe, understood she must now, she must leave us, folded her arms around the neck of all and calling our names as a last word and farewell. She called Synneva twice to her. The last word to Synneva was "Oh, it is so hard to leave you." Those words were spoken in full consciousness.

Present of neighbors were Mrs. Ricedorff and Irene Rothbun. Miss Rothbun, Signe's teacher, stopped school and offered to nurse Signe, whose last day in school was on Friday, December 4th.

Dr. Adams left for home. Death came about ¾ hour after. In the last moment her eyes took on a brilliant and happy look. I, constantly at the bed, was astonished, had only time to call the others attention, when the eyes looked dead as marble.

Our dear little Signe was gone. I had spoken to her and received an answer not over fifteen minutes before. Death came so easy that, to us, she did not seem to realize it. Signe was a most lovely child, sensible, with brilliant faculties. Her characters in school were nearly always up in the 90tees. I was surprised at her great faculties for drawing. She clung to me almost more than her mother. Her last day in school was on Friday, December 4th, 1908. The next Sunday, after we had visitors in the house, Signe was playing the organ standing in the Northwest little room and singing this song—"Shall We Meet Beyond the River". Next Monday morning she took sick. That same song was sung at her burial the next following Sunday.

At the time of the funeral, 35 to 40 carriages followed little Signe to the grave in our lot in the Waterville cemetery to place her under a monument of white marble.

Have mourned the loss very much.　　　O. Ruud

**Augusta holding Synneva – Agnes – Signe on Ole's lap
1897**

Seated: Albert, Signe, Adolph, Agnes
Standing: Oliver, Synneva
1903

Pupils at Mountain View School
3 girls on left – Synneva, Agnes, Signe. Oliver in center

Covered school wagon
School built in 1913

**One year after the death of Signe
1909**

Chapter III

Floods drown the fairest valleys; fields droop in the August blaze;
Yet rain and sun are God's angels that give us the harvest days,
And toil is the world's salvation, though stern may be its ways:
Far from the lair it has led us—far from the gloom of the cave—
Til lo, we are lords of Nature instead of her crouching slave!*

*3rd verse from *The Glory of Toil*
by Edna Dean Proctor

More Death, Continued Toil

Awaiting Ole at the post office in January of 1913 was a letter from Kristian and Olava. Since Martin had arrived nine years earlier, they had received no troubling news from Norway, even though the brothers were cognizant of the failing health of their mother. As his children gathered around the table, a saddened Ole read a letter written by Kristian.

"Brothers, Sister, and Children,

"This time it is my sad duty to inform you that our old and faithful mother received permission to leave us on the 4th of January at 1:30 in the morning. She was born on the 23rd of December 1821—a long life—91 years and a few days. She was ill—ill enough to be in bed for about three weeks. It started out with something like bronchitis, but it took over her whole body. We got some type of mixture from the doctor, and the minister came and gave her the last sacrament. The following day she was confused, saying she had to go out for something, and she kept asking us to put shoes on her. Now and then she would be sort of lucid, and she would scream for help. So it was a hard struggle. Her last evening, around 8 o'clock, she was very ill but then she calmed down and went to sleep, and she slept so peacefully that we didn't expect her to die so soon. Maren Stadum is here to help us watch over her. I noticed that her breathing became very calm, and I walked over to her bed. She was gasping for breath, and her mouth twitched a couple of times, and then everything was quiet. She was no longer with us, so the death struggle itself was apparently easy. She was fortunate in that she avoided severe pain. Lately she was getting forgetful and going back to her childhood, but she always maintained her faith in her Savior. I believe her last words were, as she reached out with her arms: "God protect me and all of mine!" Someone came today for her coffin and to report the death. She will be permitted to go to rest in the old family gravesite where our father is. I bought this for her 20 years ago.

"As far as my own illness is concerned, it is very bad, and I have to stay in bed most of the time. The neuralgia in my stomach has gotten worse during this difficult time. I keep using warm compresses, hoping that it will get better, Loving greetings to all. Kristian."

After Johanne Frederiksdatter's services, and before mailing the letter, Olava added a note. "I have to finish this," she would write, "Kristian started the letter but I was unable to write since there was so much I had to take care of because of our dear mother's passing. Mother's funeral took place on Tuesday the 14th. Our family gathered along with neighbors—40 in all—who were served a meal here in our house as is our custom. This went on from 10 o'clock in the morning until midnight, and then, on the 16th, Kristian again went to the State hospital to seek medical help. No one knows what the final outcome is going to be in regards to his illness. He has been going downhill lately. We'll have to leave everything in God's hands. It has been a difficult time for me lately. Loving greetings."

Waterville, August 3, 1913
Dear Siblings:
I received Olava's letter a couple of days ago. In regards to the monument, the pyramid shape is the best looking. The inscription may be short and something like this:

Ole Olsen Rudsødegaard
1821-1854
and wife
Johanne Frederiksdatter, born Vig
1821-1913
Peace Be With Their Memory

I suppose the last part could be omitted, but it is quite nice on a grave monument, of course. Do what you think best. It seems to me that their full names ought to remain.

It is too bad about Kristian's long illness. I told Pastor Harstad about Kristian's illness when he came to see us yesterday. He said that he had known someone out East who suffered a lot with catarrh in his stomach, but nothing helped. He then went to the coast and was cured completely by the change in climate.

Martin fixed himself up and was ready to go to Norway one of the first days of April. I guess there wasn't much preparation, but he let us know that he was leaving in a couple of days. We asked him to wait until the children had made some little things to send along to you. I had 120 dollars lying around to buy him a ticket. Without telling us where he was going, he cleared out on Monday, March 31. We thought he was going to bid good-bye to Edvart or someone else. Towards the end of the week I went over to Waterville, and then I found that he had been binge drinking all week, but as soon as he found out that I was in town, he beat it, so I was not able to get him home. About a week later, he came staggering home so sick that he could hardly walk. As usual, it took him 3 to 4 days to sleep it off. Before leaving, he severely bawled out my wife because she had asked of the bank and how much money he had there. He brags about his money and how independent he is from us and from others. The truth is that he has no money in the bank, or in his pocket, because he drinks up and squanders any money he puts his hands on. I came pretty close to giving him the 120 dollars, and if I had, those also would have been squandered.

One of the barkeepers in Waterville told me that I ought not to give him any money since all he does is drink it up, but that I ought to give him money for the ticket when he is going to leave. Since then he has not mentioned anything about the trip, saying that something hasn't worked out for him.

The pension he is getting does more harm than good for him. Since he started getting it, he has received much over 200 dollars, all of which has disappeared with only a few shoddy pieces of clothing to show for it. It is completely impossible to get him to come to his senses. If I say anything to him, he starts abusing me, using the most ferocious language which lasts as long as anyone sticks around to listen to him. When he came home, he had been expelled from town by the constable. I, myself, have seen him when he was expelled from a tavern. But that has no effect on him, it seems. Presumably, he is used to it.

Harvest season has now started, but because of the dry summer, the yield will be less than the previous year. What I depend on primarily now, is the cattle, and the prices are very good. About 3 weeks ago I sold three head of cattle for butchering:

One three-year-old ox	*1,365 lbs.*
@ 4 cents (living weight)	*$54.60*
One three-year-old steer	*1,350 lbs.*
@ 7 cents	*$94.50*
One old cow	*1,175 lbs.*
@ 6 cent	*$70.50*
	$219.60

This spring we built a new house—that is, we added to the old one so that we now have 5 rooms downstairs and 5 small rooms upstairs. The house is finished outside, but inside only 4 rooms are finished yet. It will have to remain as it is for a while. I couldn't afford to build, but I had to do it, because the children are growing up and want to have it sort of nice when they now and then have a party, and especially because other people also have started setting up nice homes. I painted it myself and did a lot of other kinds of work, saving over $200 total.

For a couple of weeks now it has been very warm so that the thermometer often has been up to 95 and almost 100 degrees. Today it is reasonably pleasant—namely 82 degrees. I see that Anders Overgjordet is back home from America. I have also been thinking about the same thing if I could sell at a good price. I'll have to wait until the Panama Canal is opened. We believe that coastal areas will rebound then.

I will close for now, hoping that Kristian will get better. He ought to try a new diet and a change in the climate if possible. Sea air is good—if he could go some place on the coast. We are all well as of this date. Greetings from my wife.

Martin was obviously becoming a thorn within the family and among some of the members of the community. His heavy alcohol intake was starting to take its toll. Heavily laden with frustration and loneliness, he wrote to his sister at Svarstad on February 12, 1914.

"Olava! I have now been ill for 3 weeks with the influenza. I was out in a terrible snowstorm. I relied on my thick and warm underwear, and they kept me warm, but the following day I started feeling some consequences. It is in my head and in one ear. I am now improving, and the doctor tells me that I'll be well soon. I asked him if this was the same illness that Brother Ole had (an ear infection), but he said it was not and that I'd soon be all right. I get up every day, but I stay inside. Ole's wife does everything she can for me and is very kind to me. But Ole! When my headache was at its worst, he started bawling me out in the worst way until I asked him to leave me alone. So much for brotherly love!

"I haven't had an answer to my last letter—too early yet anyway. Don't wait too long before you write. I wish I were home now because I am so sick and tired of everything. Loving greetings to all of you, Martin Ruud."

Kristian Ruud, who had been farming Svarstad, finally succumbed to his long-term stomach ailment in June of 1914. His death occurred just 1½ years after that of Johanne Frederiksdatter. On the 14th, two days after receiving the news, Ole wrote, *On the 12th of this month we received your letter about Kristian's death. It was not completely unexpected, of course, but nevertheless hard to take. Martin took it perhaps less hard than any of us. My wife and my children did not know him, of course, but they have always talked about him and both of you often. My wife is by nature a very sympathetic person and shares other people's sorrow.*

It was good to hear that Kristian let go of this world and was thinking of the next life. And it was kind of Maren Stadeim to help you take care of him while he was so sick.

I believe we had a kind of foreboding about Kristian's death. On the 15th and 16th of May, Martin was so ill that I thought his end was imminent. On Sunday the 17th, Edvart came, as he said, "to see Martin before he died." During those days my wife also said – many times – that she felt something was about to happen. On the 20th of May both of us went to town (Waterville). She then once more said that she felt so melancholy and unable to talk to anyone, and I said: "Well, we'll probably find out that Kristian has died." On that same day we went to Signe's grave and brought along flowers because next Saturday is Decoration Day. That same day the children went to her grave with flowers. Martin is now a little better, but he is so confused that he can't go out alone. Whether he will recover or not is hard to tell; his eyes are running now and then and he is almost completely deaf.

On that same day when we got your letter about Kristian's passing, my wife went to town again and brought back with her Mr. Malloy, who is a lawyer and a Notary Public, since we could not take Martin out of the house. I then translated the mentioned and appropriate declarations to the best of my ability in Norwegian as well as a Power of Attorney statement to you from Martin. Mr. Malloy then added his testimony, signature, and seal in English, using the customary forms, stating that he knows us as the legitimate persons signing the papers. I can't believe that anything more is needed. Malloy put the letter in the mail on Saturday morning at 10:00.

This money, which you say I am going to get from poor Kristian, will help me and my family greatly in getting my debt paid off again soon. You see, I have bought parcels of land almost every other year costing varied amounts of money. Then we had to have a better house as the children were growing up. They like to have their friends and acquaintances over, and consequently they need a lot of space. Some of the interior work on the house has not been completed, but that will have to wait for now. The interest rates are so high here now and do not at all correspond to the prices we farmers get for our produce.

We have a Norwegian boy working for us by the name of Valdemar Lindholm. His parents used to live in Langbro and also in Vigsengen, but now they have a small piece of land near Hamar. His father is Swedish and his mother, Norwegian. He came to this country last summer along with Anna Kristiansen and they are supposed to be engaged. I pay him $1.25 per day which he feels is low pay. As proof of how people like that can get big ideas when they come over here I can tell you the following: Anna is working for a family about ten miles from here and she used to call him on the telephone now and then. One day she called, my wife answered the phone. When Anna inquired about Valdemar, my wife answered, just in fun, that he was down in the yard milking. This was not true, however; he doesn't know how to milk. Anna shot back that she was not going to listen to any ridiculous comments and that we were going too far if we were having him do the milking for the low wages we were paying him. A while later she called again. Synneva told her that he had left for Waterville, to which she answered that it was too far to walk to Waterville. He has had a horse for riding a couple of times, but he was using it so hard that I told him from now on he'll have to walk.

He tells me that he saw you in Sundvolden last summer. He was there to see some of his relatives. Anna Kristiansen is the girl Kristian was there to talk to –a relative of Edvart's wife. According to what Valdemar tells me, the farmers in Norway get better profit for what they sell than we do here in America.

You'll have to write a letter and send it as soon as you can and let me know how much I'll be getting after Kristian. It's no fun paying 10% interest any longer than necessary. I guess you'll have to take care of placing an appropriate monument on the grave. It doesn't have to cost as much as the one for our parents, *of course. There is no need to let your conscience bother you because of the fact that you will be sending money from Norway to America because these days hundreds of thousands, if not millions, of dollars are sent from America to Norway. All the Norwegian Americans are sending sums of money, each to his own native community, on the occasion of the anniversary of May 17th, Independence Day, and the exhibition in Kristiania. I haven't heard that anything was to be sent to Ringerike, otherwise I ought to have participated.*

Well, you can't complain any more about your hard lot. Kristian managed everything in an excellent manner, and you and Andreas, and also Martin are reaping the benefit. If I had leased Svarstad instead of selling it to Mother, I, myself, would have been better off. But I wanted to be honest and do what was best in case something should happen to me. That was what I was thinking at that time. If Svarstad had not been sold to our mother, all of you would have been living at Rudsødegaarden, debt-ridden and in poor circumstances. I have confidence that all of you understand. Don't take it the wrong way, any of you, because I bring this up. For that matter, I have never complained, as you know.

Now Olava, you make sure that Andreas does not lose what he has received. He must admit that what he has received is not only due to his own cleverness or work, but that others have helped him. He should also think what his position would have been now if he had gone out on his own as I did. As I said, I haven't complained much, but I have suffered a lot here in this country; none of you have suffered so much pain and such need.

Olava, you think that it has been hard for you, but it cannot be compared to what my wife has been through and the work both of us do every day. This is naturally for the children's sake. We would like to set them on their feet so they can have a little to begin with. It has always been hard to start with nothing in America. Both you and Andreas must keep my children in mind so that they can think back about you and praise your name and the memory of you when they reach the age when they become responsible.

It was appreciated to receive locks of Kristian's and Mother's hair. They will be kept well and be inherited by the children. I cannot understand how Martin can be so indifferent about this as he was when we showed him the letter and the locks of hair. He threw them down and started talking about the money he should receive. The poor devil still believes that he will travel through the Panama Canal and work his way back home to Norway.

My wife and children want me to greet you and Andreas. Of course we all wish to see Norway some day. I cannot say much about my plans in relation to that or about my future plans at this point. We will see what the future will bring. Now you and Andreas should find something to work on since time is best spent in this way. I cannot suggest anything, but you should find a place where you can fish. Times are changing.

Although she had never met Kristian, Augusta was mournful over his death. Writing words of comfort in her native Swedish, she also vented concerns regarding brother Martin. Being a devout Christian, Augusta coped with the turmoil of life by relying on God's will. If the children were healthy, crops profitable, the canning of fruit and vegetables completed, or even a refreshing rain had fallen, those circumstances were gifts from the Heavenly Father. On the contrary, when life brought difficulty, she accepted His wrath, even though she said her daily prayers, bearing the burden as a deserved punishment however perplexing it seemed. Her daughter's death in 1908 tested her faith in Him, yet she remained as a devout member of His flock; nonetheless, Signe's absence left her weeping until her dying day. Augusta suffered a piercing, formidable grief, and her family would often find her clinging to a formaldehyde-filled bottle she kept hidden in a corner of a closet, containing her daughter's appendix. Wringing her hands and wiping her tears with the hanky she kept tucked in her cleavage, she audibly wept, "Oh, why, Oh, why, Oh, why—she was such a good little girl. I don't understand His reason for punishing me so!"

"Waterville,
June 17, 1914

"Dear Sister and Brother,
"With sorrow and tears we read the letter about our dear Kristian's passing. We thought it was sad that you had to go through three funerals in such a short time. But we have to be content with God's will. I am grateful to God that Kristian was glad to leave this world and that he was certain he would go to eternal bliss. He is now kept safe for all eternity, praise be to God.
"It has been very hard on you, Olava, doing the care all the time when Kristian was ill. I know it was difficult for you when he died. And you also had all the cooking and baking to do for the funeral. I hope you had help with the work as I know there is so much to tend to on such an occasion. Our children cried when we read your letter and saw Grandmother and Uncle's hair. Thanks so much for everything, Olava.
"Martin is very ill today—I believe this illness will be the end of him. It was bad for all of us that he took ill. He believes it was my fault that Ole did not lend him money last winter so that he could go home to Norway. God knows that I did everything I could so that he could go, but I could not go to the bank to get money. I had nothing I could pay with. After he took ill I have done everything I could for him and this afternoon I have to go to town to see the doctor about him.
"I have worked very hard this past winter when I had to go out in deep snow to feed the cattle and milk our 4 cows, in addition to all my other work.

"I must close for this time, dear Olava. May God comfort all of you and help all of us to achieve eternal bliss in the presence of our loving God. With the best greetings to all of you from your sister, Augusta."

Martin left for Seattle shortly thereafter in poor physical health. Yearning to return home to Norway but knowing he could not financially or physically manage the voyage, he medicated his depression with more alcohol. He tried his best to numb his headaches by consuming still more liquor, becoming increasingly malnourished and hopeless. He was diagnosed with cerebral meningitis and died in the Sisters Hospital on July 31, 1914, just six weeks after the death of his brother, Kristian. As the health law of the state required, because of the diagnosis, his body was securely bagged as a precautionary measure before it could be transferred in a casket on the Northern Pacific to Waterville. Life had been difficult for Martin. He felt unsuccessful and unloved as his alcoholism gradually took control of his life, and he died a saddened man. Buried in the family lot, Martin was 64 years old.

Johanne Frederiksdatter Ruud
Mother of Ole Ruud - widowed at age 33

Olava Ruud
Sister of Ole. Never married.
Spent her life in Norway as a caretaker

Andreas Olsen Ruud
Worked as a business man and banker
In Hønefoss, Norway

Kristian Olsen Ruud
Spent his life working the farm at
Svarstad, Norway

Martin Olsen Ruud

Workshop – Note the end addition which housed Martin

Svarstad – 1911
Left to Right: Housemaid, Andreas,Kristian,
Olava, Johanne Frederiksdatter Ruud

Kristian O. Ruud Estate upon his Death

Before the inheritance tax was withdrawn from the bank, the amount of deposit was Kr. 8276.73, of which the three heirs each owned 1/3rd with a nursery man Dynge's debt, Sheriff Nicolaisen has collected Kr. 15.00 of which each heir gets 5.00.

The total for each heir is, therefore, Kr. 2763.91

1. Olava Ruud: Inheritance tax including interest   Kr. 3741.38
   Sheriff Nicolaisen transferred to her from
   Bonsnaes Chapel along with   52.40
   the money from Dynge   <u>15.00</u>
         Kr. 3808.78

   Deduct her 1/3rd of the bank book and
   1/3rd of the Kr. 15 from Dynge, totaling   Kr. 2763.91,
   Consequently, she owes   Kr. 1044.87.

2. Andreas Ruud: His 1/3rd of the bank book and 1/3rd of the

Dynge claim	Kr. 2763.91
Inheritance tax and interest	1456.85
Consequently he has coming	Kr.1307.06

3. Ole Ruud: His 1/3rd of the bank book and 1/3rd of the

Dynge's debt as above	Kr. 2763.91
Inheritance tax and interest	1041.68
Consequently he has coming	Kr. 1722.23

These total	Kr. 3029.29
This will be covered in the following manner:	
That Olava Ruud will pay out (see above)	Kr. 1044.87
and that said bank book has an amount of	1984.42
	Totaling Kr. 3029.29

In reference to the settlement of this account it should be noted that the interest accrued on said bank book is to be divided so that each heir gets 1/3rd, and that Olava Ruud, for her expenditures for a monument etc. on the grave of the deceased, has a right to reimbursement from Andreas Ruud and Ole Ruud in the amount of 1/3rd of her expenses from each. In addition, Olava Ruud has paid me for the settlement of the estate 120 Kroner of which Ole and Andreas each will pay 40 Kroner.

Documented - Hole, August 26, 1916—A. Nicolaisen

* * *

Waterville, September 21, 1914
Siblings Olava and Andreas,

I received your letter with a promissory note in the amount of $500.00 almost 2 weeks ago. I went to the bank the following day, but could not get it cashed until they had checked to see if it was valid or not by sending it to the bank in New York. They (the bank) said everything was all right, and that the money would be available, but because of the war, they had to be more careful than usual. It would take some 30 days. I can write only a little this time because I am hauling wheat to town every day and am very busy getting it all done before winter sets in. Wheat sells at 90 cents a bushel now, but they believe it will go up to $1.00 if the war continues.

We had a good harvest this year. Many farmers have 6,000-12,000 bushels of wheat to sell. I know a German, by the name of Ihn Daling, who has more than

20,000 bushels for sale. Twenty-five years ago he worked for me for a dollar a day.

Ihn Daling was one of the largest, more prosperous wheat ranchers in the Waterville area. He had been in the Waterville country for twenty-six years, on his present location for sixteen of those, having arrived in 1888. His home, in Douglas Draw, southeast of Ole, a short distance from Alstown, was so situated that he could diversify and still maintain a large acreage in wheat. The low land of the Draw was sub-irrigated and very rich. It was there that he grew his alfalfa and other crops, and raised his stock and poultry. When he first went on the place, all the lowland was overgrown with trees. After clearing out enough for his house and barns, he left the rest for a number of years. He realized, however, from the experience of his neighbors, that this land would be very valuable if properly cleared, so he went to work on it, until nearly all of the land was cleared and put into either crop or pasture. By 1914, he would have one thousand acres in wheat with plans of buying an additional 800 acres that year. Telling his own story, in 1915, he said, "I was so wrapped up in producing wheat for a number of years that I didn't realize what this low land was worth. It was quite a task to clean it off, but I simplified it by cutting the trees off at the ground and letting the roots rot. When I had them cleared off, I used a disk with which to break up the ground. There was a fine seedbed there already so I did not have to take much pains with it. I have about thirty acres of alfalfa and grew upwards of one hundred tons this year.

"There is a good market for the hay around here and I have sold considerable and am feeding it to my stock. Just now I have fifty head of cattle, part of which are calves, and ten head of milk cows. We make butter, which we sell in town. Our calves get some of the skimmed milk, as do the chickens, and four pigs. Another feature we have is bees. We have five hives now and have good results, supplying our wants.

"As a rule we have about four hundred fifty chickens, grow carrots, pumpkins, lettuce, squash and other vegetables. Last year we raised about fifteen hundred pounds of fine celery which we have buried, some of which we will sell. We sold, from our small patch, about $80 worth of delicious strawberries.

"In connection with the wheat, I think the use of a combine is not the proper thing. We always cut our grain and thresh it in the old way. The straw is very valuable around the place in connection with the stock, as it furnishes a lot of roughage and when used for bedding makes good fertilizer in the shape of manure. To illustrate how valuable I have found it, I will say that a neighbor of mine, who has a combine, wanted some straw, and was willing to pay, and did pay me $10.00 each for three small stacks and hauled it quite a distance to his place."[28]

Ole's letter to Olava and Andreas continues: *I have about 2,000 bushels of wheat to sell, and I have enough oats and barley for home use. Of cattle, I have 9 oxen, 3½ years old and some cows for sale, but I am waiting for the prices to go up. The butchers are offering 6 cents a pound for oxen, and 5 cents for fat cows, "living weight" (on the hoof). In Chicago the price of oxen is 10 cents per pound on the hoof. We will have about 80 animals that we intend to keep this winter. We have recently mowed and put in stacks 75 tons of hay. We have only about 50 tons of straw so I will have to buy some.*

School started last Monday. Agnes and Oliver will have to stay home now and help with the work. The others are attending school in Waterville. A school wagon that has been covered and remodeled for that purpose comes and picks them up every morning at 7:30 and brings them back in the evening.

Martin, I suppose, we will have to leave in peace and not say anything more bad about him. I am including a copy of a document I was given in Seattle, confirming that his body had been left in my charge. I am also sending a translation of the most important part, which I have penciled in with a circle. The rest you will have to figure out the best you can since I don't have time to write. It isn't really an official death certificate, but it will do quite well as such. Down below, Mr. M. B. Malloy, the Notary Public, has certified that this is a correct copy and that he knows me well and that he also knew Martin, witnessed his funeral, and knows that he is dead, etc.

And now we'll have to see what happens as far as getting the money you sent. If it turns out that it takes a lot of trouble, then it is best to leave my money in the bank until the war is over and all international business is back in proper order. The German Army has pulled out of Paris and has fortified itself on the hills along the river Aisne in the northwestern part of France where there was a terrible battle these last days and the week before—without any decisive victory. The Germans claim that the Allied British, French, and Belgian forces are showing signs of weakening. The Allies are saying the same thing about the Germans! The Hungarian forces are said to have suffered severe defeats in battles against the Russians. News from Berlin claims that the German Army in Prussia has beaten back the Russians.

We are all well, as of today, and are working every day. I have planted 60 acres of winter wheat, which is beginning to sprout. Today I sold 6 loads of wheat for $318, but that will pay only for the cost of harvesting.

Although most farmers in the Big Bend devoted the greater portion of their time to their principal crop, wheat, they diversified to some extent for home use, raising everything they ate, except for staples like coffee and sugar, and to keep up the fertility of the soil. Some added esthetics as well. An avid promoter of tree planting, Charles W. Hensel, who came to Waterville in 1887, took considerable pride in the appearance of his home five miles north of town. Within a few years, Hensel, an admirable, handsome man, became widely known because his farm, distinguished by its surrounding beauty, was visible from miles around. He advocated planting trees that were either transplanted from the mountains nearby or grown from seed. His intention was to beautify the land, to minimize the wind erosion of valuable topsoil, and to provide warmer quarters for the stock. The quality of his land was no better than that of others, but Hensel made a study of horticulture and put his knowledge into application, giving his land the finest yield resulting from his agricultural practices.

John McKay, the local County Commissioner, had his home ranch on 240 acres north of Waterville. A promoter of diversification, he wrote, "Stock should always be kept on the ranch to use up the waste products and to fertilize the soil. Every rancher should keep stock as it will keep him at home to tend to it and he will always find something to do about the place, so both the man and the place are benefited. Raising about five tons of carrots, which are fed to the stock during the winter months, is better for them than the patented stock foods. Practically every place in this district has a draw or low place in it where alfalfa can be grown profitably. It is one of the best feeds obtainable for a change. Six or seven years ago I planted ten acres which generally bears about a ton and a half per acre a year, although I have gotten as high as two tons and a half in favorable years. My usual practice is to cut it about July 1st, pasture it later in the year when it has dried out some. The horses and hogs are let in first and the cattle afterward. Great care should be taken that the cattle do not get on it before it is dried out thoroughly, as they are very liable to bloat if they eat it green."[29]

Surrounding farmers varied in their specialties. The Lovejoy dairy on 200 acres south of town utilized steel stanchions, cement floors, and a separate sanitary washhouse, and milked 17 Holstein cows, marketing butter, cream, and milk. Frank Malfa, owner of a forty-two acre farm just west of the town, was known as the poultry king of the Waterville country. Raising about 400 chickens, Rhode Island Reds and White Rock, he sold eggs and ran a profitable business. If they weren't good layers, the hens soon went to market. His barns were clean and dry. If the floors were not cement, he kept 8 inches of straw over the dirt floor and covered the roof with straw as well to absorb the moisture, as a dry, comfortable atmosphere was essential if good laying was expected during the winter when eggs were scarce and prices high. Malfa raised about 2,000 heads of cabbage and a large quantity of carrots, and fed them to his flock during their winter confinement. He also raised about 3 acres of wheat, which he cut, but did not thresh, allowing the chickens to scratch the grain out for themselves. It was good to "keep them busy," he would say, and tell his friends that "there was nothing nicer to hear than the singing of a flock of well-kept and happy chickens."

Ole supplemented his income by selling cut firewood to the town folk, by selling slabs of salted pork from the smokehouse, or by surveying for the County or private landowners. His acreage of wheat was small compared to that of most of his neighbors. But no matter the size of field, when the grain is golden, the kernels ripe, the weather dry, priorities center on harvest time.

With the help of his five growing sons and two hired men, Ole would begin cutting each late August. By using a type of combine called a Header, the crew could harvest up to about 15 acres per day. The equipment cost $700-$800 and was operated by push power consisting of three to four teams of horses harnessed to the back of the header. The horses were hitched to a powerful beam that reached back from the machine far enough to make room to put the doubletree. Underneath the rear end of this beam, was a six-foot wheel called a "bull wheel" with a long handle above it. The bull wheel drove a long "bull chain" operating the eight-foot sickle bar that cut the crop. From the handle, the header driver could guide the machine in front of him, as he stood and drove the horses.

The header had a long running canvas, called a draper, with little sticks riveted across it, about a foot apart for the entire length. After the ends were buckled together, this canvas went around pulleys at each end of a platform built into the machine to catch the heads of grain being severed as the machine moved forward. Then a reel brushed the grain back onto another canvas draper which carried it to the "header box."

The specially constructed header box, built with one side lower than the other, was driven alongside the header, and was able to collect a good-sized load before pulling out to unload at the stack-yard. There were usually three or four of these wagons in an outfit, so the header could keep right on going, and there would be an empty wagon ready to pull up under the spout. Header wagons, pulled by a two-or three-horse team, all had long axles under the rear to keep them from tipping over.

The headed grain was stacked, either near the barn where the farmer would want his straw stack, or else in some convenient place in the field, putting enough stacks in a place to make a setting. Sometime later, a stationary threshing outfit would come along and thresh the grain out. The threshing machine would be staked down in the most desirable spot near the setting, close to where they wanted to stack the straw, and also where there was room for the horsepower.

The horsepower was a part of the outfit to be staked down where several spans of horses could be hitched to it, and go around and around in a good-sized circle, pulling all the time, furnishing power to run the threshing machine. This horsepower had to be staked in just the right spot, so a tumbling rod could connect it with the separator, which would go fast or slow, depending on how fast the power driver made his horses go. There was a platform built inside the circle, over the top of the horsepower. The driver stood on this platform with a whip in his hand to speed up the horses, if need be.

As the grain shot out of the separator, the "sack jigger" would shake and level each filled sack and pass it over to the "sack sewer," who sat upon a couple of full sacks of wheat. Having his threaded needle always ready, as speed was essential, the sewer would quickly twist and roll each corner of the sack. With a quick twist of the wrist he would slip a double half-hitch of twine around one corner of the sack to form an ear. Then, zig-zagging the twine across the top, he would finish with another double half-hitch to form a second ear. As grain harvesters do to this day, Ole and his sons worked swiftly in the hot weather to complete their harvest before any unforeseen weather pattern would roll in, disrupting their labors and ruining the crop.

Other important parts of the outfit were the derrick, and the derrick fork. The derrick, with a pulley in the top of it, would be set up just where a fork-load of heads could be dumped for the man who was feeding the separator. He was the one to keep the grain going in a steady stream into the cylinder of the threshing machine. The derrick fork was about four feet wide at the back, with four long, strong iron arms on the fork, running from the outside corners of the frame, and connected with each other by a ring in front. From the ring, a long rope ran up through the pulley at the top of the derrick, then off to one side where a team could be attached. This would furnish power to drag the headed grain up with the derrick fork.

When it had been lifted to just the proper spot, the fork-man would signal to the driver to stop. Then he would pull a small trip-rope attached to the fork, but long enough to reach back to him. The fork would dump its load, and the fork-man could pull it back after another load. The driver of the team of horses would then lift up the doubletrees with one hand, and keeping his eye on the fork-man, he would pull the team back with the other hand. It was vital for this two-man team to synchronize their work, as well as watch out for dangerous mishaps.

Each sack of wheat weighed between 125-140 pounds. The farmers would haul it to town, at their convenience, with two or four-horse teams, and unload at the warehouses where it would be weighed five sacks at a time. After the sacks were weighed, graded, and recorded, they were stored in the warehouse for later sale at market price, or hauled to the tram on the plateau west of Waterville to the Columbia River, where they were transferred to the steamboat at Bray's Landing, three miles north of Orondo, then hauled farther down the river by boat for railroad shipment.

Extending about two miles from the top to bottom, and across two canyons, the cable tram, built in 1902, consisted of a moving cable supported on wooden towers carrying 4 ft. long, 3 ft. wide steel buckets. The return trip would haul freight or lumber, and occasionally a daring rider who chanced a long night in the bucket, as one fellow had already suffered consequences from a halt in the operation of the tram until he was rescued the following morning. At first, the weight of the downward buckets operated the tram, but this proved unsatisfactory, so an engine and drum were installed at the top loading point on the plateau. The tram ran day and night carrying thousands of bushels of wheat from the Big Bend, continuing operation until 1910.

In the early days of the tram operation, the traveling superintendent of the Seattle Grain Company, F.H. McKay, whose office was located in the Centennial Mill in Spokane, was sent to Wenatchee in the spring to buy and ship bulk wheat to the east. What he found was a poor grade of wheat brought down the Columbia from the Waterville Plateau. Due to an unpredicted early snowfall, leaving much of the threshing undone, many farmers on the plateau had been forced to leave the wheat standing in stacks throughout the winter. The farmers needed to sell their crops, and took a gamble when threshing resumed in the spring. They didn't take enough off the outside layer of their stacks. As a result, an occasional sprouted kernel was spotted in the wheat sent to market. The superintendent kept asking for the best, and only the best, to mix in and bring up his grades. Still, the wheat with sprouts and whiskers kept coming, so he went up to the wheat country to investigate. McKay soon found himself in a battle with the farmers who had contracts with the Seattle Grain Company. They would hear him say that only No. 1 wheat would be bought at the agreed price; No. 2, or No. 3 wheat would get the regular reduction. But if it had sprouts or whiskers in it, it would be rejected. The farmers argued, and threatened lawsuits, but none were started. They lost income. Bills were not paid. The wheat buyer went back to Spokane.

McKay had a challenging job. His career as a wheat buyer had begun with the Northern Pacific Elevator Company in Rosalia, Washington in 1890, where his salary was $65 per month. His business school training in Iowa emphasized profit and loss, so he spent a considerable amount of time on the mathematics of farming. McKay's job demanded detail, honesty, friendliness, and firmness, so much of his time was spent getting to know hundreds of farmers in the Inland Northwest, as well as recognize and grade dozens of different varieties of grown wheat.

He learned that each variety had its own peculiarities. In the Palouse country, the farmers grew principally Club wheat, so called because of the shape of the head. There was Big Club, Little Club, and Red Chaff Club. These all had short stubby heads and kernels of a yellowish color, and were high in starch content. McKay found that when he chewed a mouthful of any variety of Club wheat, it was soon all gone, except for the bran (the outside covering of the kernel).

In the Big Bend country, a harder type of wheat was grown. There, they grew Bluestem, Red Allen, White Australian, and Early Bart, as spring wheat. All of these, except White Australian were high in protein value and were eagerly sought after by the mills. After chewing a mouthful of any of the hard varieties, McKay would soon have a nice wad of gluten gum. This proved the protein content.

He also learned that there were several kinds of winter wheat, usually reddish in color, planted in the Big Bend. Jones-Fife, which produced abundant

118

straw and had no beards on the chaff, made excellent hay. The farmers usually planted a strip of it, a rod or two wide, around their wheat fields to cut green for hay before harvest and, in that way, made a road around the field. Another variety was Turkey Red, sometimes called Shoepeg. This had a bearded head, and the straw was not so good for feed because those beards would stick in the throats of the cattle and horses, but the wheat itself was strong in protein and commanded a premium from the buyer.

There was another variety of wheat grown, for a while, in the Palouse country, called Sonora. It was a beautiful yellow color with even grains, and was much sought-after by the breakfast food factories of the East. But this brand did not yield well, and the farmers soon quit raising it in Washington.

Each variety of wheat had a definite price on the market for number one quality. A premium was paid, sometimes as much as ten or twelve cents a bushel above number one price for that variety, especially if it had strong gluten content.

To become a successful wheat buyer, McKay had to recognize all varieties at sight, and know the market value of each one. As he learned the business, he found himself chewing wheat from morning to night in order to evaluate the protein content and the market value. One day, he noticed that he was slowly wearing out his teeth! He would finally visit a dentist in Spokane to have those teeth capped with gold. Although his friends laughed at him, the teeth stopped wearing out, and he still had his own after many of his contemporaries were depending on false ones.

When Waterville connected itself to the railroad line in Douglas, the mode of transporting wheat changed, more land was cultivated, and as a result, productivity increased.

Warehouses were built with one receiving door, and had a scale which would weigh one thousand pounds built just inside the entrance where wheat could be weighed as it came off the farmers' wagons. A five-sack lot weighed from 650-700 pounds. Three or four doors on the railroad side of the warehouse made it easy to transfer wheat out into boxcars on the track, since the warehouses had been constructed with the floor at the same level as the floor of any freight car stopped at the loading doors.

There were many companies buying wheat, and this was the type of warehouse that they all used, with one exception. The Northern Pacific Elevator Company had grain elevators in the East. When they built warehouses in the West, they built them so that they could handle bulk wheat. A strong bridge was constructed on the receiving side, so that the farmers could drive their teams pulling a wagon-load of filled sacks clear up to the level of the eaves beside the elevator. Here, a big wagon scale had been built into the driveway bridge where the receiving agent could weigh a load all at once. The wagon would then be unloaded, one sack at a time, onto a five-sack hand-truck, and trucked back over a narrow runway built to the center, through the entire length of the warehouse.

The wheat would be dumped up five sacks high at the very end of the building. After the wagon had been unloaded, and weighed once again, the farmer would drive his wagon down, off the other end of the bridge, and then back home for another load.

Whenever the sack-buckers had time to spare, they would go back to where they had dumped the sacks of wheat. Here, they would cut strings, empty the grain out, pile up the sacks, and tie them together into bundles of fifty to be sold back to the farmers.

Midway up the sides, for their entire length of about twenty feet, these elevators had cross-rods with blocks and nuts outside the walls of the buildings to keep the sides from bulging, letting the wheat spill out as they were filled. On the railroad side, each elevator had several little built-in loading spouts with slides inside the warehouse to close them. When the operator wanted to load a railroad car with wheat, all he had to do was to cooper the boxcar, then place a longer connecting spout from one of the smaller spouts across to the boxcar. After he had opened the slide, letting the grain out, he would go back to the boxcar to shovel the wheat into the ends, filling the car to a level of about four feet.

Each year, a partial amount of the farmers' harvested crop was saved for seed, stored in a dry corner of the granary. The roof was checked carefully for possible leakage, since any sign of mold would require disposal of the seed. Some of the grain was ground into flour, sacked for use in baking, or lightly ground for the cracked wheat mush eaten at the breakfast table.

After a long blistering day of harvesting one August, a weary Ole Ruud left a stack of about 30 sacks of wheat by the thresher, planning to transport them to the warehouse the following morning. But when he went outside after breakfast, they were gone. He didn't mention it to his wife because he didn't want to cause her worry. He didn't mention it to his boys or even the hired man. He mentioned it to no one, but the incident caused him worry and stress. He, like all immigrants, was aware of some prejudices within and around the settlements. He knew that occasionally there was competition, distrust, jealously, and even dislike among the Swedes, Norwegians, Irish, Scots, and Germans, usually between the men, and, from time to time, even within the women's social groups. He was well aware of the fact that generally, Catholics, Lutherans, and Methodists kept to their own kind for similar reasons. Several days later he went to town. A local farmer walked up to him. As they reached out to shake each other's hand in greeting, the sly farmer asked, "Say, Ole, did you ever find out who stole your wheat?" "Ja," replied Ole, "I just did."

* * *

It would be a few years before the general-use tractor would revolutionize agriculture and change the face of farming. This shift in horticulture practices would bring financial disaster to those men on Badger Mountain engaged in the business of raising horses. These men, who were often lone bachelors, had prospered up to this time, as their herds drank from the fresh-water springs and pastured in the green valleys of the mountain. It had been profitable to breed horses and sell or trade them off to the wheat farmer, who required multiple teams, or to the fruit growers by the Columbia River, who cultivated the orchards. But with the advent of the tractor, in the '20s, many of these good horses were sold to the army, or sent off to the glue factory, as the horse-dealers, one by one, gave up and sold or lost their land.

When it became financially feasible, a large three wheeled 1928 model Harris combine with a gasoline motor was purchased by Oliver in 1929, but 12 horses were required to pull from the front hitch. This 16 ft. combine was much heavier, had a longer header to cut the grain and a separator on the machine, and would require five men to maintain operation. The crew consisted of the "driver," the "header tender," the "machine operator" who rode on the top to level the combine and also released the accumulated straw, the "sack jigger," and the "sack sewer," who worked on a platform on the side of the combine sewing then sliding the tied sacks onto the field. Again, times were tough with the start of the Great Depression and fifteen years would pass before Oliver would finally pay for his side-hill combine.

The dry land wheat farmers were totally dependent on the rainfall and weather patterns in determining the yield from their crop. By the first of June, they became like flesh-barometers with sensors always directed toward the sky, the wind, and the moisture around them. Rainfall ranged from 11-14 inches per year in Douglas County. An August thunderstorm, with an accompanying cloudburst, was the harvester's worst nightmare. A winter without adequate snowfall, a spring lacking in sufficient rainfall, a late freeze in the spring, mold resulting from a heavy rainstorm before cutting—all could substantially decrease their income, causing financial misery. The harvest of 1915 brought discouragement. Ole wrote to his family back in Norway.

For us here, the harvest this year has been the poorest in all the 36 years I have been here. The yield of spring wheat and other grains was hardly 1/3 of a normal year. Fortunately, I had 30 acres of winter wheat with a yield of about 350 bushels, most of which I sold for seed to many whose harvest was worse than mine. The price is $2.15 a bushel of 60 pounds. We got little hay, so I have already bought hay for $200.00 for the winter. We'll hardly have enough potatoes for our own use, but we made the mistake of planting them a little late. I will probably not sell enough vegetables to break even. However, we sold cattle this past summer for $1,800.00, so we won't have more than 50 cows and horses to feed throughout the winter. Of hogs, we have about 12, and we have to butcher or sell most of them for lack of feed for them.

The County Fair is taking place this week, only for Douglas County. The entire family went there today—except I; I had to stay home and take care of the house. I am going there tomorrow. The children brought over miscellaneous items, such as a variety of garden seeds, beans and peas, and other little stuff they have harvested themselves.

I sent over 4 swine—good breeders, some of the best, I'm sure. It is an improved race, the best I have had, and they go by the name of <u>Duroc-Jersey,</u> and they are red, that is, their bristle is red, as red as any redhead you have seen. And then, a fine one-year-old ox, of the Hereford race. The boys also took over two horses for racing. Albert rode one today, one named Dick; he didn't win, but his horse wasn't the last one of the six either. The other horse is called Frank, and they are going to ride both of them tomorrow. There are small prizes for those who win. However, the entire horse race is only for entertainment of a lot of curious spectators coming from all over to attend the County Fair.

We are getting more apples from the orchard by Orondo this year than we can use ourselves, and we'll sell some. They are offering a dollar a box. These apple boxes aren't big, only 11" x 11" x 17½", and they hold hardly 40 pounds of apples. Synneva and a German girl are down by the Columbia River, not far from our orchard, picking apples to earn some money. They are getting paid $4.50 a day if they are able to pick 100 boxes a day. The orchard belongs to a family by the name McGinnis who also used to be our neighbors, but sold out for $27,000 and moved to the Columbia Valley. They expect to harvest 25,000 boxes of apples which they expect to sell for $1 to $2 a box, and they expect to make about $6,000 in clear profit after all expenses have been paid. The truck farming in the Columbia Valley is expanding immensely, and between four and six thousand railroad cars of apples are shipped out every year. Apples from this area are considered the best of all apples in the United States, and this year they sell for $1½ to $3 per box for the best kinds, such as Delicious, Winesap and Stayman.

Next spring I intend to plant some trees of a new kind of Delicious, called Golden Delicious, which are golden yellow in color. You can't believe what a fine taste they have. They are almost as good as the Grandma Apples, but they are also slightly sour and have, in addition, a special aromatic taste not found in other apples.

Couldn't you send me a few twigs for grafting from the "Grandmother Apple Tree"? If it is no longer in existence, maybe you have grafts of it. I am sure that over here, those would be something new. New varieties are only arrived at accidentally from seed. Grandmother planted those trees when Father was a young boy. She bought them from Elsebeth Sundoen.

By the way, ask Kristian Ruud if he wants to know anything about the old days. I can tell him what old Maria Sundet, Paul Sundet's mother, related about the big flood in the fjord when she was young. I guess it happened in 1860. Maria Sundet and several other grownups were sitting at Flaberja by the sound, and I was sitting there also, listening, for it was always my habit to listen when grownups were talking, and I remember many things that were said when no one believed I understood or paid any attention. Old Maria was about 80 years old when she told this story, and I was about 12. Maria said: "one summer it rained so hard—it was before the Sund Bridge had been built, and I was rowing travelers across because often there was no one else to do it. Well, when the flood was at its worst, I rowed... ... ..."

What happened to Maria? Obviously, she lived to tell about it—but how it all came out, or any chilling circumstances will forever remain a mystery as the last page of the letter is missing! But old Maria had weathered many storms and was told to have spent an entire night, during an early fall freeze, rowing back and forth across those same waters dividing the two farms, frantically smashing at the forming ice. The animals on both sides needed fodder and she was determined to keep the waterway open so the men could do their job.

$$*\quad*\quad*$$

Whenever guests would be invited to the home for supper, they would often bring along their fiddles, extra food, and nightclothes, planning to spend the night, or perhaps even a few days. If several neighbors were present for such a party, Ole and Augusta would open up the doors, exposing the parlor and dining areas along the entry hall. A lively dance would follow the feast. The Andersons, the Jensens, the Nelsons, the Ruuds, along with the Mitchells, the Millers, and the Oaklands, all would dance the two-step until late into the night. These families would take turns sharing their homes to entertain their friends and fellow immigrants. It was at such a gathering at the home of the Andersons that twenty-two-year-old Agnes was introduced to a handsome, dark-haired immigrant from Norway.

In October, 1915, the spacious parlor with its dark green walls and high white ceiling was decorated with colorful flowers, green leaves, and hanging lamps for the wedding of Agnes to John Ingolf Berg. The twenty-nine guests filled the room as Ole, now 68, escorted his lovely daughter, dressed in her delicate, handmade white wedding gown with a bouquet of roses in her arms.

BERG-RUUD [30]

"One of the prettiest of fall weddings took place at the home of Mr. and Mrs. Ole Ruud, Wednesday afternoon, October 27, when their daughter, Agnes, was married to Mr. John Ingolf Berg of San Francisco, the Rev. Sterns of Mansfield performing the ceremony, using the Lutheran service.

"Promptly at 4 o'clock the groom entered the parlor from a side door and advanced to the altar at one corner of the room where he was met by the bride, who had entered the room from an opposite door on the arm of her father, accompanied by her sister, Miss Synneva, and also Ardis Anderson and they took their places, Miss Joy Welby playing the wedding march. The Reverend Sterns then proceeded to unite them in the holy bonds of matrimony.

"The bride is the oldest daughter of Mr. and Mrs. Ruud, pioneers of the Waterville country, and was born and raised here, graduating from the Waterville High School. The groom is a prosperous young man of San Francisco, where he holds a lucrative position with the American Canning Company, spending his winters there and during the summer months in Alaska. They will make their home in San Francisco where a handsome home awaits them."

Wedding of Agnes Ruud to Ingolf Berg 1915

Family dinner prior to wedding of Agnes and Ingolf Berg

Harvest 1919

Twelve-horse team   Five-man crew

**Tramway near the loading point on the
Waterville Plateau**

**Near the Tramway north of Orondo, WA
In operation from 1902-1910**

**Waterville, Washington - 1917
Photo courtesy of Douglas County Museum**

* * *

November 1, 1916
Andreas and Olava,

  I was in Waterville on Monday the 20th but did not manage to send a letter so I will write a few words this day. On that same day I sold a little over 800 bushels of wheat for $1.52 per bushel. The highest price that has been paid so far! It is possible that it will go higher because it seems like the whole world has too little to live on. I still have another 300 bushels to sell but I want to see where the price will end up. For what I sold I got $1322.00 and paid all of my minor debts, both to the bank and to the stores and that amounted to $800 but then there was also so many high priced things to buy for the winter that I did not go home with more then $300.00.

  This coming spring I must buy around $300 worth of farm equipment and saddles for 4 horses. A pair of saddles cost $45-60. But that is not the end of my purchases. A new plow has been invented that plows 2-3 furrows. I would like to have one of those, even if it costs $700.00. I am sending a page of a catalog so you can see what it looks like. A few gas-powered tractors are used here now to pull loads on the roads. One tractor can pull two wagons loaded with 150 sacks of wheat or more!

  Now we have ready for the market $1500.00 worth of livestock to be butchered. I hope to become in the near future again free of debt. The weather is still nice and dry, without snow. We are bringing out and spreading manure with two wagons but it goes slowly since we have a lot of it. I bought in the summer a wagon for $150.00 that is only for this use—called a "manure spreader". It has a moving bottom that brings the manure to the back and a wheel that throws the manure.

  Not far from where he had built the hotel in Orondo, Ole purchased land, a few acres at a time next to the Columbia River. After making several attempts to establish a fruit-producing orchard in the meadowland next to the mountain, he realized the elevation and the weather patterns were not conducive to sufficient productivity, as only a few hardy trees—crab apple, pie cherry, plum, and apricot—sustained the cold temperatures of winter. On the acreage by the river, an elevation drop from the farm of around 2100 feet, the warmer climate would produce a pleasing crop of fruit and berries. By the month of June 1917, he was anxious to try grafting from twigs from Svarstad.

  Your letters, written January 22, I received about the 5th of March. The little bits of news Andreas is telling about are quite amusing for me to read. I thank you for the letters and for the little twigs for grafting which arrived at the same time. They were nicely packaged and undamaged. I didn't see any sign indicating that anything had been opened on the trip. However, I believe that it had been a little too dry for them because the paper was completely dried out and the twigs looked a bit dry. We placed them in water immediately and later in damp sand *until the 10ᵗʰ of May when I did the grafting. They are not going to live, all of them, but I looked at them today, and one twig from Bestemorapalen (*Grandmother's apple) *tree was sprouting, and one other one shows signs of life. Whether they'll live or not we'll find out about later, but in case we are not successful this time, I'm going to send you a tin tube with a tight cover and bottom so that it will keep the moisture inside. I can send something in it, either a new kind of potato, seed, or some twigs of our most popular apple trees for grafting.*

The Duchess apple is the earliest to ripen. I have some good ones, and they would do well in Norway. My best ones, and the best tasting, are Spitzenburg. They are among the highest priced on the market. Thousands of cases of those are sent out from the Columbia Valley each year. In addition, there are many other varieties that are good looking and pleasant tasting apples. I'll name some of them: Yellow Neuton Pippin—those are yellow like wax and tasty; Golden, Maiden Blush—those are dark red all over and very good; Jonathan and Western Spy, and a lot of others. I could come up with something to send that wouldn't be contraband or subject to customs. It will cost the same. We'll see if those I got are going to work out.

The orchard we have by Orondo looks great now, and this year it will provide us with all the fruit and berries we need, such as apples, cherries, plums, apricots, and peaches. We may possibly also get as much as 100 lbs. of wine grapes. You see, it takes about 4-5 years before they really start bearing fruit. This spring I planted more than 40 grapevines, and I have space for a lot more. So, we can have whatever we want when it comes to grapes and whatever can be done with them if we are able to do the necessary work. I have about 20 acres of orchard in Orondo right next to the river because I buy a little more off and on.

Dr. Smith, who was the original owner of Orondo and whom I have mentioned previously in my letters, passed away, 80 years old, this spring about the end of April. I was down there about that time along with a carpenter and one of my little boys, putting up a small house so that we can have a place to stay when we go down there to take care of the orchard. I then went to see John Brown Smith, (that was his full name), several times. I tried to talk to him about Eternity and Religion and said that in case he wanted to accept a minister, I would go and get one for him. But he answered that he had no faith in any minister and was not afraid to die. He was a spiritualist, you see. I knew quite well that he did not believe in any other teachings, for throughout the many years--more than 30—that I have known him and been with him many, many times, we have talked a lot about teachings, and it seems to me that the spirits have deceived him, just as they are said to have deceived others who have become involved in Spiritualism. My own experience seems to prove that true.

Dr. J. B. Smith served, along with Ole, in Douglas County as its coroner for four years. Their compatible friendship is recognizable in the fact that both men were literary advocates and independent thinkers possessing curious minds. A civil war veteran, Smith had studied and practiced medicine in the east before coming to Douglas County, arriving in Old Okanogan in 1884. He was known for his honesty and claimed that he found so much "humbuggery" in the practice of medicine that he quit the profession.

After trying to raise a small crop of wheat in the land near the dry town, he became discouraged, left his un-harvested field suffering from drought, and went farther west to the Columbia River. Finding Orondo Grove a pleasant place, he decided to settle in. After making friends with the Indians, who took him across the river and surrounding area, he felt the area had great potential, giving him reason to establish a townsite. Along with other early settlers, forty-six-year-old Dr. Smith erroneously predicted a railroad line on the east side of the river as well as a large city in Orondo. His mistaken assumptions would, within eight years, materialize in a more appropriate area farther down the river, facilitating easier access in all directions and bringing population growth and industry to Wenatchee.

Ole's letter continues, *We were working down there for several weeks, and one morning I was just thinking about going to look in on him when his 18 year-old only son came by. In answer to my question about his father, he answered that he was about as usual. Consequently, I waited too long because an hour later we heard that he had died. I was fully aware of what I would need, so I had brought along my Sunday suit, and I attended the funeral a few days later. A woman, one who was a believer in Spiritualism, performed the graveside services. All the old settlers were present; some of them I hadn't seen in more than 20 years—at the time I was traveling around, doing surveying in the Entiat Valley on the west side of the Columbia River where many of them live. There was a Norwegian there from Kristiania by the name of Eriksen. When I asked about Hettie Bonar, a girl I had known, an old lady answered. "That's me." She was the one who had performed the graveside services!*

* * *

Forty years had passed since Ole had emigrated from Norway. Since 1919 had been a difficult year for all farmers in America, he debated with himself about whether to return to Svarstad. Olava, who never married, had spent the majority of her life on Svarstad, working part-time as a housekeeper for the local Lutheran minister. Her death, in 1919 at the age of 64, left the farm to her two surviving brothers. Andreas, a banker, was working in nearby Hønefoss. Ole pondered, weighing the pros and cons. He finally concluded remaining at the site he had homesteaded in Washington State was in the best interest of all, as he knew his children, all approaching adulthood, would not approve such a change. He realized there were many things for which to be grateful. He was thankful his boys, too young to serve in the war in Europe, had also escaped the devastating influenza epidemic, which killed millions of people—more than the war itself. He was bonded to his farm in the Big Bend and his family depended on him, so he knew he would never return to Norway. Realizing this, he signed total ownership of Svarstad over to Andreas. Rarely did he feel downhearted, but at this time his heart ached for his homeland.

Breidablikk Farm
January 5, 1920

Brother Andreas,

Your letter of November 3rd was received right after a little over three weeks en route—along with the two photographs of the Svarstad farm and surroundings. Yes, it is very interesting to see these well-known areas again. I also see Hans Fjeld's house and barn on our old flat land. Wouldn't these two be a splendid farm together? On many occasions I have yearned to see my old home again—the mountains, the fjords, go fishing in the lakes. Except for in my dreams I know that will never again be a possibility. But many good memories remain vivid and fresh in my mind. I belong here now, but I will continue, for the rest of my days, to also love Norway. Even the children enjoyed the pictures and think it is so beautiful there. Wouldn't it be fun for them to see pictures from Rudsødegaarden and more places along the coast that we traveled as children? Nothing pleases them more than when they can go to the water and try their luck if there is at least a brook with small trout in it. Every time I go to Orondo on the Columbia River, they almost always come along. Lewis Andreas is the most eager fisherman. All of them are hunters. I gave the boys each a little Winchester magazine rifle that they take along when they hike over the hills, but they rarely get anything, because there is always something in the way such as a rock or a tree.

I have enclosed the two documents you sent, signed by me with a notary certification. Now you own your own farm in your own name. It is large enough for you and you can now do with it what you will. But <u>hold on to what you have and stay where you are as there is no better place.</u> You aren't really far from your neighbors—say hello to Han Thomason for me.

I have also received a letter from bank manager Jensen with a full account of everything, and I may correspond with him now and then, as most of my inheritance from Olava is in the bank, and my papers are left in your security box. This can be left until later. I have decided, so far, that everything that comes from Norway will be divided amongst my children and only used in helping them to acquire a home. Ingolf Berg and Agnes are now scouring around California to buy something, but all the land is sold and almost unreasonable. I have promised *them not more than $1,000.00 if they buy something. Ingolf is healthy again and is earning good money.*

Synneva is with them in the winter and will come home in the summer. She was in Seattle for a few weeks in the fall and helped out in the house of a family of our friends. From this she got enough money to take the steamship to San Francisco and from there traveled to Colfax—a mountain chalet in northeastern California where Agnes is. They have a little Ford automobile to drive around in and Synneva drives it well. She writes that they had a Christmas tree and visitors for Christmas, namely Ingolf's brother Einar and a girl, Emma Schneider, of German origin who is studying to become a nurse. The Schneider family lived in our neighborhood for several years but sold out for around $40,000. It looks like Synneva is on good terms with Harry Schneider, the youngest son of the old man, who is a widower and lives in northern California.

We are having now the finest winter weather we could hope for but in the beginning of November we had a very strong cold like the coldest day in Norway. There are only six thumbs of snow, but we wish more would come, since this will help with next year's harvest. Last summer was the driest of the last four drought years and our harvest was poor. They say that the position in conjunction with six or seven planets has something to do with both the drought and many other unusual things in the world. When the position of the planets came to its high point this last December 17th, 1919, a frightful storm, an earthquake and volcanic eruptions were predicted, and I read many went and committed suicide in fright of that day. But the day came and went and nothing out of the ordinary happened.

Oliver and Albert are now spreading straw for the livestock. I had to get $300.00 worth of straw this fall. We now have only 50 animals and 20 horses. I had to sell more than I wanted last summer because the oat crop dried up but the prices are still good. Just today I sold a calf that arrived in the spring of 1919. It weighed together with the skin and without the intestines, head and feet, 300 pounds and sold for $51.00. The price of wheat is now over $3.00 per bushel now that we don't have any to sell. Clothes and other things are also getting more expensive. It doesn't help that the government is tightening its fist in our pockets.

People complain about the high cost of living, but those that <u>should</u> work go on strike and wander around and say there is no work to be found. But the truth is that they <u>won't</u> work. There are many questions I would like to ask if I could get answers to them. What is the address to Tinfos Iron works? Do you know the number of my shares?

Have all the German children gone home again? I have seen in the Norwegian newspapers that it pleased the parents very much to see their children so well taken care of and they looked so well that, in some cases, they almost couldn't recognize them and they brought so many good things with them. I think it was so honorable of Norway that it will never be forgotten and will find a place in both Norwegian and German history. Here, we hear the most shameless lies about "The Huns" from the pro-British side. But not all the Americans are on the British side on this issue. Those that brought America into this war are the most hated by the general public. It is claimed that the Allied forces, including the United States, have not only broken their promise against the 14 points and the Armistice Treaty (a ceasefire agreement), but also in many other directions.

Innumerable people, old and young, perished during and following WWI. In 1920 the International Red Cross asked the League of Nations to appoint Fridtjof Nansen, the well-known Norwegian explorer of the Fram expedition, scientist, and diplomat, as High Commissioner for refugees. Suffering in prison camps in Europe and Asia were half a million forgotten men, prisoners of war, who had fought for Germany and its allies. Many of these prisoners no longer had a homeland, knew nothing of the fate of their families, and they were dying by the thousands from cold and hunger. Nansen abhorred warfare and its senseless slaughter. Through his untiring humanitarian actions an enormous amount of relief took place, saving hundreds of thousands of forgotten prisoners and refugees in Germany, Russia, and Austria, all desperate in their sufferings. Nansen, honored with the Nobel Prize for Peace in 1922, would continue his heartfelt work, devoting his life to the promotion of human welfare, until his death in 1930.

During World War I, the neutral European countries, Denmark, Holland, Switzerland, Norway, and Sweden all received refugees seeking safety. Norway, because of its neutrality and tolerance, always a country with a high sense of justice and humanitarianism, provided a safe haven for many children following the war. Austria, for example, an impoverished nation of 7 million, appealed to the League of Nations for help. Norwegian families responded with spontaneous support for rescue operations, taking in Austrian and German children of the starving and oppressed populations. As the tragedy of war unfortunately dictated, some of these same children, fed, cared for, and protected by the kind-hearted Norwegians would, in the early '30s, join the German Nationalist Youth Organization and be among those in the German Nazi Army who would return as conquering oppressors in WWII following orders of Adolf Hitler.

For the first three years of the war, beginning in 1914, the U.S. had proclaimed itself neutral, although, by the time it entered the battle in 1917, the Allies in Europe had come to depend on munitions being supplied to them from factories in the United States. After a German submarine torpedoed and sank the passenger ship *Lusitania* off the coast of Ireland in 1915, taking the lives of many Americans, anger built in many people in the U.S. The British ship, carrying around 1200 passengers, mostly women and children, was also carrying a delivery of munitions in its cargo. Although the general American public did not favor joining the fight overseas, President Wilson convinced Congress that it was morally the "right thing to do," to act as Europe's policeman in order to put a halt to the hateful brawl going on, thereby securing the safety of their right to establish a Democratic government.

Ole's letter to Andreas continues: *Too many lives have been tragically lost resulting from the senseless war and many people here, not always agreeing in philosophy, continue to discuss the circumstances. Let us hope that all of Europe can begin to rebuild itself now and war tactics of any kind are erased from countries all over the world until the end of time.*

Our three youngest boys are going to school every day in Waterville. A covered sled picks them up in the morning and brings them home in the afternoon. Lewis Andreas is working in Fyrable making small electric batteries, and has made them so strong that they can light a lamp. We haven't gotten electric light amongst us farmers yet, but it will come. Many farmers have their own light apparatus, made of a gas-powered motor, a dynamo and storage battery. I have read and studied a lot all winter to learn how to thoroughly understand these remarkable discoveries that can be at least partly understood by studying electricity. Now I know so well the principles of how it all works that I can build these instruments if I had the necessary materials and tools. For the children's sake I have thought of trying something in that direction, and am now corresponding with the companies that have these things for sale. And there are many.

You say in your letter that you were going to send buds in the winter, but they haven't arrived yet. The Granny Smith apple buds are the ones I really want. I am sure these will get a good price here. The sweetest we have aren't nearly as sweet as the Granny Smith apples. In this excellent apple climate by the Columbia River and along the whole Columbia Valley, it would turn into something very significant, if not of national renown, then maybe for Norway. We don't know what this could come to without trying. Every remarkable type of fruit has its own history from the very beginning. Granny Smith apples will also begin with Eslebet Sundøen. Whatever great name they will have after many years is not for me to say. Do what you can and send them in the tin crate I sent you last winter. Put a little damp paper or moss in both ends of the crate. Don't wait until spring when the weather gets warm.

I don't have more to tell except that everything continues the same. Nils Øvergjordet died some years ago, Anne and Ragne, too. I haven't heard anything from the Wilbergs in 20-30 years. Have you heard from Johanne? It has been so long ago since I visited her in San Francisco, but she went back to Norway after nothing came of what we had planned for her and I. It was probably the best for me as Augusta has been a good wife. Have you heard anything from Marie Rudsødegaarden, Soffie's sister? How are things with Soffie and Petter Øverby? Say hello to them for me. Have they begun to fish again? Greet Kristian Ruud if you are going there yourself for the buds. Also, Nathan Vig, and them on the hill.

If you have some small things from Kristian and Olava, then take care of them as they can be sent to the children one day and be cherished by them. I realize you are now in the midst of winter, but are crops expected to do well this year? Write back in a few days and don't wait as long as I did. You must have more time than I do.

"Haying is in full swing on Svarstad this August," Andreas wrote to his brother Ole and family, "but the gathering is delayed somewhat by a shower now and then. My neighbor, Kristoffersen, has bought grassland at Hov, Røsholm's property. The workers are striking on some of the farms in Haug. It is doubly difficult to get the work done. Røsholm is selling his hay on the root at 50 or 60 kroner per mål (¼ of an acre) which is very cheap, considering that hay sells for up to 55 kroner ($13.75) per Skp. (skippund, about 350 pounds) this year. (1920). The grain and potato fields are doing well everywhere in Hole, and in all European countries as far as that goes, but the worker strikes all around are affecting the whole economy.

"By the way, the little German girls who came here last winter are going home in a few days. Marie Haug stopped by last week to help me clean, and had two of them with her. One of them, by the name of Lotte Gartner from Breslau had just arrived, and she is going to stay at Haug for the winter. The other, whose name is Eli Pillati, attends the Buskerud School where Marie is teaching. She attends the classes, but is exempt from learning religion since she is Catholic. She knows enough Norwegian now so that we can converse. Her first cousin, Marie Ratter, has come here to stay with the engineer of the Nickel Works in Tyristrand.

"Olaf Haug was here two weeks ago; he is still working on his potato harvester which is supposed to dig the potatoes out of the ground, sort them in 3 different sizes, eliminate rocks and potato stalks, and put them in bags, and he has secured the patent to the machine in America as well as in Canada and several European countries. He is hoping to take out a patent here in Norway, also. He has set up a corporation and two merchants from Drammen have signed on for 15,000 kroner each, and some from Haug also have signed on so that they now have 90,000 kroner all together. I didn't have that much and couldn't afford to buy shares, but I signed as a guarantor for 5,000 kroner. He has two men helping him in a workshop in Drammen. A man from Aas Agricultural School had inspected the machine in the shop and he believed that the principle was correctly applied, but could not give any more details until the machine has been tried in the field.

"I have a new tenant—a man and his wife. They came here from Rjukan, but earlier lived in Hønefoss. His name is Gabriel Jørgensen and they have grown children—a son in Hønefoss who is going to be a chauffeur, a married daughter near Ask, and an unmarried daughter someplace. The wife mends my clothes and is a seamstress. They have a little kitchen and a woodshed and they are going to pay 15 kroner a month. It is not so quiet when there are people in the house.

"There is a lot of car traffic these days so that it is difficult for pedestrians to use the road because of all the dust that gets right in your mouth and covers the clothes. It is predicted that in 5-10 years there will be more than 30,000 cars here in Norway. The people in Hønefoss have formed a corporation and are constructing a big brick building about in the middle of town, and it will house a repair shop and a garage for automobiles. There are 70 who have signed up to buy shares. Hønefoss Private Bank is also putting up a big brick building. Since we are part owners in the bank, we might also reckon that we are part owners in this building. I guess it is supposed to be three stories high, and located right next to the market place, so it ought to provide a good income when it is finished."

Norwegian banking went through a difficult period, especially during the years 1921-24. Many farmers got badly into debt during the war, and the years immediately following, and nearly all were in connection with some private bank or another. A number of bank failures disrupted much business and worked the usual hardships on society because of it. It led to new laws in the field of banking. The government, at that time, was given the power to put banks, which were very weak and beginning to totter, under public administration before the crash could occur. Around 1924, a large number of private banks were under public administration. The result of this put private banks under a strict system of public control and inspection, and put large powers in the hands of both the Bank of Norway and the government to intervene in all cases where a private bank was in trouble.

Andreas's letter continues. "I may be able to take a trip to Rudsødegaarden this summer. I already went to the Hole Cemetery and put flowers on Mother's grave and asked the caretaker to water them. Olava's and Kristian's gravestone was tilting a little and I asked the caretaker to take care of that also. I am including a photo of me, and one of us all at Svarstad. It was taken about two years before Mother died. Greet Edvart Berg from me and all of you are greeted also. Andreas."

Chapter IV

And slowly it brings us nearer to the ultimate
soul of things:
We are weighing the atoms, and wending the seas,
and cleaving the air with wings;
And draining the tropic marshes where death had
lain in wait,
And piercing the polar solitudes, for all their icy state;
And luring the subtle electric flame to set us free from
the clod—
O toiling Brothers, the earth around, we are working
together with God!
With God, the infinite Toiler, who dwells with His humblest ones,
And tints the dawn and the lily, and flies with the
flying suns,
And forever, through love and service, though days
may be drear and dim,
Is guiding the whole creation up from the deeps to Him!*

*4th verse from *The Glory of Toil*
by Edna Dean Proctor

Steadfast Principles and Reflections

Having been on the farm for the past thirty-eight years, Ole, now 74 years old, was starting to slow down. His two daughters, married to the Berg brothers, were living in California. Synneva had given birth to the first grandchild, Ellen Christine, on May 18, 1921. *We have Ellen's portrait,* Ole would write his brother Andreas. *She is a very beautiful child with proportionate facial features and a high forehead just like mother's. We are surely going to get more portraits over time so we can send you one. Einar and Synneva are now in San Francisco, where he practices his profession as a painter and gets $8.00 a day.*

Ingolf and Agnes are at the farm in Auburn and I think they are doing quite well. They are clearing their land in order to plant a pear orchard as fast as they can. But they complained about the intense heat in the summer. They are saying that eventually, they want to travel back North. They also say that I was right when I said that California's climate is not suitable for people of Northern descent. I have sent the $1,000 more than a year ago from the last amount of money that you sent through Olava. I am soon going to send them more for the same amount. They would be in need of it since the orchard is still a big expense for them. But they are off to a good start. They also have 6 milk cows and are paid well for butter and cream.

We are now getting 50 cents per pound—a little less than a Norwegian skaalpund for butter and a similar price for cream. So, often it is not worth it for us to make butter. During the whole summer we have sold regularly one 5-gallon container and sometimes an 8-gallon container and each one brings in $7 to $10 dollars. (We send it by train to the Wenatchee Dairy—a butter factory). The payment comes just as regularly in a form of a check or a money order, after which we withdraw cash from the bank in Waterville.

This year we got an average crop and sold 1,020 bushels of wheat, but we only got an advance payment of 65 cents per bushel. The rest we will get in one year and that would be according to the average price for wheat for that year. This rule has been implemented by a farmer's union of three western states, namely Washington, Idaho and Oregon, that I and thousands of farmers have joined. This is to prevent rich speculators and dishonest scoundrels from driving the prices up or down as they wish. We think that the average price will be one dollar per bushel. The wheat prices are still determined in Liverpool, England, but the goal is that we, the farmers, can set our own prices. With this goal in mind the farmers are getting organized now, not just here in America and Canada but also in Australia, New Zealand and South America. If it were not for this farmer's union, wheat prices would most likely be as low as 50 cents per bushel or less.

* * *

In the fall of that same year, 1921, Oliver went to an annual dance at the local school to welcome and meet the new teachers. Without a proper introduction, he took a chance and asked Eloise McKay, a twenty-four-year-old graduate of the University of Washington, for a dance. That very evening he would confide in his friends that he just "might marry that brunette English teacher who danced like an angel." Oliver had courted many local girls but, in Eloise, he found the epitome of womanly dignity, a female who analyzed all aspects of life, an unpredictable challenge, a female like no other. She fell in love with him before the school year was out, later saying she quickly recognized his basic good character, healthy body, strong hands, and his honest and humble nature. After she left her $100-a-month job in Waterville in June, he would write over one hundred letters to "My Darling Queen" with poor sentence structure and misspelled words, but somehow the romantic tone held her devotion to him.

On November 27, 1923, Eloise, who loved opera, beauty, and poetical writings, married Oliver, the down-to-earth farmer. With her home in Spokane filled with bouquets of lilies of the valley and musical presentations, the ceremony united an unlikely couple with opposite backgrounds. The 70-year union would be filled with hard work and many sacrifices for the seven children they would bring into the world. Maintaining a respect for education, always cognizant of and self-conscious about his own lack in liberal arts, Oliver supported her adamant determination to give all their offspring a college education.

Ole liked his new daughter-in-law. He thought she was a beautiful woman with her chiseled profile, perfect posture, and waist-long head of thick, dark hair styled high in a French roll that emphasized her long smooth neck. He showed her a calendar picture he had saved many years previous to meeting her, remarking on the facial resemblance and cameo complexion. She impressed him with her spunk and agility as she kicked her laced high-heeled shoe to touch the top of the doorway in the dining room with the tip of her toe. He found her intellect to blend well with his own philosophies as they discussed the state of the world or the life of the farmer, giving them many stimulating conversations in agreement with each other.

They spent hours discussing the admirable qualities of the Scandinavian greats: Henrik Ibsen, the Norwegian dramatist, Gustav Vigeland, Oslo's notable sculptor, Edvard Munch, the contemporary painter, and Roald Amundsen, the renowned explorer. They shared admiration for Jenny Lind, the Swedish Nightingale, Ole Bull, a notable fiddler, and ventured further into the scientific world discussing Carolus Linnaeus, the Swedish botanist who provided a simple system of nomenclature in plants, giving them two names, genus and species. They discussed Alfred Nobel of Sweden who devised a safe way to handle nitroglycerin by producing dynamite, and who later gave $9 million to set up a fund to award yearly prizes for merit in the sciences, literature, and world peace. Even the milk separator, Ole boasted, was invented by a Swede. Eloise admired his curious mind and told him she planned to fill his big house up with children and raise them all to be thinkers with ideas and dreams. Ole knew Oliver had married a full deck and he might have his hands full trying to satisfy all of her intellectual and artistic demands, but he had to admit that she was a fascinating woman.

Eloise McKay

Oliver Ruud 1923

Oliver Ruud

Augusta, on the other hand, didn't think Oliver had married the kind of wife he needed. She refused to attend the Spokane wedding, so none of Oliver's family witnessed the marriage. To Augusta, reading Shakespeare, studying the classics, practicing pianoforte, singing favorite arias, and discussing subjects which should be left to the men, such as politics or farming practices, were all a waste of time—especially if there were floors to scrub or housework of any kind left undone. She wanted her son to marry someone who was not so citified but knew how to use a shovel, milk a cow, and maintain an immaculate house—a woman more like herself. A woman's place, according to Eloise's new mother-in-law, was unquestionably tending to her man, reading her Bible, and keeping up with the Lord's work.

Following the marriage of Oliver and Eloise, Ole found himself corresponding over several issues with his son's father-in-law. F.H. McKay, an arrogant, 6'3" redheaded Scotsman, had met many farmers in the Big Bend, both as wheat buyer for the Seattle Grain Company in the early 1900s, and as a farm mortgage inspector for the Old National Bank & Union Trust Company in Spokane. Some of his acquaintances knew him to be a "wheeler-dealer" businessman whose overbearing demeanor occluded any believable compassion. After his statuesque and cultured daughter married what he referred to as "a common farmer," McKay started pressuring Ole to deed some of his property in the fruit growing area of Orondo over to the newlyweds.

Frederick McKay, an atheist, also delighted in political debates. Any kind of argument stimulated him, giving him an opportunity to boastfully pontificate his opinions. After the raging World War I had ended, most people were feeling the devastation from the loss of millions of lives. Many Americans were voicing or writing their opinions on how the world could prevent such a global tragedy from recurring. McKay obviously had addressed that subject in conversation or letter. The content of the exchange is unknown; however, he received a reply shortly thereafter, dated February 14, 1924.

Dear Mr. McKay:

Your letter of February 9 was received a few days ago. Am enclosing a copy of the Bok Peace Plan, and two blanks for warranty deeds. (In 1923, Edward W. Bok, a philanthropist from Philadelphia, announced the American Peace Award of $100,000 for "the best practicable plan by which the United States could cooperate with other nations to achieve and preserve the peace of the world.") *My intention is to make out a deed to Oliver on the Orondo fruit farm as soon as I can—but first, I must do a little surveying to ascertain with reference to some permanent initial point, the exact location of three small lots that must be excluded from the tract. This is the lot that John H. D. Smith's house stands on and two pumping stations down at the Columbia River.*

I have received this river land in various ways, some by warranty deeds, some by quit-claim and some by tax title. I don't know how safe it would be to give a warranty deed on lots that had been quit-claimed to me. In the case of Oliver, it would be no trouble, but if he should sell and my title to any of it comes in question, what could possibly happen then? Well, most likely nothing.

Since I come to think it over, I am a little at a loss how to word a description when this is to be a grant or gift counted off on his inheritance to the amount of $1,000. Could I write this way: For a consideration of $1,000 to me in a note due to me when no money would be turned over from him to me, or in what other way could it be written? The rest of it would be very simple. I have made out deeds before. I will be down there to do the surveying and some other work as soon as the roads and the weather be good.

The Bok Peace Plan I have read carefully and studied to the best of my ability. It may be the best and most practical plan for the United States to follow in as much as this country ought to keep on the outside of entangling alliances and as neutral as possible.

They put forth the "Monroe Doctrine" again. But as the United States was the first to violate it, what else would the world make out of it except to put it in line with the 14 points, something like a pill for others to take, but not for us. The concluding sum and substance seems to be to "stop making war materials". But this will not stop wars as long as causes for war exist and as long as domineering, grasping and dishonest men can command whole nations to go murdering one another, and then they will soon find the tools to do it with. Therefore, I would commence the game at the beginning and not at the end. That is, <u>stop causes</u> and those that make causes out of whole cloth.

The first thing seems to me would be to curb national and international liars (purify the press). Write the true story of everything, history as well as the true owner, strips of provinces, necks of land, passes, & etc. Curb the so-called "International Bankers", Traders and those that profit by plunging nations into war. As it is now, these overlords of usurers, usurpers and other criminals seem to play with courts, law making bodies, people's money and fruit of toil the same as we play with cards and checkers. Stop all this outrage and war will stop and also the making of war materials. But the doings at Versailles is all rambling because they made more causes for war than there was before. War will not stop before "the battle of Armageddon is fought". "They shall cry 'Peace, Peace', but there shall be no peace". (Bible) "Know the Truth and the Truth shall make you free". When this is done, war will stop, not before.

When out this way, drop in. Yours truly, O. Ruud

Complexity and frustration were occurring among many crop growers. Ole was aware of the widening gap between the urban citizenry and the farmer. For the first time more Americans were living in cities as many farmers had quit working the land in the 1920s, moving to the urban areas, some suffering foreclosure. During the war farmers profited by increasing cultivation, even plowed marginal lands to supply enough food for the country and its war-torn allies. However, following the war, farmers found themselves with surpluses of goods without profitable market value. Society was undergoing great change. America was no longer thought of as a frontier land, but as one of industry. The ending of WWI left many Americans with great hope and promise and a carefree feeling of exhilaration, but the struggling farmer was suffering from economic depression.

Ole was no exception. He, as many others in the country, mortgaged his 1924 crop to try to save his farm. The Chattel Mortgage, filed with the Auditor of Douglas County, September 18, 1923, for the sum of $1210 was clearly spelled out. After combining, sacking, and hauling expenses were satisfied the balance went to the bank, but the farm, with its 80 acres of wheat land, was saved. He wrote the figures in pencil on the back of the agreement.

Acres	*80*
Bushels per acre	*20*
	$1600
Price- 80c	*.80*
	$1280.00

Less combining, $220; less Sacks, $120; less $600 to F. M. Powers;

Totals	*$940*
Balance	*$340*
Less hauling of 800 Sacks @10c	
Balance	*$260*
Less other expenses	*260*
O. Ruud share	*000.00*

The new era began handing out immense progress along with some revised turmoil. Immigration was at a high, as was racial discrimination. The Ku Klux Klan had been renewed, stirring up a mistrust of foreigners with vigorous actions against the Germans, Jews, Italians, and Russians, as well as the Blacks, which caused Congress, under President Warren G. Harding, to cut immigration from an unlimited number to a few. In contrast, thousands of Model-T Fords were being produced and the privileged were enjoying a Sunday drive to the countryside for a picnic and a game of croquet. Electricity was lighting movie theaters attended by throngs of city dwellers. The fascination of the airplane excited all Americans, instilling wonder and amazement. Tractors had begun replacing horse-drawn machinery and radios were making their way into thousands of homes. The women's suffrage movement was in full force and women were speaking openly, promoting birth control. The younger, and often brazen women, were shortening their skirts, bobbing their tresses, dancing the Charleston, and smoking in public. It was a new America.

Esther Ruud Stradling

In the Big Bend of Washington State, life for Ole Ruud remained conservative, unaffected by newspaper articles on the social frivolity in the cities. He and his family continued their daily work from sunup to sundown, as did their neighbors. Kerosene lamps lit the homes at night. No one had electricity. Every farm family relieved themselves in their outhouses and only heard or read about the luxury of a room with a bathtub and a flushing toilet. Progress in matching the city-folk was slow-coming to farmers in the area. Burying pipe under the ground from the cold-water spring up the canyon to the house would finally bring running water to the sink in the kitchen in 1923.

During this time of the early '20s, Prohibition was in full swing. The Temperance Movement claimed partaking of intoxicating drink was not only sinful, but was also the greatest danger to society, a devastating threat to family structure. History has been written that Prohibition increased the crime rate, corruption in government, and expanded disrespect for the law. Neighborhood gossip on Badger Mountain claimed that tucked within the shelter of the pine trees next to water springs, several stills produced "a mighty fine drink," and even the local sheriff was said to have dropped by on occasion "just to check it out, take a few swigs, making sure it wasn't going to poison the folks who took a sip from time to time." One poor old homesteader, taking advantage of making a few extra bucks bootlegging, was turned in to the authorities, arrested, thrown in jail and lost his land.

At the base of the canyon, Ole maintained his strong work ethic, always hoping for enough profit from his crops to help his children obtain a good start in their adult life, but he deeply felt the consequences of the economic depression of the farmer and knew he couldn't do anything about it. He held strongly to his political values and his dedication to his occupation. Newspaper articles describing the prosperity of the country, along with the carefree attitudes of the flapper era, enhanced his caution with his own finances. Some thought the U.S. had the world by the tail even though production of goods began to exceed consumption. Many people thought urban prosperity would go on forever. Ole doubted it.

Waterville, Wash., U.S.A.
November 17, 1925

Brother Andreas,

Almost half of the farmers have gone bankrupt here on the coast these last years, and nearly all of them have a lot of debt. The reasons are the same as in Norway—exorbitant taxes and sky-high prices on everything we must buy, including what we have to pay in wages to workers. The financial affairs of every country in the entire world are in the hands of a relatively small group of people. In my opinion, all countries have a few so-called scoundrels who try to control the majority by paying off congressmen and other lawgivers. Groups of this kind have for many years tried to accumulate the wealth of the entire world.

This year we had the poorest harvest we have had in a long time; we had only 500 bushels of wheat for sale, but I sold cattle and pigs last summer for well over $1000.00. However, taxes and everything we must buy are so high that it feels like throwing money in the ocean. But then we have also built a big shed for 8 to 12 horses at the cost of $250, not including our own work. Last fall, we put up a new hen house. It cost us a little over $500.00, not including our labor.

I still have some 300 bushels of wheat to sell, but I expect the price to go up to $1.50 per bushel after Christmas. I also need this money for a lot of other things. Lewis Andreas needs $250 for tuition in January. He is named after you, and you couldn't spend your money in a better way than by helping him. He also will be able to pay you back sometime in case it is needed. There is a lot of demand for people in his profession, and the pay is good, but it will be several years before he will be earning any money. He was 20 years old May 10 and is doing extremely well for his age.

I see in the paper that the Norwegian krone is increasing in value rapidly and is approaching par with American money, namely, 27 cents for 1 krone. Par is 28.70 cents per krone. Ask in the bank how much in American money I can get for 1 krone, or more correctly, how many kroner and øre it takes to buy 1 American dollar. In other words, what is the rate of exchange between American and Norwegian money?

This fall we planted 145 acres of winter wheat, and we are hoping for a good harvest next year. We also have 25 acres for planting various types of seeds in the spring. We now have 28 horses and 35 head of cattle, the least I have had of cattle for many years, mainly because of the poor harvest and the drought for the last 9 years, so I have had to buy fodder at high prices. I have bought this for over $100 already this winter.

We often hear from our folks in California. They are doing very well. Synneva's husband, Einar Berg, is building houses and selling them. He has built and sold 2 houses and is working on the 3rd one, all that in a little over a year. Agnes's husband, Ingolf Berg, Einar's brother, is working in his orchard. They are raising mostly pears, and they also have 7 or 8 milking cows and sell milk to the hotel in Auburn. Albert is living with them and works in a meat and butcher shop, earning $20 a week, also in the city of Auburn. Lewis Andreas is living with Synneva in San Francisco and is attending San Francisco University studying electrical engineering. It will take him three years to graduate, beginning in August of this past summer. He always gets excellent grades and is a great guy. However, it costs me a lot of money.

Andreas, your last letter of July 6 I received and answered the same day. However, since then, I have heard nothing from you. I started thinking that in case there is something wrong, I'd better send you a few lines anyway and I see from your letter that you have had an eye operation and that you now see quite well. Be careful now so that you don't get a relapse! Never read in poor light!

My own eyes are worse, especially the right one; I can't read the biggest letters with that one. It is by using the left eye that I am able to write this, and I read a little by using a big magnifying glass, but it is like being in the twilight. My left eye has never been good. Edvart has told me that his mother had said that I had stuck the point of the scissors in my eye when I was sitting on her lap.

Now I have decided to go to Seattle in a couple of days to see Dr. Pontius who operated on both of my ears in 1905, in other words, twenty years ago. He is an excellent eye and ear doctor. I got a letter from him today. He wants me to come and see him as soon as possible because he is leaving on a trip to Europe on the 10th of December. The operation on my ears consisted of cutting a hole through the bone behind the ear and cleaning out all the matter that had formed back of the eardrum. Only the best doctors have courage enough to attempt this operation. I was very ill and near death, and am a little hard of hearing. However, I can hear ordinary speech close by.

Greet the neighbors, the Haugs, for me. You must write soon. When I am ready to leave for Seattle, I will send you a few words again. O.R.

(Sunday, November 22) Since I wrote the first part of this letter it just so happened that I couldn't get enough money for the trip to Seattle, so I had to postpone it for a while. I had to borrow $300 for the expenses of the operation, and I wasn't able to get it from the bank here in Waterville, which I had expected, and consequently, I have written to a bank in Spokane (the Old National Bank) where Oliver's wife's father is working. However, I expect to hear from them in 2 or 3 days.

*   *   *

By 1926 the farm had slowly grown to one thousand twenty acres—320 acres in tillage, 700 acres of mountain grazing land holding a few valley hay fields, as neighbors sold Ole their small patches of land and moved away to greener pastures. Or some, who simply became discouraged with the lack of substantial gain in financial security, gave up farming entirely. This would be a year to bring many changes. It would be the last harvest for Ole and his sons, as pyramidal health problems began to affect both him and Augusta, requiring that they rest their tired and worn bodies. From his desk in the northwest room of his house, on September 1st he wrote again to his brother: *Your last letter, written early last spring, I received a long time ago, and I also wrote several weeks ago, but have heard nothing from you. I hope good health continues to be with you.*

A doctor said to me recently, as I shook his hand to say good-bye: "Send us a few words when you are 100 years old!" Well, I promised to do that and added that I wouldn't object to getting to be 100 if I could remain reasonably healthy. I mentioned my mother's high age and he said, "You can beat her by 7 years!" However, I got a kind of paralysis in my left hand and left arm in the month of June. Both I and my wife, Augusta, then went to a spa located at a distance of 2 hours by car from here, and both of us had 2 weeks of treatment by an osteopathic doctor. It consisted of warm baths in water from Soap Lake, which is the name of the spa. Next, we received a hard rubdown all over our body, especially the back. After that, an electric current for 15-20 minutes. He said I tolerated a strong current. He administered 25 volts, but I don't know how many amperes. My hand was completely cured. After 4 treatments, my blood pressure went down from 150 to 120, which he said was a little too low. My blood pressure ought to be 135 for my age, he said. After that, I took 4 more treatments, but that was too much, and made me very nervous. However, I am now almost back to normal. He said it would prevent a repeat of the paralysis. My wife had 6 treatments, which he said would avert a repeat of stones in her gall bladder as well as relieve her rheumatism. It cost us $2.30 per treatment. The doctor is German and his name is Schrag. It was he who said I would live to be 100.

Soap Lake, also known as Sanitarium Lake, located in central Washington, was called "Smokiam" by the Indians, meaning "healing waters". The buoyant, mineral-rich, soapy-textured, alkaline water from the 3 mile long, 1½ mile wide lake was used by the Native Americans for the same reasons it was used by the throngs of people who came from long distances in the 1900s. Rheumatism and skin disorders, such as psoriasis, were relieved as the sufferers soaked in the water, or coated their joints with the mud from the lake bottom or shore. Muscular pains, circulatory ailments, nervousness and depression, even syphilitic disorders were claimed by many to be eased as the vacationer mudded, soaked, and carried on therapeutic conversations sharing personal suffering with other visitors. Ole and Augusta believed in the healing power of the minerals and, when their treatments were completed, filled the extra jugs brought along for use in their home bath when they returned to the farmhouse. Augusta claimed drinking a few sips of the water was an effective way of "cleaning out the body." "It didn't take much," she would say, "it worked every time." The soapy water had multiple uses.

Ole's letter to Andreas continues: *These treatments didn't help Edvart Berg much. He waited too long before going to Soap Lake. He is a little better, but his right hand is still paralyzed. It is said that good living and not enough exercise make the blood thick, absorbing minerals, which causes hardening of the arteries, making it more difficult for the heart to pump the blood through the body, and this is the reason for the strong, or high, blood pressure. And if it goes so far that an artery is almost completely clogged, paralysis follows. And if it goes far enough so that the heart can no longer carry out its heavy work, the whole thing shuts down, and that's death. Consequently, there are many who collapse and die or are found dead in their bed in the morning. It seems to me that there are more and more of those around here these days. So go to the doctor and have your blood pressure checked! You can get medication for it.*

We have now finished harvesting and threshing for this year. The harvest was as good as could be expected after a summer without rain whatsoever. The fall wheat was nevertheless pretty good; we got 1,958 bushels of wheat of a variety called Turkey Red and 146 bushels of a variety called Jones Fife. We plant this (Jones Fife) mainly in order to cut it for hay or fodder and we probably have some 30 tons of hay of that kind. But we thresh enough so we have seed for another year and then we sell the remainder. We got 70 sacks of that kind, and since we only need 10 sacks, or 20 bushels for seed we have left 60 bushels at $3.00 a sack. What I sold of the other kind I got $1.10 a bushel, but when all expenses are taken into consideration, we have probably barely 75 cents left.

The buyers are now driving the wheat prices down daily. In spite of the fact that we have a variety of things to sell, we still have a hard time meeting all expenses. The orchard did fairly well because I have it rigged up so that I can irrigate. We probably got a ton (2,000 pounds) of cherries. Of those, and of apricots, we sold for about $60.00.

I am sending a package of newspapers, and inside, there are some dried cherries of a kind called Bing Cherries, named after a Chinese who first brought them from China. They are the biggest and best to be had here in this country and they are selling in the market this fall for 10 cents a pound. But we only get 5 cents and let people pick their own. Let some of them soak in water overnight, and you'll see what they taste like. They are dark brown, almost black in color, and the biggest ones are about ¾ of an inch in diameter. The big pits are from apricots. They are yellow in color and about the size of a small egg of a hen, somewhat sour and very good. I am not sending these for you to eat, but to plant. I dried the cherries in the sun because I believe that is nature's way of planting them. Plant both pits this fall as soon as you get them—about 2 inches deep in sandy soil where they will get sun in the spring. However, now and then it happens that fruit with pits may take 2 years before they emerge. Mark the place where you planted them! And don't think you are too old for planting trees. You can still live long enough to eat fruit from them. I think I'll be planting something as long as I live.

We often hear from our children in California. Lewis Andreas is now at the University of California. It is an excellent institution with 15,000 students. He is now enrolled in 18 different subjects and is working hard to advance. During vacation he worked in a fruit packing plant for almost 3 months, making $325.00. But that is not sufficient. I don't have enough money to help him. He thinks he can manage on his own, he says. A few of the others are doing it. But I believe it will be insufficient. He is now working 3 hours a day at a boardinghouse for girls who are attending the school. He does dishes and sets tables and waits on the *tables one hour each for breakfast, lunch and supper. For this he gets room and board. But he says it is a noisy place with lots of din and uproar. And that is not hard to believe—with all those energetic girls. They are all around 20 years old. He can't study there, but has to go to the school library. Albert is working in a butcher shop in Auburn and is doing well. He has his own automobile and is living with Agnes and Ingolf, about 7 miles from town. Einar, Synneva's husband, is still building houses and selling them and is doing well. The university is in Berkeley on the other side of a bay in San Francisco, a good distance from Synneva, and it would cost Lewis too much to travel back and forth, that is why he lives at the boardinghouse. Synneva has two girls—Agnes and Ingolf have no children.*

Adolph and Otto are working at home now, but they absolutely want to leave and get a higher education. It seems that all young people are getting to be afraid of farming. And no wonder—the shameless way farmers are being treated by greedy speculators who buy up the produce, and greedy loan sharks and merchants of all stripes, not to mention labor unions. All of those, more or less, belong to the class we used to call grafters or parasites in Norway.

It is difficult for me to write because of my eyes. I am now totally blind in my right eye so I can't see my hand a foot away. My left eye has never been good. I believe I told you why I didn't have an operation when I was in Seattle before Christmas last year. But now I am going back there soon. I stagger around here. My glasses don't help much for my left eye, and as far as the right one is concerned, the lens might just as well be made of wood.

Andreas, I have now scraped together a long letter to you. You might come up with one half as long and send me as soon as you get this one. Greet Gabriel Jørgensen and his family, and finally you, yourself are greeted.

Feeling weary from his life of hard work and constant battle with mastoid infections, and now poor eyesight, Ole, at the age of 78, knew it was time to quit. He moved with Augusta to the warmer climate of Auburn, California to live with their daughter, Agnes, and her husband Ingolf. Augusta had yearned to make the change since the move would also bring them closer to Synneva, Einar, and granddaughters Ellen and Evelyn. Adolph entered Business College in California while Otto studied at the University of Washington. Ole had confidence in his decision to lease his farm to Oliver, who, as the eldest son, had traditionally given up his schooling after the eighth grade to work beside his father.

So Oliver sold his small fruit farm in Orondo on the Columbia River and moved with his wife Eloise and baby Frederick Olin to Waterville, giving his father a promise to keep him up-to-date on the conditions of the wheat fields and animals, in addition to the financial circumstances of the farm. "It's the only life I know," Oliver would always say, "the only life I ever wanted." And he would be content there for the next 68 years, slowly increasing his ownership, mainly rangeland for cattle, to a total of three sections.

Prior to the move to Auburn, California – 1926
Back row: Oliver, Albert, Adolph, Lewis, Otto
Front row: Ingolf Berg, Agnes, Ole holding Ellen Berg,
Augusta, Synneva, Einar Berg

*   *   *

Following a drive through the Redwood Valley to visit friends, Ole compared the land in a letter to Oliver. *I have seen mostly grape and orchard plantations and but a few wheat fields. They were very nice, but not better than I have had in Douglas County, Washington. There are round-topped hills, and wide valleys with considerable areas of level country only partly under cultivation, and few wild birds to be seen. All yesterday afternoon the country was over-laid with a thick smoke and Nels said it was probably burning to the northwest somewhere. The grass vegetation, which has been rich, is now dried up, brown, and would burn easily. As I am writing it is 95 degrees!*

I think this part of the valley is, at least, an ideal place for grapes. The land here at Nels's grape plantation is one of the finest and his crop grows without irrigation. Although the well is 20 feet deep, it would perhaps be only 10-15 feet down to raise water for sub-irrigation. This level land is of very good soil, alluvial, loose and deep. The level valley runs only a few miles further north and the whole valley contains approximately 1000 acres. A railroad, the Northwestern Pacific, runs close by to the coast to a place called Uricka (Eureka), a distance, in

152

a straight line, of about 25 miles. After that the country runs into mostly stock and sheep ranges. Hops are also grown in places.

A little Indian reservation to the north a few miles has only about five families. They cultivate or raise nothing but work for the whites, picking grapes, hops, etc. The price for picking grapes will now be about $4.50 per ton or 5c per box.

You better write to Lewis and Otto to see what they may do. I don't hardly think that Lewis could come home to Waterville while going to the military camp at Tacoma for lack of time and it will cost $15-20 going and coming. From next fall Lewis will have a year left, and it will be the hardest one, too. He will get and need exercise, but rather not on the farm at present. He must put all his energy in to what he is doing now and I think he will get the best of grades. He is on the Roll of Honor now and must stay there. He will have all he can do, but the boys can write you and talk for themselves.

The Port Townsend boom was unexpected to me. No telling what will come after the paper mill. I think it is located on a point I was looking at, with the intent of buying, over 30 years ago when a friend of mine, Lars Johnsen, and I were speculating about the purchase of land on the coast. And now the areas over there seem to have a limitless future for industry. As everyone knows, hindsight does one no good, but with no doubt in my mind, I know now I should have gone ahead and invested in property over there.

In January, Ole shared some deep concerns regarding his observations on the economy with his brother Andreas. *Otto, the youngest boy, is not 20 years old yet, and he is staying home, helping Oliver. Next winter, or around the 1st of January 1928, the intention is that he too will come to California, to San Francisco, to attend school. Oliver must then hire a stranger, one who demands an almost unbelievable amount of pay. People here have lost their common sense. Carpenters are now demanding—and getting--$10.00 a day. Masons, or bricklayers, I believe they are getting $12.00 a day, and the more they get, the less they want to do for the pay they get. But they are all out to crush the farmer, to grind him into powder. From one bushel of wheat, $10.00 worth of bread can be made, and of cakes and fine bakery goods, $15.00 or $20.00 worth. A lot of men are loafing around, half starved, while demanding $6.00 a day for work. A farmer has no daily wages and gets no interest from the money he has invested in land and other things. But taxes on everything are high. Bankers and owners of State Obligations and cash on hand pay* **no** *taxes. A lot of wealthy landowners and factory owners are able to wiggle themselves out of paying much in taxes. Consequently, it falls back on the little farmer. However, everything is now being done to get rid of this inhuman tax system. The farmers are going through bankruptcy by the hundreds of thousands.*

I have been fortunate in that I have not been lacking so far and Oliver sends money after he has received his pay for what he has sold or for the crops.

The prices are good, especially the cattle prices and he has hopes for an excellent harvest from the farm up in Waterville. I am also writing to the bank in Hønefoss about sending me $500.00. As soon as you get this, will you go up and take care of sending this money as soon as possible? This is for the boys' schooling. I know I'll take a loss on this since the krone is not at par, but it doesn't pay for those who are in school to go out and work their way through school in the interval. There are, however, many enterprising boys who work a few hours a day in order to get some money. Lewis has done that, too.

Ingolf Berg has a huge orchard—about 1000 pear trees, a big grape plantation, and a lot of fruit trees of various kinds, such as figs, plums, and some kinds which I can't remember. I work in the orchard every day, pruning pear trees. A great many trees will soon be planted. We have virtually no winter, but it rains often, and we have warm sunshine during the day. Vegetables like cabbage, carrots, turnips, salad, etc. are growing all winter. Einar Berg is building houses to sell.

In your letter last fall you say that just the day before you had planted the cherry trees I sent you. Since then I have heard nothing from you. When I answered your letter I also wrote to Kristian Ruud and sent cherry twigs for grafting to him in a tin tube which I wanted him to return to me with twigs for grafting from the Grandmother and Aakero trees in order to try grafting one more time. The worst part about this is the packing and the long trip, causing them to dry out. I suppose Kristian is getting feeble and ill now, being more than 90 years old, and I imagine he is getting tired of cutting off twigs and sending them to me for grafting. I have not heard from him yet. Neither have I heard from Haug or anyone else in Norway in a long time. What's going on with them? I suppose they are forgetting me more and more, and there are probably few who would recognize me if I came home. If you can manage to take a trip to Rørvigen in the summer, ask Kristian, or his daughter if he is away, if they received that tin crate full of dried cherries for planting last fall. And, if the buds are being sent soon, you can send them to Oliver at my old address in Washington State. He will use them as if I was there.

That 71 year-old woman you have taken into your house, who you say is the mother to Mrs. Skraeder Engen at Benterud, I don't know in the least, continued 79½-year-old Ole to his 78-year-old brother. *The only Benterud I know is in Faekjaraasen, where Mrs. Olia Benterud lived. It is probably good for you to have someone in the house, who can also help if you get sick, etc. It is illegal here in America for two unmarried people to live alone in the same house and cook and eat together. But Norway isn't America. If you got married to this old woman then people wouldn't have anything to say. They probably won't anyway. But if something like this should happen, then make sure not to sign any papers where the old woman or her heirs will get a hold of everything you have. Have a contract written in such a way that each has their own separate estate. You don't know who will need medical help first—you or her. If it is her, then you will have to pay a woman to help. If it is you, then someone still needs to be paid.*

Few of those that are 71 years old can depend on their health and life for very long. Our grandmother was 74 when she died and she had been bedridden for a year. In this case, it is best not to be married and obliged to anything. Make sure that nobody makes a fool of you, Andreas. It would be fine for Mrs. Skraeder Engen to divide things with you after her mother's death. On the other hand, if you have a separate estate, then you can have the power to give the woman or her heirs what they deserve, and someone else what they deserve.

You should remember that with the purchase of Svarstad, our estate became worth at least 10,000 Kr., of which I didn't get anything. Also, that when father and mother were married, father was nearly bankrupt and every shilling of mother's 700 spesidaler of inheritance went to pay old debts. She also brought in all the furniture that was in the house when we were small. She told me all this many times. Although our family fortune began 200 or more years before, it was because of mother's work and effort and good guidance that we didn't become poor and in the same class with Jens Tangen, Iver Madsen, Ole Hagebraaten and thousands of others. You must not take the wrong direction, as you know it's a long way down. My point is you shouldn't set things up so that everything you have shall go to strangers and intruders that haven't done any work. Our good Mother would gladly have made it easy for us all, and I think the same about my own children.

The fact that Andreas had moved a woman into his house must have gnawed at Ole. Only a few weeks passed when he sent still more advice to his brother, this time a bit more caustic: *I have been thinking a lot about that old woman you took into your house—whether there might be some plans behind it which you are unaware of or do not understand. You may be quite sure that there are those who would like to wrestle away from you everything you have if they could, or at least some of it. I'll warn you against this once more. Do you know, for instance, what would happen if you married this woman and Alf Vestern, your guardian, relinquished his rights and someone, in one way or another were able to wriggle it around in such a way that she took his place? What would happen then? Couldn't she in that way acquire such power over what is yours that she could proceed as she wanted? And, in addition, you do not know what advisers she has to fall back on, or what their intentions are. How far is it from you to Benterud, where her daughter lives? What other relatives does she have close by? I am sure that those who might have certain plans are more afraid of me than anyone else, although I am far away. And that they are setting you up so that you will not reveal anything about your affairs to me! Write soon and let me know about this woman! I can assure you that someone who is 71 years old has little value as a wife. My wife is 17 years younger than me, but she looks older and she **is** older when you consider her health. Both of us are now getting old, and we may not have 10 years* *left to live—either one of us. The important thing now is to arrange it in such a way that those who come after us have some little thing to start with and thus be able to honor our memory, just as we honored our parents' memory. All of this is an important matter, which ought to be considered seriously.*

Here in this country a lot of peculiar things happen when there is money involved. Hardly an issue of the paper is published without an article about some abomination; murders, robberies, divorces are part of daily life, mainly for the sake of money. Young girls are hanging around older men in order to get hold of their millions. Recently, the newspapers have been full of stories about a 15 year-old who married a wealthy man of 65, then sued for divorce based on cruelty on his part, and as long as the case was in court, she was getting $200.00 a week in alimony since she ran away saying she was afraid for her life if she continued to live with him. However, she couldn't prove one single thing that he had done to her. His servants testified that she had lived in an abundance of luxuries, frills, and money with never an unpleasant word from his side. So, instead of getting all the millions in compensation, which she demanded, she got no divorce by law, and a choice between going back to her old husband or stay away and get nothing! Now and then such schemes succeed, based on mistreatment, unfaithfulness, drunkenness, and a lot of stuff that doesn't exist.

Now I want you to pay attention to what I am writing, and don't let anyone cheat you, because they could make a beggar out of you. Perhaps you should burn this letter immediately and then don't say a word. You don't know who might be going through your papers!

After settling in California, Ole refocused and began to study his genealogy, the line which had molded his traits, features, and character, and it was imperative to him to record his ancestors with accurate documentation. None of the siblings had married, leaving his seven surviving children as the only descendents of his father Ole Olsen Rudsødegaard. The image of his parents had been carried within his thoughts throughout his life, so with time on his hands, possibly feeling somewhat useless, he began to reflect. Perhaps, since moving off the Washington farm, he began to feel a sense of mortality as letters referred back to the beauty of his childhood home near Oslo, the experiences of his youth, the touch and smell of his good mother. He reminisced about his young father, senselessly made lifeless so long ago. He recalled how much he was like his dead father, how some of his sons and daughters resembled himself and his brothers, in both facial features and temperament, aware that these characteristics such as tone of voice, hairline, nose, gifts of art and learning would carry on down through the generations, thus giving him a feeling of satisfaction and joy. Being such a record keeper of every penny, every cow, every business deal, every fence post, every bushel of wheat, he was determined to have his Norwegian bloodline written with as much detail as could be found. Studying his roots was perhaps the beginning of a transitional path—the beginning of the conclusion for this quiet mannered, hard working Norwegian who had had one goal in life—to be a good, respectable man. But whatever the reason, he was adamant about keeping the family records in the hands of the rightful owners. In an attempt to retrieve a hymnbook in which the records had been inscribed back to the original purchase date of Rudsøgaarden by his great-grandfather, Ole Anderson Rørvigen, in 1751, he wrote again to Andreas.

*January 27, 1927: Your last letter, written in October last fall, I received a long time ago. However, you did not mention the old hymn book in Rørvigen. It may never find itself in our hands, the rightful family. That old "Hayseed", Kristian Ruud, is probably not interested in having their names included in our family register here in America. **Now you must try!** Next spring, on a beautiful day, take a trip to his house, then you borrow his boat and row across to Rørvigen. Demand to see the hymn book. Stick it in your pocket and leave! Let them know what I'm telling you here, that I am the legitimate owner of it as the **oldest son** going down in a straight line from the first owner, namely (1) Anders Olsen, (2) his oldest son, Ole Andersen, who bought the Lower Rudsødegaard and married Rolf Rudsødegaarden's oldest daughter (her name I do not know), (3) His oldest son, Ole Olsen, our grandfather, (4) his oldest son, Ole Olsen, our father, (5) his oldest son, Ole Olsen, myself. Then on to my oldest son, (6) Carl Oliver. Next (7) to his oldest son, Frederick Olin Ruud, who now is a brave little boy less than two years old. Now don't forget to do what I am asking you.*

Possibly, Ole took his mind off Andreas and his live-in housekeeper after receiving a letter on March 29th, 1927 from Marie Rørvik, who was living at Rørvigen with her husband Karl and six children. "I would like to introduce myself," she wrote. "My name is Marie Kristiansen Rørvik married to Andreas Rørviken's oldest son Karl. As you well know, Karl's father, Andreas, died a year ago, the burial held here in Rørvika. His son, Karl, who as I said is my husband, was then responsible for the property. We moved into the place on the 25th of March 1926.

"I wanted to write to you about the psalm book. Mr. Gabriel Jørgensen who lives with your brother in Hønefoss visited us once last year soon after we had arrived. He came because of this psalm book. Yes, I promised to write to you and send the book but it turned out later that it was not the right one anyway. I highly regret our carelessness. There are so many books and papers here, and we have looked through a lot of it but we have not found the correct psalm book yet. Andreas, my father-in-law, surely looked for it himself. The psalm book we have found is from 1846. In it there is a family register which reads:

Kristian Hansen Rørviken—born December 1821, died February 23, 1907.

His wife Karen Nilsen Rørviken—born 15th December 1815, died January 1875.

157

Their children are: Marie, who was married to Andreas Johannesen Rørviken. Nils Kristiansen married to Elise Marie Hansen Vigg and Johan Rørvik who live in Oslo.

"We cannot, therefore, give you any further clarification on your grandfather, or great-grandfather. We will still try to look through some loose papers and books, if no one else in the family has found it. If we can find it in the summer or if we come across it during spring-cleaning we will gladly send it to you as soon as possible. But I hope all the same that you send us some lines.

"I will finish with thanks for your writing and will send you, Mr. Ruud, our best wishes, both from my husband Karl Rørvik, my children and myself Marie Rørvik. We have six children – 3 girls, Reidun, Gerda, and Ingrid, and 3 boys, Willy, Finn, and Kristian. My husband will be 50 on Christmas Eve, 1927. I will be 47 on July 12th, 1927. I am just writing this for fun. I will possibly send you a picture of us later if I can correspond with you.

"Best regards to all of you from us. And to you who were so nice to write to us—many thousand greetings. All the best! I hope you forgive me for being so late with my response. The address is Karl Rørvik Krokklen, Ringerike. Sincerely, Marie Rørvik"

Five months later, on September 25th, another letter came from Norway,

"You would probably be somewhat surprised to get a letter from someone you probably don't remember, but I will promptly reveal who I am. My name is Johan Rørvik, and I am the youngest son of Kristian Rørvigen and his wife Karen. The reason I am writing is that we apparently have interests in common since I am also currently collecting information about my family, but it is going slowly, because one always lacks birth years, dates and birth places for these old folks.

"I stayed this summer at Ringerike—am living in Oslo—and during this stay I learned from my brother's daughter Marie that you had written to her and asked for some information. I was also able to read your letter, which was very interesting, and I have in this connection undertaken some research at Ringerike, amongst others at Elstangen and at Kristian Ruud's place, but the research at these places did not yield any results.

"At home in Rørvigen, I have dug through all the papers, but I only found an old will, that you probably already know about—I'll come back to that later, since it is best to tell things in order. I have also visited your brother a couple of times in Hønefoss and there looked through all his old documents, but that did not yield much result either. Here I will mention the different names and data, which were there: October 20, 1736 – an Ole Rolfsen is the owner of Rudsødegaarden. He must be Rolf's father. Then comes 1755--Ole Olsen has inherited Rudsødegaarden, the same year that your grandfather was born, as you know-- he was born 1755, died December 13, 1836 and your father was born April 10, 1821. But then comes something unclear. On April 4, 1766, Ole Andersen Rusdødegaarden transferred half of Rørviken to his stepmother Bodil, the widow of Anders Olsen Rørvigen, and her two sons Erik and Jens. This seems to mean that Ole Andersen also must have lived at Rørvigen. It must also be certain that Anders Olsen had been married twice, and that Ole is from the first marriage.

"There was also a document from which it appears that your grandfather must have been married three times, because with the transfer of Onsaker on March 12, 1789 the following information appears: "The inheritance of the deceased Anne Andersdatter, daughter of Anders Olsen Onsaker, goes over to her surviving husband Ole Olsen Rudsødegaarden and their two children Anders 7 years and Marie 4 years." And then comes the old will, mentioned earlier, which was found at home in Rørvigen, dated July 13, 1882 in which an Erik Andersen transfers to his half-brother, Ole Andersen Rudsødegaarden—half of Rørvigen. Erik must have inherited this half from his mother.

"This is all I have found at Ringerike. The sought after psalm book cannot be found in Rørvigen. However, I was planning to research the archives here in the city as one could possibly find something more there, but since I have been back from the country for only a week, I have not yet had the opportunity to start on that and that is why I will send this in the meantime. Your brother asked me to greet you warmly, and tell you that things are going fine. All the best regards from an old 'homesteader', Johan Rørvik----Address: Sofiesgate 10, Oslo."

In the fall of 1927, and as she promised, Marie followed up with another letter to Ole in Auburn, California. "Dear all of you! Good day to you and thanks for the letter with pictures. I suppose you are waiting to hear something from the old country, Norway. Well, letter writing is not taken care of quickly here. We think about writing, that's all. It's a great shame that I have not written earlier. Time flies so fast, and we hardly know how late it is, until we have gotten old.

"Well, this is how it is: I was going to visit your brother Andreas before I wrote back to you. It turned out that it took a while before I got around to going. Now I have been there twice. He has a very beautiful home and a very capable old housekeeper who is attentive and clean. He himself is in good shape and in good health, and he remembers a lot of things from the old days—it's real fun, listening to his tales. But he had no additional news about the family. He had sent you all the information you can expect. All you have to do is to read through carefully what he had sent, he said, and "he will find out what he is looking for". He was going to write to you. Maybe you'll get his letter before you get mine.

"My uncle, Johan Rørvik, came to see us this summer. I told him about this family. He asked if I wanted him to help me with it, and he would write to you. Uncle, you see, is into such things, and he is acquainted with many of those old families. Then one day I got a letter from my first cousin Martha (Uncle's oldest daughter). She told me that Uncle had sent you a letter and is waiting for a response from you. So I hope, Mr. Ruud that you will get more definite information about a variety of questions you are posing. But that doesn't mean that I want to terminate my correspondence with you. We should like to continue to hear from you over there about you and yours.

"I hope you get this letter before Christmas or that it gets there by that time. May everything go well with you—that is my sincere wish. We read in your letter that on Christmas Eve day, the 24th, you, Mr. Ruud, can celebrate your 80th birthday. Looking at your picture, we find that hard to believe. At the same time my husband will celebrate his 50th birthday. It is great to be able to reach 80 years and still look the way you do, Mr. Ruud. I hope you can keep going and stay well for a while yet. Merry Christmas and a really good New Year is our wish for all of you from us. All is well here. This winter has good snow for sledding—8-10 degrees Reaumur.

"Congratulations on your day of celebration, and we wish you everything good for the time you have left to spend with your loved ones. We shall probably never have the great honor of meeting you personally. However, we feel that we know you anyway from your picture. We'll send one of us later – we have nothing suitable right now. Greet your family from us. And you, Mr. Ruud and your wife are hereby greeted most sincerely. Yours, Maria Rørvik"

*   *   *

After Ole and Augusta moved to Auburn, Oliver kept them up to date with the progress, if any, made on the farm in Waterville. He wrote his father often, sending a percentage of the profit as had been originally agreed upon. After settling into the big house, he continued the farming practices common for that time and kept up frequent correspondence with his parents; however, only a few letters will be included in this narrative.

"April, 1927
Dear Papa, Mama and all:
"Many thanks for the presents you sent which we received O.K. Synneva sent some candy and that went fine, too. We have 14 little chicks, and 14 setting hens. One on turkey eggs! We will set 5 more tomorrow or the next day. We have 5 colts and 7 calves—4 of them are heifers. The sows will have pigs most any day now. I think there is good money in selling young pigs at $6.00 each. The sow will bring about $30.00, so with 5 pigs each--that makes her worth $60.00. Up to now they haven't cost a cent to feed. We let them run with the cattle and fed them two dead old horses that we got from Leslie Clark.

"We are ready to start plowing. The wheat looks good but the Turkey Red isn't as thick as I'd like, but it may stool out if we get a little cool weather. I also planted about ¾ pound of carrot seed to feed the cows this winter, so we should

160

have plenty of milk. We have been spending the last two days fixing up the water pipes as they were in bad shape, then it will be time to plant the garden.

"We had a radio here for a while but took it back to town as we didn't think we could afford one yet—besides being a time killer, a sleep stealer, definitely it was not a labor saver, but was a liability. Although, I could sit beside one for hours and listen to the music and so could Eloise, if there was time to do so.

"It doesn't look much like spring yet up on the mountain, as there is lots of snow. The snow is nearly all gone off the home pasture and the grass looks good. We won't use it much, if any at all, this year—we'll just forget that it's there. The wind is blowing and I can see the dust starting up out in the east. Send me a gold nugget if you find more than you can sell!
Love to all, Oliver"

I think you have done very well this year with your crops, Ole wrote that fall. *I never used to get any more in bushels out of those two fields and some years less. As to the bothersome showers in harvest time, I was well used to having sometimes as many as 12-14 horses standing and tramping and dirtying down more grain than they could eat in 3-4 days. I think on the average we had these showers every other harvest.*

Much of this horrible waste could be prevented if those crews would do the work as required from those things that grow from the ground. But this is in line with all American wastefulness. Do you remember that fall in the wartime when we had a crew of I. W. W.'s to thresh on the other side of the creek? First, I had to pay them $40 extra to go over there. Then a heavy shower came and they had to lay off about by noon. I thought they would clean up a little before they went from the machine and up to camp. Next morning I came down and found all the horses standing in the grain stack with 2 ft. of grain under them, eating from the top of the stack, with harnesses on. The men had dragged grain out, not yet threshed, and pitched their tent upon a foot deep of it. The only one outside was the foreman. I got mad on seeing such a mess and called his attention to it and also to the horses. He merely looked up and said, "Hoo, Hoo, I thought they was all tied up to the wagon." A sack, well-filled, but not sewed had fallen over, some of the wheat had run out and they, the horses, went forth and back tramping the beautiful grain down in the dirt. I think I have had my share of the reckless abuse of threshing crews and also of threshing machine owners. When Minneck done the threshing, they fixed it so I had to have them over every Sunday for three years in succession and I would have gotten them the 4th year if they had not broke down.

About my share of the crop, you better sell it when you sell your own and send me the money. Do the best you can about it. I put the money in the bank in Auburn and get a few dollars interest. Wheat is not likely to go up much as long as the farmers have any of it left. Not over a month ago it was $1.51 in Portland.

I have the boys to help through school, and the taxes. I also would like to see if we could pay the taxes early enough next year to get the rebate. This is another grist the privileged class has provided for themselves, as they always have money on hand and draw an extra burden on the farmer, who has money only in the fall. Now try to keep this in mind, so we can pay, if possible, soon after New Years.

You may not get much of the wheat crop this year, but see to pay your father-in-law, McKay, or the bank, and be that much ahead. When you sell the horse, or any horse, you better take a mortgage if they don't pay all cash. And don't trust any man too far. You might do like I did one time in a deal. I said, "I think that perhaps you are a rascal and the same can you think of me!" And he found that quite reasonable. Your gain will mainly be in cattle and what you can make out of milk cows. I found it that way. For this reason, save all the straw you can, rather than buy straw then waste it.

I can't see the idea your neighbor Clark has about getting a combine, unless it's one that would also elevate the straw or deliver it in a header box or light rake made for it. The price they ask of you, $450, for ½ interest in the old tractor is entirely too much. They paid only $500 for it themselves and that must be 10 or 15 years ago. They were telling me of their bargain many times. It's hard to give any advice, but you better look it carefully over, as they can well afford to sell it much cheaper. If you can get ½ interest in the whole outfit, tractor and threshing machine for $450, it is not so bad. And you could take it home and do a thorough overhauling. To get along any old way may be all right, if any old way can be found. Inquire into what new machines can be had for by this time. It seems to me that these manufacturing trusts should come to their senses soon, hearing and knowing of the desperate condition of the farmers. This will be the greatest issue of the next election. Everybody here will now vote the Socialist ticket. I believe California will all go socialist.

Don't let that father-in-law of yours, McKay, boss you too much! Perhaps he thinks that when about 5 years is out that you should clear out of there and go to Spokane. But I say, bring your children up on the farm. It will be a blessing to them. Farm life will change to the better some day, and city life rather to the worse. Now remember, the present conditions cannot last if the American people are not absolutely struck blind and become dumbfounded morons!

Would farm life change for the better, and city life for the worse as Ole predicted? On the whole, his presumption was correct. The entire country, as well as Europe, was still suffering from the aftermath of WWI. When the Great Depression hit in 1929, hundreds of thousands of urbanites lost jobs, homes, and life-savings. Twenty-five percent of the nation's work force was unemployed by 1933. Bread lines grew and grew. The homeless built shacks out of old crates, and called the dwellings "Hoovervilles" after President Hoover, who refused to provide government aid to the unemployed. City dwellers, from all classes, suffered from misery and desperation.

The plight of the American farmer worsened as well as thousands lost their farms in foreclosures. But many hung on during those depression years, lived off the land, and bought nothing except bare necessities. Of the two places of existence, farm or city, the farm brought more assurance of sustenance during the economic crisis. Families took in hired men, who worked for mere board and room, and welcomed them at their table as they nourished themselves on simple homegrown foods.

Ole's letter continues. *As I have no immediate use for the money, you can take time to fatten and sell the cows. But make up an account so I will know what I can depend upon. We must also have some clothes and a little for other things, though we work for part of the living. We are glad to learn that all is well so far and that the children is so nice.*

Since the oppressive summer here is over, I feel much better. The heat even upset my stomach and I felt sick so I could not eat or digest properly. I am thinking much about looking over a place up along the coast where stock raising and dairying especially flourish.

Albert is doing well in the butcher shop and is with us today, coming home every Sunday. Adolph is also doing well in the Business and Bookkeeping College, and he earns a little extra money working on Saturdays in an Italian grocery market for which he gets about $6.00 a day, sometimes a little more. Lewis is getting good grades and earning some extra money so he nearly can help himself now.

Today is the first time I have seen any cloud for several months so we will soon have showers again. I am glad when every stormy season is over and lightening has not struck the houses. We ought to see what can be done to prevent such disasters. Now write often and tell about the business. You know I am interested.

"Well, I've fooled around with the balance of your wheat money and this is the way it sets," wrote Oliver in November.

"Your share of the crop $983.63

Sent on Sept. 7, 1927 ....750.00
Paid for county paper..4.00
Paid last half of tax 162.58
Paid Dr. Gerhardt 50.00
Licensing and advertising of the Stallion Hector........................17.05
$983.63

"The license for Hector will cost only $15.00 but I can use the other $2.05 for advertising. It may be more or less but I called it that to make the crop account balance! Have you any account of what you have paid Dr. Gerhardt? He charged $200.00 for his work on you. According to their account book you owe $113.00. I paid him $50, so that leaves about $63.00. I didn't see the Dr. until afterwards, out on the street and he was in a big hurry.

"The old fellow that is here and helps with the chores sure is a prince— nothing is undone when he comes in at night. He was broke and had no home, so I told him I'd give him $10.00 a month for the winter. He is handy and willing to work. He is an old miner and railroad man, spent most of his time in Minnesota and Kansas. He walked most of the way here from his last job in Montana.

"We had about 10 inches of snow which is nearly all gone, although, we have fair sleighing yet. The summer fallow is wet as can be—clear to the bottom. A horse would mire down in it.

"I may buy Frank Brook's bunch of purebred shorthorns if we can agree on the price. His price is $90 a head and mine is $75, so I think it is as good as off, although cattle are like gold. The Quincy butcher offers 11c on foot for steers, something no one ever heard of before at this time of year. What is more, they will go higher. I've had a cash offer of $300 for your Percheron stallion Hector, but I'll try to get more than that before I talk business for that sum.

"We are starting to fatten the hogs to butcher, so you'll have a couple of nice porks down there pretty soon. They are getting like a ball of butter and so ought to be good to eat. I am keeping four nice red sows for next year, maybe it's a mistake, but I believe that next fall we'll see hogs at a premium. They are only 9c or 10c on foot here now. I got 20c per lb. on what chickens I sold. The coyotes must have taken a lot of what I had. Anyway, I haven't got very many left—only about 75. I am keeping a few old hens so as to have a few early setters as I like to get most of them hatched in April if I can.

"Uncle Edvart Berg is about the same but slowly getting weaker. He is helpless as a child but can feed himself now with one hand and between trying to talk and making motions he can make himself understood pretty well. We have given him nearly all the wine, as he loves it, and also the goat cheese that Synneva sent. If you could send him a little cheese each month or two I'll help pay for it as he loves it so. He seemed to improve after he had some, but whether it was the cheese or not, I don't know.

"We cook potatoes for the chickens every day in hopes that they will soon start to lay. I am going to grind some barley to have ready for them, as soon the corn feed will be gone.

"All is good nowadays. The babies are 500% better; in fact, they are well again. Freddy is a perfect gentleman when he wants to be but he's an outlaw when he's naughty. He is some boy—he packs his suitcase with dolls, caps, balls, and plays he is going some place. One day he was 'going to the mountain after wood,' also 'to Waterville to get a bull,' then 'to California to see Papa and Gamma', so he seems to remember you alright. Little Lois talks or laughs a lot now when we play with her. She is a pretty girl. We took pictures yesterday and will send you one soon.

"Eloise seems happy and contented. She sang two solos at the Pomona Grange last night. She sang "Schubert's Serenade" and "At Peace With The World." It was a wonderful success. The cellar is full of spuds, fruit and carrots, the wood shed is full, we'll have 4 fat hogs to butcher for you and I weigh about 180 lbs., so why shouldn't I feel good! Love to all, Oliver"

At the end of December Oliver finished the butchering, putting a large portion of it in the smokehouse. By February he put 163 pounds of smoked pork on the Southern Pacific Railway for shipment to his parents in California, along with 100 pounds of ground rye harvested that fall from the field, sending four sacks of flour along with the meat.

With instructions from his father, Oliver sold 11 lots in Orondo for $150 and Hector was sold for $450 cash. "If I had held Hector for another two months I might of gotten $500 but, yet, I might not of sold him at all and he might of died as he was entirely too fat," Oliver wrote. "The old fellow who stays here enjoys pitching all the good hay to the horses that they can possibly eat. The team, Carrie and Hoc, are as fat as I've ever seen them but they work every single day. From the cash received from the sale of Hector, the yearly real estate taxes were deducted and so these are the calculations from that.

Total real estate tax-----$361.01
Rebate--------------------- 11.83
Less rebate----------------349.18
My share-pasture tax------49.88
Your share of tax-------$299.30

"So $450 less $299.30 leaves you a balance of $150.70 which I will send. I paid all the tax including my own as I thought the bank was none too safe and the bills would be out of the way at the same time."

I have been very busy helping Ingolf, doing what I can in the fruit harvest, wrote Ole in the late fall of that same year. *The yield is not very great yet on account of the trees being young. The last now are the grapes, and we expect a man here today to get about 800 lbs., or 16 boxes, which is all we have sold so far. He offered only $30 per ton, but the price is really about $50. It is the same here as for the wheat growers. Buyers and speculators take advantage of cramping conditions for the farmer, artificially brought on.*

My writing is poor because my eyes are. I must get glasses for between short and long distances before I can work with comfort at a bench or drive a nail good. I see you went to Spokane to have operation on your nose. Don't you pay any $150 for it. I had polyps cut out twice. The first time, Dr. Holic in Seattle, charged me $5.00, the second time Dr. Martin charged me $15.00 and no hospital or after-treatment needed. The doctors could not tell me what causes the polyps, but people, both men and women of all classes and walks of life are subject to them. Even sailors who breathe saltwater fumes get them. Dust and heat, I think bring them on as quick as anything. But your headache may disappear simply by correcting hurtful and unnecessary habits, like overeating, for example.

You say in your letter that you have decided that Otto be a farmer. Now it is not easy to decide for others, as you may regret it. Let him rather decide for himself. If he is tired of studying and thinks he would like the farm better, let us help him to it. The best suggestion I could make for him is architecture and building. In taking such a course he will learn many things besides construction and mechanical engineering. He could become a good draftsman, learn surveying, how to lay out a townsite, and spread himself out for many things according to his genius, liking and energy. I have an old drawing instrument, and he knows it, but I have not heard from him regarding this.

He wrote that he is taking a test for air service. Lewis did not pass this test. I will most intensely advise both of them to let this flimsy sport alone. A sort of hazardous sport is all it will amount to. As long as it cannot carry freight or heavy burdens, its greatest usefulness is ended. We have all the swift ways for travel and communications that humanity needs or ought to have. All the loud talk is carried on by the aviation trusts already formed for moneymaking schemes. They want lots of young men trained and to risk their lives for their benefit and further experimental purposes. Its only usefulness, if I can call it so, is in case of war, which is sure to come, maybe in less than 100 years. And then, those in the air will be the winners. Some scientific facts of importance have been discovered through aviation, so it is here to stay, the same as many other things we used to get along nicely without. So far as I can see during this 80 years of my life, the producing classes are no better off, but worse. *Who could now in these days of grate and toil afford to celebrate at a wedding feast for a whole week as was done in Norway and other countries 150 to 200, or more, years ago. No, our substance must now go to those that neither spin nor weave but only gather, store and lay up treasures that moth and rust may consume.*

You think this must be a nice country here in California? Well, it would if one could enjoy 100-105 degrees of heat for weeks in the summer. But I would take the place where you are, the soil and scenery, and I would also take cream, butter, and cheese of the North much before the numerous sweet fruits and vines of the South. The more I read about Alaska and the North, the more I regret I didn't see it. Here the grass and soil are dry as a bone, but the fires in the grass and brush have ceased. They tell me it is customary to insure the pasture, then set fire to it and collect the insurance.

I suppose you will remember that the taxes are to be paid before December 1. If one day goes over they charge full interest of 12%. I put some of the money, $500, in the bank in Auburn at 4% and if I can keep it there for a year I will have $20 earned in interest, but the rest of my money will not last the year out. Otto must have more help, also Lewis, and I don't know what else. Mamma and I ought to have a woolen blanket for winter and soon some clothing. Ingolf and I together bought a nice Sedan automobile that had been in a wreck. It has cost $40 so far, but when fully repaired we will have a nearly new sedan for about $150.

If you have good sleighing this November it would be well to get some wood for next year and saw it up early. Have you got a man for help for part of next summer? Write soon so we can keep track of what is going on. My best word to Eloise's father, Mr. McKay.

* * *

At the University of Washington, 20 year-old Otto was studying forestry, keeping up his grades, but becoming restless. In the early spring of 1928, his 80-year-old-father, ailing physically, but remaining sharp in mind, wrote: *Am glad you are doing well in your studies, Otto, that is what you are there for. It is all right to be on good terms and well thought of by the girls and the rest, but if you neglect your studies, be sure it will soon be noticed by the girls especially, as they don't look kindly to a "skirt-chaser", as those men were called in the old country. On the other hand, one who can appear well in their company and also be high or even their superior in his mental work, they invariably look up to these men. It is a woman's nature to look up to men as a superior both mentally as well as physically. Then they think he is something to lean upon and they will seek his company. Sensible girls are very keen and quick to see man's qualities. A small wrecking of a scrub don't take well with girls of able understandings. They like heroes. Charles Lindberg could get most anyone.*

Who is this Martha Hjermstad you write about? Where do her folks live? In the country or city? May I caution you that there are girl spendthrifts, as well as boys, and the good looking ones are often the worst and make the poorest of wives and most often become the runaway flappies. They depend too much on their good looks, while the homely ones only can depend on their good domestic qualities, and therefore, often make the best life partners. But it also may be visa versa. This ought to be enough on this delicate subject. You have the best time of your life right now, and if you don't make proper use of it, you will regret it in time to come.

Adolph is now done and got his examination with credit—92. He found no employment yet. It is queer that none of you should like to be mechanical workers, architects, or engineers of some kind. You may find out in time that the farm or the soil will be the surest and best standby, and more so as times roll on. Cities grow bigger and population as a whole more numerous. It is estimated that by 1930 the U. S. will have 122 million. When I came here in 1879, the population in the U. S. was 54 million. In a few decades more there will be no surplus farm products. There is no more new country for the grabbers to exploit, and they better call a halt now that usurers and profiteers and grafters have brought an interest bearing debt upon the people's shoulders—principally the farmers amounting to a little sum of 130 billion dollars. Can you comprehend the amount? I asked Ingolf how long he thought it would take to count to a billion. He guessed 6 months.

I think it would be handy if you could fix it as to come this way and then continue your schooling at the University of California. You ought to get grades good enough now to get in. As far as working as a salesman, I doubt if you would make more than your salt and it must be a tiresome and tedious job to go from house to house and chaw the same thing over and over again all day long, and saying many things that are not always so. But if you should go anyway, you better study out some good jokes, and also tell them that you do it to earn money for schooling.

It is very important for you to get good grades, so this is what you must work for. Even if you think the study in Economics is some hocus-pocus, learn it anyway. You will someday learn to understand right from wrong. We would not like to have you taking flying or air service as your main study for many reasons. First, it is the <u>most dangerous</u> service there is. I have clippings of about 11 that have been killed in this month, and that is not near all. Second, the air service is absolutely impractical for industrial purposes of any kind. This you ought to readily understand. But the airship has come and will be kept up for <u>war purposes</u> only. The establishing of mail routes and passenger routes at big expense is for keeping an air army in training. How many are getting killed or maimed is not considered. Guggenheim and international grafters are keeping up the Lindberg

*boom as a bait for young men to go into it. If they can wiggle this country into
another war, they shall have this army to fight for them. Look at the private war in
Mexico, how they forced the American boys to fly and drop bombs on the Mexicans
trying to defend themselves. But now, aerial torpedoes have been invented that
can be steered from the ground by radioactive forces to hit the mark—how would
you like to be the mark? And then again, is it anything to depend upon for a living
in old age, or before, if a person succeeds to live a few years?*

*If you could go home in the vacation after June 10 and help Oliver on the
farm, then Freddy will remember you after that. Us, he doesn't know anymore.
Your military training is all right, for in case of war you will then be an officer
and not a common soldier. But you must select something for your main study that
you can make a living by even into old age. You have already learnt to work with
your hands. In this respect you have a great advantage on the city boys that never
drove or harnessed a horse, never had hold of an ax handle, shovel, plow nor any
other kind of industrial tool. Let them go into the air, they like to be birds anyway.
Let the city boys be the birds of the air and envy them not. Maybe the air service is
made for them and let them have it.*

*If Oliver wants you to come and help him in the vacation time you ought
to do it. You will keep healthier there. Am going to town tomorrow and send you
$40. Use them careful. But if you could help Oliver, it would be a help to him in
getting a reliable worker, and also the children not forgetting you. I am afraid that
all of us here will be complete strangers to them by the time we get back. As I have
said before to all of you boys, never lose sight of the farm. It is the safest of all
pursuits. The old farm up there at Badger Mountain has fed all of us through for
many years, and without serious hardship or risk of life, such as a seaman working
around machinery. That same old farm would have continued to feed every one of
us the rest of our lifetime if we would have stayed with it.*

*Albert is here now, being temporarily out of work. There are lots of idle
people in San Francisco and other cities, also Seattle. The prediction by some
prominent economist is that a tremendous world crisis is due for next spring of
1929. If this comes it will affect us as well, and many things may change.*

*I guess you know that little Evelyn is dead and buried. Einar, Synneva and
Ellen came home here with Mamma and left for San Francisco again yesterday the
28th. This is a difficult time for all of us.*

The sorrowful news had arrived from California in March of 1928. Evelyn,
the second daughter of Synneva and Einar, had died from heart failure resulting
from the effects of rheumatic fever. Evelyn was 3½ years old at the time of her
death.

When the letter arrived in Waterville, F.H. McKay was visiting the farm.
A new business deal was in the making, subtly addressed by Oliver in his next
letter to his parents.

"Dear Papa, Mamma, and all:

"Just received yours and Synneva's letter. It was somewhat of a shock, although I expected it more or less since I learned that it was her heart. Poor little girl, her troubles are over. Ellen is right, death comes to all of us sooner or later. It was hard for Synneva. It was nice, Mamma, that you could be there.

"I talked to sister Signe the other night in a dream. It was a wonderful meeting but a sad parting. And yes, I remember how she was dressed in the dream. She wore long curls, and a cream colored dress with a lace yoke and cuffs and also had lace around the bottom of the skirt. When I woke up, my eyes were filled with tears, but such is life—full of many sorrows—but many joys, also, to keep us going.

"Our wheat looks wonderful here—never have seen it so nice. It is hardly thick enough to harrow, although I may harrow it to warm up the ground and help hold the moisture. It looks much better than it did the year we got 45 bushels per acre and the ground is full of water, soaked to the bottom and then some.

"We have one little colt and a dandy too! Will get four more. But it seems as though everything has an end. Carrie had hers. We put her under the sod today. On Wednesday morning she had her colt and yesterday morning she was dead. I had slept in the barn for two nights so as to be sure her and the colt would be all right. About 2:30 Wednesday morning I heard her making a fuss, so I lit the lantern and dressed. I waited for about ¾ of an hour. She didn't make any progress so I decided to investigate. The colt was sort of doubled up so she had to have help. We saved the colt so far, a fine big horse colt and are feeding it on cow's milk. It can't stand by itself yet, so I doubt if there is any hope for it. I was sure surprised to find the mare dead in the morning. She had only been dead about an hour when I came out. She acted more or less restless in the evening but I didn't think it was a bit serious when I checked on her again at 10 p.m. But she won't have to work anymore. She is one horse that I hated to give up.

"I don't know whether I told you that we were piping the water down from one of the little springs. We found it just opposite the little rocky hill about 425 feet from the picnic grove. I got the ditch dug for 3 cents per foot, which I thought was cheap enough. The hired man George dug it. Thank heavens we won't have to fix any more busted pipes. It is all going down from 30" to 3ft. so it won't freeze. We struck a nice little spring, which runs now about 10 gallons per minute. I have to buy about 200 feet of 1" pipe to fill in the extra space. I hope you will not be dissatisfied with me doing this as I do it at my own expense.

"By the way, what do you think of the Colt Carbide lighting system? I wish you would investigate it and see what you think of it. There are several systems around the country and they all like them fine. The address is J. B. Colt Co. 599 Eighth St. San Francisco.

"Freddy says "I'm going to ride the gray mare down to California to Grandpa Ruud!" He weighs 41 pounds now.

Oliver   (P.S. We have just taken on a land deal. Mr. McKay will explain it to you, as he intends to write to you very soon. He says we've got it all to win and very little chance to lose.)"

F.H. McKay decided Oliver should be farming more land in order to increase his financial status. His daughter, Eloise, deserved a life of greater affluence and he had arranged a perfect deal, he thought. Through his prominent bank in Spokane, he arranged a loan in his son-in-law's name for $18,000 for land north of Waterville and instructed Oliver to farm it. Shortly afterwards, he informed Ole of the plan: "Mr. O. Ruud, Dear Sir: You will be glad to know, I am sure, that I have been able to arrange it for Oliver so that he gets to farm the land that Harmon Wilcox had (400 acres) over northwest of Waterville in sections 1 and 12, TWP 25 R 21 EWM. We are going to have to take it for the mortgage ($18,000) and have it fixed so that Oliver gets title subject to the mortgage without having to assume and agree to pay the mortgage. That lets him rent it for just the interest on the mortgage at 6% and the taxes, and if he has any kind of an average crop that will be cheaper for him than paying 1/3 of the crop as rent, and, in addition, gives him a chance to resell the land if it goes up a little and make some easy money.

"He has stock enough here so that he can do the necessary work, and it is enough later than your place so that he can finish his work here at home before it is time to go over there to plow or harvest. There are 120 acres in winter wheat over there now and he gets 1/3 of that delivered in Waterville this fall, and he will summer fallow 280 acres over there this year for crop next year. After harvest in 1929, if he doesn't think it pays to keep it, he will let us have it back again.

"The winter wheat looks good, has a nice even stand. The stock looks good. Oliver has a man here that seems to take an interest in everything. Both Oliver and Eloise seem well and the children, too, are husky and happy.

"Remember me to Mrs. Ruud and tell Synneva that I was very sorry to hear that her baby had been taken by death. But she should not grieve. The distance from the cradle to the grave is only a short one for any of us. And when a child is called to the heavenly home, we know there is no more sorrow or suffering for it. When our turn comes to go, it is easier if some of our dear ones are already on the other side, than it would be if we were leaving them all here on earth without our protection and care. So tell her not to grieve but to live for the other little girl. I think that they can look back from heaven and if *we* are unhappy, it makes *them* unhappy also.

"I saw Otto when I was in Seattle a few weeks ago. I like that boy. Don't worry over his inclination to fly. He is only getting it out of his system when he writes such stuff. I have a son (Francis) who writes that way, too. But he never really *does* anything of the kind. Otto has been working pretty good this last quarter. It was a little hard for him to get at it again at first after having been out of school for a year.

"I am selling a lot of land for the bank this year. Sold a $70,000 farm near Genessee, Idaho last week. If our Columbia Basin bill gets through congress, and it looks now as though it will pass, it will revive interest in the dry lands down around Lind and similar dry districts.

"Oliver tells me you like California. I may come down there and live myself some time before long. I only started in to tell you about the 400 acres of land that Oliver is going to operate. I hope I made it plain to you that I have fixed it for him so he can't lose any money and stands a very good chance to make some. I am yours truly, F.H. McKay"

Fred McKay, employed by the Old National Bank in Spokane as a land appraiser, kept his mind centered on money, profit, and easy land deals. Ole Ruud understood the chemistry of soil, climate, capabilities of physical labor and advocated peace of mind. Within the week McKay received a biting response.

Auburn, California
April 3, 1928

Mr. McKay, Dear Sir:

    Yours of March 26 last received. I thank you very much for helping Oliver to broaden his activities in farming, and have done it so that he may wiggle out of it without serious loss if necessary. But the layout is not better than what he has for several reasons. First, that whole flat out there, though big in crops, is as a rule, gotten more or less frosty. Second, there is no outside pasture, water must be pumped from deep wells, and there are no fruit trees or a good house to live in.

    And most likely, the ground is in bad cultivation, so it may take at least two good plowings to bring it up to its full capacity. By good plowing I mean eight inches deep and no "cut and cover" as they call it. That is to plow a furrow every two or three feet and turn a little dirt over the stubble. Plowing must be done right if you expect results. Oliver knows what I mean by that. And also, all cultivations and work after. All this takes twice the work generally done by renters. In some cases, it may take three, four to five years to get a badly used piece of land into cultivation. All this Oliver ought to know from the time we took over the old Ben Eker's place east to what we had before. Though the land was plowed the same the first year, we could see the difference in the crop as if it had been clipped with a clipper.

    You, of course, must do well for the bank to be a good servant, but no bank should loan $18,000 on any 400 acres out there. It is probably interest and taxes and costs and the rest of it added to the principal to be some check on the grain gamblers, transportation companies, milling trusts, farm implement trusts, if not *the money trust itself before anyone could pay $18,000 for it and hope to be out of debt in his lifetime.*

Merely a land boom, like what we had the five years before the war will not make it. That boom, in my opinion, was made by the big bankers throwing a few extra millions of easy money loose into circulation and starting a paper boom. Sand was sold north of Waterville in that time as high as $110 per acre, but, of course, it got back in a few years. This artificial boom was made by the bankers to sell the land they had stole during the panic of 1893 and after, when we farmers, including myself, had to sell our wheat for 22 cents a bushel. I was in debt for $600 and for this I would have lost all I had if the Governor had not given after-taxes for 3 years, but which we had to pay later. Having beef cattle was the only thing that helped me out, though a four-year old fat steer brought only $15. The panic of 1893 was, as all other panics and financial flurries, artificially gotten up by the money trusts for their own benefit.

We are living in scaly times and dangerous to go in debt even to a small amount. A world or local crisis may come any time. I wonder much over what will be the end of the gambling of Bank of Italy and Bank-Italy stock and other bank stocks here in San Francisco that has gone up in a short time several hundred per cent. If you know anything about it, tell me. Banking certainly is a fat business with the farmer at the other extremity. Now election is at hand and I think the same old gang will go in again, though Socialism runs high here.

I have not seen much of California yet, but I know the best part of it is owned by big men and corporations and held at prohibitive prices. Here, near and around Auburn, the country is covered with scathing timbers and must be cleared. The soil is a heavy reddish-yellow clay and heavy to cultivate, but good crops are raised when properly handled. Fruits are the main crops. I can readily see that for ordinary farming, a scientific rotating system could fare and easier be employed here than in the Big Bend. Such a system requires tame grasses, clover, and timothy. Without these, then farming is a hard success. If I could find a tract with soil that suits me and not have too hot summers, I would have no objection to sell out in the Big Bend and move down here but have not found it yet.

I consider the fruit farmer here to be in a worse fix than the wheat farmers in the Big Bend. A raisin grower told me that at this time he could only get 2 cents a pound when we had to pay 15 cents in the store. The rice growers have entered into a combination and ship their surplus rice to China and Japan and sell it at $3.00 per 100 lbs., or any old price in order to hold the prices up here at home, which you are well acquainted with. Only the choicest selected fruit can stand shipment to New York for the grower to get the cost of picking and packing. The false financial system is the first cause. The Jap rice growers are undersold to their great astonishment.

My boys here are doing well for their age. Lewis, at the University of California, is doing better than the average student and I hope will be a man someday, if nothing happens to him. I would like very much to see the country to the south of Eureka along the coast where the summers is not so hot.
Excuse blunders. Yours Truly, O. Ruud

Oliver tried for several years to yield a profitable wheat crop from the 400 acres, but the land proved to be as Ole predicted during those years of drought. Arising at 4 a.m. each morning, he worked until dark. Unable to continue the grueling schedule or maintain any profit, he lost the land back to the Old National Bank in Spokane. McKay, of course, was disappointed. But since no money had been required for a down payment, Oliver lost nothing except wheat seed, time, energy, and a bit of pride. He, like his father, loved the land by the mountain with its natural spring water flowing from the hills and preferred to center his life there. This devotion would hold fast. So would the financial strains.

Farmers, all over America, always seem to be struggling—foreclosed on by bankers, ruined by crop failure, droughts, or simply depleted funds and low profits. Some give up because they simply can't afford to continue. Today, farming costs continue to rise. Many owners have too little land to make a living, or have debts they can't pay off with wheat prices low, taking inflation into account.

When Ole leased his farm to Oliver in 1926, it concerned him that the never-ending toil and financial struggles might prevail. He was right. Keeping the promise to his father to stay on the farm, and always keep it under the Ruud family name, would fill Oliver's heart, but never his pocketbook. In 1981, when he turned the land over with a sale contract to his grandson, James Ruud, he knew the U.S. rural economy had totally changed, and no longer could the small profits of the rotating 300 acres of wheat land sustain a family.

Some have said that it used to take up to a thousand acres of wheat land to support a family of four. Now, with the continual rise in the cost of living, a family needs 2,000 acres or more. Since the 1970s, the state of Washington has lost more than 3,600 wheat farms—nearly half the number that existed 30 years ago. The small farmers have disappeared, one by one, bought up by a larger operation. A farm in Eastern Washington containing several thousand acres could, at one time, have been divided by more than fifty family farms.

Since the first pioneers settled in Washington State over 200 years ago, agriculture has played a substantial role in the state's economy. According to the Washington Wheat Commission Market and Production Information, Washington ranks fifth in wheat production in the nation. Combined with production from Oregon and Idaho, it is sold as Pacific Northwest (PNW) wheat. Only fifteen percent is sold into the domestic market. About eighty-five percent of Washington and PNW wheat is exported, the top importers being Japan, Philippines, and Korea. But competition is high with the European Union.

The EU, a group of 15 nations organized in 1993, opened internal borders to ease the flow of people, goods, and services, creating a common market of over 350 million people. With the eastward expansion in May 2004, adding an additional 10 nations, the fusion of East and West now covers 455 million people. Last year, Europe and the Black Sea area exported more wheat than the U.S. for the first time in nearly a century. Rich soil, abundant fertilizer, and cheap labor and land, plus weak environmental regulations gave Central and Eastern Europe a big edge over the U.S. Their wheat cost less than half per bushel of U.S. wheat. The fact that the grain is lesser in quality than that grown in the U.S. does not factor in, as needy, hungry countries buy affordable food products.

In an effort to save the U.S. farmer, the government offers a subsidy program to qualified farmers. According to the EWG (Environmental Working Group, per 2002 Census of Agriculture,) 70% of the farms in Iowa, North Dakota, and South Dakota are receiving government payments, whereas, in Washington State, only 20% receive subsidies. Washington's neighboring state of Idaho has 35% of the farms on the subsidy program. Oregon has less, with 13%.

Who gets subsidies? Only farmers who grow one of the eight program crops are eligible for farm subsidy checks. Even then, they are eligible only if their land has been enrolled in the program to establish an official production history.

In Douglas County 196,000 acres are planted to wheat each year. Of those, about 25,000 are spring re-crop acreage. 171,000 acres are held in summer fallow, planted to wheat the following year. Presently, 186,362 acres of land within the county are under the Conservation Reserve Program.

The CRP is a voluntary program for agricultural landowners. All farmers are eligible for conservation program payments providing the land has been owned, or operated, for at least 12 months. To be eligible for placement in CRP, land must be either cropland that is planted, or considered planted to an agricultural commodity four of the previous six crop years, and is physically and legally capable of being planted in a normal manner to an agricultural commodity. Or, the land must be certain marginal pastureland that is enrolled in the Water Bank Program.

Participants enroll in CRP contracts for 10-15 years. The purpose of the CRP is to protect topsoil from erosion and safeguard the natural resources. By reducing water runoff and sedimentation, CRP protects groundwater and helps improve the overall condition of lakes, rivers, ponds, and streams. Acreage enrolled in the CRP is planted to resource-conserving vegetative covers, making the program a major contributor to increased wildlife populations in many parts of the country.

To foresee into a future of such land reserve practices, and accelerated costs in farming operations was, in 1928, incomprehensible to both Ole and Oliver.

As a result, advancements in farming practices were slow-coming after Oliver took over the farm. The team of horses held power enough to pull the plow. It would take a surge of distemper, a highly infectious viral disease in animals, to nearly wipe out his entire12-horse team of Percherons before Oliver would purchase a tractor in 1939. New ways of lighting the farmhouse were explored, but the kerosene lamp would not be replaced with a Delco system until 1935. Lines bringing electricity to the house would not materialize until 1947.

Don't let the slippery agents fool you on the Carbide light, Ole wrote to Oliver the second week of April, 1928. *The light is fine and perhaps cheap, but what I object to is the tube system and the generating system that must be outside and requires constant care and looking after lest something happens to it. And it was this that made Kamholtz and Kimball and others in Douglas go back to the kerosene lamp. It was over 25 years ago they had it. Ingolf has lately bought a big Delco outfit that is to be taken out of a large summer resort hotel at Lake Tahoe in the higher foothills of the Sierra Mountains about 80 miles east from here. The hotel is owned by a millionaire, and the Delco system, similar to Corderman's with 16 cells and 32 volts, has over 60 cells and 120 volts and cost $3,000 to install not very long ago. Ingolf got it for $150. The rich owner wanted to get the electric light from a dynamo. Ingolf cannot go after it before the snow is off in the mountain by June lst. Spring is now here.*

It was too bad about Carrie. She was a good horse, but all we can do is to forget, the same as we had to do after the loss of Fanny. Cause unknown and nothing to be done. But I doubt very much if you can succeed in raising her colt by using cow milk. We tried it at home in Norway when I was young. I was the one to feed the colt. We finally did not have milk enough and had to mix it with water, flax and barley meal, the best we had. All we got out of it was a small undersized pony with a belly as big as a cow. He became a perfect nuisance, running after us always to get something. He learned to open the doors, especially the cellar door, get in, upset things and get his nose into everything. Finally we had to sell him for almost nothing. We had bought him for a calf skin and called him "the calf-skin horse". I have heard others say the same—no luck with raising a colt on cow milk. Better if you could find a mare that had lost her colt, if she will take it.

The almond trees have been in blossom for over two weeks. Now plum and prune trees are turning white. But many people around here have been sick with the flu for weeks. I have been sick for a week myself and am not well yet but feel better. I cannot give any plans for the future and prefer to tell the stories after.

There is another thing I now wish to write a little about. You mentioned in your letter that you have had an uncommon dream—that you met Signe, had a talk and a sad departure. Now without fastening yourself to these things, I wish you to understand that such uncommon dreams are not to be counted as merely meaningless gush. I have studied Spiritualism for nearly forty years. First, some of Swedenborg's most remarkable writings, then many other writings on the same subject. And just now I am reading a book of 400 pages called The Sacred Book of Death—Hindu Spiritualism—Soul Transition and Soul Reincarnation by Dr. L. W. DeLaurance, a Hindu himself. He says his writings are partly from his own experience, but mainly from the experiences and teachings of great gifted Hindus in ages and ages past—something similar to Swedenborg. The trend of the teachings of these two named are so near similar that there seems to be something in it. Swedenborg's writings were made about 200 years ago, all in Latin, and since translated into English. It is not likely that he had much knowledge of Hinduism, though he was a very learned man of the upper class and a good friend and adviser to Charles XII, King of Sweden, who fell in battle at Fredrikshald, Norway in 1718.

If I had not had so many queer trances, dreams and other unusual experiences myself from the time I was young till not very long ago, I would not hardly write this. My belief is that if I had not had invisible or spiritual help, I would have been dead sixty years ago. I have had most of the experiences both by broad daylight and in the night by what they call trance-dreams, and this has a meaning in my experience. I know there is something in telepathy. The Hindu writer says when a thought comes into our head that seems common, it may be of ourselves or led on by a friendly or malicious spirit. But under certain conditions when something actually is at stake and we hear a plain whisper in our ear, it is done by a spirit. I have heard these whispers on occasions, when something serious might have happened both by broad daylight and at night. I know there is something in what is called "second-sight", for I have had the experience. I think I could count 10-12-15 times when I have been within a hairs breath of being killed and once of killing another one, unintentionally, by taking him for a game animal. That the cap on my gun had got wet saved me, and I cannot remember the cap did not go off more than that time. And in a similar way from getting killed myself—in handling horses, working in the timbers, on open water, and on ice. I have had escapes that I would not like to try over again, but so far have escaped without crumbling a hair on my head.

I have been, as it were, forced to walk <u>against my will</u> in a certain direction and do something I knew was wrong without being able to turn around and walk the other way. The Hindu writer says that, in such cases, a loud and intense prayer is the only help. When a somnambulistic condition is brought on to a person, whether by day or night, it may be caused by spiritual influence and called a "trance or trance-dream". When brought on by another person, it is called "mesmerism" after the discoverer Mesmer, also "artificial somnambulism" or some other name. The Hindu says that spirits even have power over matter and can even cause wind to blow.

177

Under a "trance-dream" a person dreams and he suddenly wakes up and sees everything around him as he would by daylight. That is when the inner or spiritual light is opened. Under "second-sight", by daylight, I have seen a person so plain as I see my hand now, when upon close investigation, nobody was there. If by night, then it is called a ghost, for spirits sometimes are given power to partly materialize. I never saw a ghost.

The Hindu says that those having experiences as mentioned above may be somewhat gifted that way and will not deny a life after this. But those that do deny must be stupid or have no clairvoyant gift or power of imagination. The old Vikings had a God they called Bure, and when they prayed to him the wind would turn and blow the way they wanted to sail. It is a common word with us Norwegian men to say when we want to row across the lake, "wait till we get Bår-vind". I said it myself many times, but never prayed to the God Bure.

Now as to your dream of meeting Signe. Could you describe it again in detail? How did she look? How dressed? What was said and etc.? It might have been a trance-dream brought on by her or some spirit friend for a purpose and so have a meaning. Have you ever read anything on Spiritualism? Or occultism? All of my experiences I remember in the smallest detail, though some of it happened in the old country before I had ever read a word on the subject.

It is good you got the water piped down. Where did you find the little spring? Was it there where we took water at the picnic ground or lower down below the steep hill? Where did you lay the pipe? I had intended to lay the pipe line above the little three cornered field for irrigation purposes at the same time, as the water could have been brought to the 2nd story of the house. But the cost held me back.

Able to help out with little jobs here and there, their basic needs cared for, the situation in California was satisfactory for both Ole and Augusta, but Ole pined for the Pacific Northwest. He had referred to his farm in every single letter mailed to Washington inquiring of details regarding financial, climatic, and even social happenings. Soon he would be taking a trip to Breidablikk, but it would be his final return. As he sat at his desk on April 19th, 1928, he unknowingly wrote his last, and perhaps premonitory, letter to Oliver in Waterville.

I feel I ought to be there and help what I could, but Mamma thinks I ought not go alone on the train. I feel better now than when I came down here. In 1926, and before, the doctors had told me that my blood pressure at 150 was too high, indicating hardening of the veins. This is caused by taking up calcareous matter in the veins and system. And you remember I had a stroke in the left arm before going to take treatments at Soap Lake. The pressure was brought down to 120, but may not stay down. So last summer, when in San Francisco, I bought an apparatus, a new invention, a new discovery. Its principle merit is to take down blood pressure and much more. I have used it off and on until a few weeks ago when the doctor here tested my blood pressure and it was down to 100 and too low. He gave me some medicine to take and told me to come back. It must have had a good effect since I feel good now, in fact, so good that I want to come home to Washington. It would do me a world of good to be on my farm once again and breathe the fresh cool air coming from the mountains.

The blood pressure instrument is so simple that anyone can make it. It is about 6 lbs. of No. 20 insulated copper wire, wound like a skein of yarn and big enough to roll through easy, and wrapped with some cloth or skin. An electric current from a light socket runs through it to create a magnetic current going into the body. It cannot be felt but must have healing influence. I will send a closer description of the named electric apparatus if anyone wants it.

I hope you, with the help of Eloise, keep a strict system of the accounts on correct bookkeeping principles. She must find the time for it. And you must also find the time in the evenings to write me often on your doings, financial and working as a whole. It is necessary in order that I can properly cooperate with you in the time I have left. You must remember that our whole family fortune is now in your hands. Therefore, to successfully carry things out, I think it is necessary for me to know. Also remember that you are only a beginner and have lots to learn, while I, with practically 70 years of never forgotten experience on the farm—and that in two different countries and under three different climatic conditions. And now, I am fast learning under the fourth climate, and still I don't think I know it all, but have yet much to learn. Climate makes the farming as much as the soil and experience and work. I have, besides all this, been to 3½ years of school to learn it—1½ years in practical hard work, getting up 5 o'clock in the morning, both winter and summer before I was 20 years old. And then, two years of theoretical study of the hardest kind having no vacations, only about a week in the holy days. Don't overlook that my schooling is 60 years old, and that it took place in Norway. I feel right now that I would like to go into the timbers and start anew, if I could find the land of <u>my dreams</u>, which must be far off across some big ocean perhaps. No, No, hardly there either! But be contented and do the best you can in lot and vocation.

Just two days later, on April 21, Agnes sat at her desk in Auburn and wrote a grievous yet inevitable message:

"Dear Oliver, Eloise and Babies,

"Mama says thanks for the pictures—they are too sweet for words. The children look so well and happy. Wish we could say that of Papa right now. He has been feeling fine up until today and that is why I am writing this letter. He came in from the vineyard at 11:30 this morning not feeling very good. Had pains in his chest, arms and the back of his neck. Became worse about 5 o'clock so sent for the Dr. who said it was a heart attack. He gave him a hypo and some pills. At

6 o'clock the Dr. had supper with us and left at 9:20 p.m. Says that at Papa's age, one never knows when such an attack will come on. Papa has been resting easier all evening. It is now 12:50 midnight and Mama and I are sitting up.

"Now I would not worry if I were you, as he may get over this attack and not have another for a long time. Dr. says that at his age we can expect such attacks and all he needs now is plenty of rest and he will pull through. We hope to see him much improved by morning. We must trust in God above all to save him. This is the first heart attack he has had since he had his teeth pulled and has been feeling so well since he got over his cold. We were planning to go to San Francisco in May for a couple of months.

"Albert is still here. Went in town and phoned Synneva and Adolph. They, in turn, will let Louis know. He is so busy now studying for his exams. Have written to Otto so am sending it when I send this one to you.

"Rest is the main thing now. All he can have to eat is milk for two or three days. Must close for now but will add a few lines in the morning. With love from us all, Agnes"

"10:30 a.m., Oliver: Papa spent a very good night considering the pain he had suffered yesterday. Seems to feel much better this morning, voice clearer, pulse stronger, slight pain in the chest, but resting easier. If he has no more attacks, we have great hopes of him being well again. Agnes"

Ole's declining health, with a failing heart and frequent mastoid infections, had taken its toll. Two years and four months after leaving his home and farmland on the Waterville Plateau in the Pacific Northwest, he was returned to the land he loved. On April 28, 1928, at the age of 80 years, 4 months, he was buried beside little Signe in the family lot in Waterville, Washington. Agnes and other members of his family who were at his bedside prior to his death recalled his saying, "I have lived a long life. I have always done what I thought was right. I am ready to go." His long journey came to its end as death stopped softly by for him the following day, quietly enfolding him as he fearlessly received his final peace.

In remembrance of his father on each Memorial Day, Oliver would walk across the sunny side of the mountain early on those mornings accompanied by one of his own children. They would talk about the fresh air, the beauty of the view from the mountain and the goodness of his beloved father. Carrying several empty buckets, they would fill each one with the wildflowers of the land to place on the gravesite. The red fluorescent Indian paintbrush, the deep blue and violet lupine, and the abundant bright yellow sunflowers all held a remarkable significance in bonding Ole to his treasured land.

When gazing upon the gravestone of Ole, who would have 86 year-old Augusta at his side in 1950, the engraved words reach out. "Be Faithful Unto Death and I Will Give Thee A Crown Of Life." Many of his one hundred sixteen surviving descendents, all of whom in their own way strive to maintain some part of the decent and prideful character of their grandfather, often reflect on his work ethics, his liberal or conservative opinions, his common sense values, and wonder what he would have to say during present day times. *"Keep steadfast in your principles,"* he'd probably say, *"and do not, under any circumstances, waver from these teachings. Learn new knowledge, utilizing the applicable, and adamantly work to protect the backbone of us all—the land and its farmers.   Be true to yourself, be honest and fair—it will filter through to your children. And when you shake your neighbor's hand, look him in the eye and let him feel your character. Above all, take care of each other, it's your duty, you know, and, Ja, probably you would be better off just leaving the rest to the Man upstairs!"*

The Ruud Home completed in 1913

Endnotes

1. *World Book Encyclopedia*, Vol. 3, s.v. "Gunter's chain."

2. Richard F. Steele and Arthur P. Rose, Contributors, *History of the Big Bend Country* (Spokane, WA: Western Historical Publishing Co., 1904), 529-530.

3. Robert H. Ruby and John A. Brown, *A Guide to the Indian Tribes of the Pacific Northwest* (Norman and London: Northwest University of Oklahoma Press, 1986), 204.

4. Ibid., 205.

5. Ibid.

6. Steele and Rose, *History of the Big Bend Country*, 522.

7. Waterville Historical Society, *Beginnings: Waterville, Washington* (Wenatchee, WA: Commercial Printing Co., 1989), 24.

8. Alvaro L. Corbaley, diary, January-February 1885.

9. William Stanley Lewis, *Early Days in the Big Bend Country* (Spokane, WA: W.D. Allen Publishing, 1965).

10. Charles Kerr, "Survey Notes Tell History," *Wenatchee Daily World*, 11 April 1973.

11. Steele and Rose, *History of the Big Bend*, 544.

12. Lindley M. Hall, ed., *History of Central Washington: A History of Wenatchee, Entiat, Chelan and Columbia Valleys* (Spokane, WA: Shaw and Borden Co., 1929), 289.

13. Ibid., 29.

14. Ibid., 104.

15. Alvaro L. Corbaley, diary, January-February 1885.

16. Lewis, *Early Days*.

17. Ole Ruud to East Lansing, Michigan newspaper, letter, reprinted in the *Big Bend Empire*, 8 February 1894.

18. J.Q. Tuttle to the *Big Bend Empire*, editorial, 8 February 1894.

19. Ibid.

20. Ibid.

21. Alvaro L. Corbaley, diary, January-February 1885.

22. Charles Kerr, "First Orondo Hotel," *Wenatchee Daily World*, 10 October 1971.

23. Steele and Rose, *History of the Big Bend*, 551.

24. Ibid., 551-552.

25. Ibid., 553.

26. Alexander Watt, *The Art of Leather Manufacture*, rev. 4th ed. (London: Crosby, Lockwood and Son, 1897), 213-214.

27. Ibid., 68-69.

28. *What Your Neighbor Is Doing* (Spokane, WA; Day & Hansen Security Company Publishing, 1915), 84.

29. Ibid., 59-60.

30. "Berg-Ruud," *Douglas County Press*, 28 October 1915, reprinted in the *Waterville Empire Press*, 31 October 1985.

Bibliography

Brandt, Willy. *My Road to Berlin,* as told to Leo Lania. New York: Doubleday, 1960.

Brandt, Willy. *In Exile: Essays, Reflections and Letters, 1933-1947.* Translated from the German by R.W. Last. Philadelphia: University of Pennsylvania Press, 1971.

Burg, David F. *The Great Depression: An Eyewitness History.* New York: Facts on File, 1996.

Corbaley, Alvaro L. "Diary." January-February 1885.

Daniels, Roger. *Coming to America: A History of Immigration and Ethnicity in American Life.* New York: HarperCollins, 1990.

Grimley, O.H. *The New Norway.* Olso, Norway: P.M. Bye & Co., 1937.

Hale, Frederick, ed. *Their Own Saga: Letters from the Norwegian Global Migration.* Minneapolis: Minnesota Press, 1986.

Hall, Lindley M., ed. *History of Central Washington: A History of Wenatchee, Entiat, Chelan, and Columbia Valleys.* Spokane, WA: Shaw and Borden Publishing Co., 1929.

Johnson, Paul. *A History of the American People.* New York: HarperCollins, 1997.

Koht, Halvdan, and Sigmund Skard. *The Voice of Norway.* New York: Columbia University Press, 1944.

Larsen, Karen. *A History of Norway.* New York: Princeton University Press, 1948.

Lewis, William S. *Early Days in the Big Bend Country.* Spokane, WA: W.D. Allen Publishing, 1965.

McKay, Frederic Harrison. "Memoirs." 1946.

Paludeine, David Sean. *Land of the Free: A Journey to the American Dream*. New York: Gramercy Publishing, 1998.

Ruby, Robert H., and John A. Brown. *A Guide to the Indian Tribes of the Pacific Northwest*. Norman and London: University of Oklahoma Press, 1986.

-----. *Half-Sun on the Columbia: A Biography of Chief Moses*. Norman and London: University of Oklahoma Press, 1965.

Steele, Richard F., contributor, assisted by Arthur P. Rose. *History of the Big Bend Country*. Spokane, WA: Western Historical Publishing Co., 1904.

Strachan, Hew, ed. *World War I-A History*. New York: Oxford University Press, 1998.

Warner, Philip. *World War I: A Chronological Narrative*. London: Arms and Armour Press; New York: Sterling Publishing Co., Inc., 1995.

Waterville Historical Society. *Beginnings: Waterville, WA*. Wenatchee, WA: Commercial Printing Co., 1989.

What Your Neighbor Is Doing. Spokane, WA: Day & Hansen Security Company Publishing, 1915.

Online Sources

"Ancestors from Norway," "Ships of our Ancestors," by Odd S. Lovoll. *Journal of American Ethnic History*, Vol. 13.
http://homepages.rootsweb.com/norway/na26.html

"Norway," Microsoft Encarta Online Encyclopedia, 2003.
http://encarta.msn.com, 1997-2003.

"Fridtjof Nansen: Man of Many Facets," by Linn Ryne.
http://www.mnc.net/norway/Nansen.htm

Elevations

(As recorded by Oliver Ruud in the 1960s)

Wenatchee, Washington	672 ft
Orondo fire station	745 ft.
Waterville, Washington	2740 ft.
Mountain View school site	2734 ft
Ruud farm	2900 ft.
McGinnis's place	3046 ft.
Top of the mountain where Ole climbed to observe the view in 1883	3400 ft.
Sanstroms' place	3500 ft.
Top of Ruud Canyon	3794 ft.
N.W. Corner of section 16	3806 ft.
Top of the hill on Hanson Road	3968 ft.
Radio towers—Badger Mountain on the Ruud property	4143 ft.
Top of Badger Mountain	4444 ft

Time Line

Dec. 24, 1847   Ole Olsen of Rudsødegaard was born in Norway.

1848-1853   The Northwest (present Washington, Oregon, Idaho, parts of Montana and Wyoming all were known as the Oregon Territory).

1853   The Oregon Territory was divided. Became the Washington Territory and Oregon Territory.

1859   Oregon became a state, leaving the remaining land as Washington Territory.

1863   Washington and Idaho were divided into separate Territories.

1870   Ole Olsen Ruud graduated from agricultural college in Norway.

1875   Ole purchased Svarstad. Began his study of opportunities in America.

1879   Rudsødegaarden was sold. Svarstad signed over to Ole's mother. Family moved to Svarstad. Ole arrived in New York-- traveled to Minnesota and Iowa.

1882   Ole traveled to San Francisco, then north to Walla Walla. Arrived at Brents Post Office near Creston, Spokane County, Washington Territory.

1883   Christina Augusta Larson arrived in New York from Sweden. Ole Ruud homesteaded in May at the foot of Badger Mountain in the Big Bend country.

1884   Waterville was named county seat of Douglas County, Washington Territory. Ole was elected County Surveyor.

1889   Washington became a state.

1890   Idaho became a state.

1892	Ole placed ad in "Lonely Hearts" column in Chicago paper. Augusta Larson traveled to Waterville, Washington and married Ole Ruud on November 24th.
1893	The economic panic began.
1898	The Alaska Gold Rush began.
1907	The eighth child, Otto Fredrick, was born to Ole and Augusta.
1908	Signe died after an operation for appendicitis.
1913	Ole's mother, Johanna Frederiksdatter died at Svarstad in Norway (age 92).
1914	Kristian Ruud died in June at Svarstad. Martin Ruud died on July 31 in Seattle (age 64).
1915	Agnes Ruud married Ingolf Berg
1917	U.S. joins WWI.
1919	Olava died at Svarstad in Norway (age 64).
1920	Prohibition, Industrialization, and the Flappers dominated the newspapers. Farmers suffered another economic depression. Synneva Ruud married Einar Berg and moved to California
1923	Oliver Ruud, the oldest son, married Eloise McKay.
1926	Ole and Augusta Ruud moved to Auburn, California: Oliver took over the farm in Waterville.
1928	Ole Ruud died in California on April 22nd, following a heart attack (age 80 years, 4 months). Buried at Waterville, Washington on April 28th.
1932	Andreas Ruud died in Hønefoss, Norway (age 83).
1950	Augusta Ruud died in California (age 86). Buried in Waterville, Washington.

Kinfolk

Many people in America closely identify with their Norwegian heritage. It is true, however, that opinions are divided on whether, or not, those Norwegian-Americans relish a steaming bowl of lutefisk covered with melted butter, a side plate of pickled herring, and a thick slice of rye bread heavily laden with limburger cheese. One group will claim that even the slightest aroma of such a meal makes them retch, while others insist it's a palate pleaser and can cure anything—a headache, depression, even some intestinal problems. These same promoters proclaim such delicious nourishment stimulates brain cell growth, enhances body strength, and keeps one in a pleasant frame-of-mind. The following named kin of Ole and Augusta Ruud were, or presently are, vastly divided when subjected to a table filled with such offerings. But one fact has always stood, and continues to stand firmly in agreement among them; that the Scandinavian genes passed on to them by Bestefar and Bestemor Ruud planted a solid and prideful foundation. One hundred and twenty-eight offspring have evolved from the marriage of the immigrant from Norway and his Swedish catalog bride!

To those who are no longer among us, "Thank you for the love you gave to your families. You will forever be remembered."*

Agnes Inga Johanne Berg*
Synneva Augusta Olava Berg*
Diane Planchon Lovejoy
Daniel Andrew Lovejoy
Linda Planchon Seeno
Michael Vincent Seeno
Evelyn Agnes Berg*
Eric Christopher Berg
Peter Nikolai Berg
John Anton Lubimir
John Gordon Lubimir
David Anton Hixon
Samuel Wentworth Hixon
Tina Lubimir Byrd
Carl Oliver Ruud*
Kathryn Rae Keenan
John Frederick Keenan
Eric Olin Ruud
Erica Rae Ruud

Signe Kristiana Jane Ruud*
Ellen Berg Kilham
James Arthur Lovejoy
Carol Christine Planchon
Claire Luna Lundberg
Elizabeth Anne Seeno
Raymond Einar Berg
Jon Nelson Berg
Mildred Berg Lubimir
Margaret Jean Lubimir
Karen Lubimir Hixon
Adin Allen Hixon
Liam Lubimir Hixon
Christopher Stuart Byrd
Frederick Olin Ruud
Sonya Rae Keenan
Sylvan Oliver Ruud
Alexander Ruud
Lois Ruud Stinson

Christine Gray-Walker*
Joseph Scott Osborn
Eloise Christine Gray
Cameron W.B. Wiggens
Christopher James Wiggens
Olivia Claire Schroeder
Ava Galina Schroeder
John Oliver Ruud
Carol Ruud Strong
Kenneth John Ruud
Christian Otto Ruud
David Keith Ruud
Chandler Louise Ruud
Otto Francis Ruud
Donald Allen Ruud
Cassie Alexandra Ruud
Theresa Ruud Cole
Mary Irene Ruud
Carl Edward Ruud
James Lawrence Thompson
Claire Pauline Thompson
Lonna Ruud Welch
Makayla Anne Welch
Rhonda Stradling Lara
Dianne Stradling Denenny
Derek John Denenny
Nicholas Mark Stradling
Ryan Thomas-Keith Stradling
Seth Thomas Stradling
Randall Keith Stradling
Eric Samuel Allen Rupley
Anne Babcock Ruud
Delana Cavitt Ruud
Robert Albert Ruud
Louis Andreas Ruud*
Paul Gregory Ruud
Emily Karter Ruud
Quentin Ruud Kuhlman
Laurel Eliane Kuhlman
Nels Christian Ruud
Eric Phillip Ruud

Lara Ellen Osborn
Joshua Ronald Gray
Claudia Moody Wiggens
Chelsea Elizabeth Wiggens
Cara Moody Schroeder
Natasha Christine Schroeder
Alexis Cordell Schroeder
James Howard Ruud
Whitney Nicole Strong
Carson Oliver Ruud
Saige Isabella Ruud
Caitlin Keely Ruud
Nolan Nicholas Ruud
Dean Francis Ruud
Dorothy Frace Ruud
Donald Allen Ruud, Jr.
Martin Karl Ruud
Theresa Keeara Ruud
Lisa Ruud Thompson
Emma Louise Thompson
Tana Ruud Urizar
Makenzie Diane Welch
Esther Ruud Stradling
Danielle Louisa Ellis
David Timothy Denenny
Mark Howard Stradling
Jeffrey Oliver Stradling
Thomas Dale Stradling
Jessica Lee Lenore Stradling
Ila Ruud Rupley
Otto Fredrick Ruud*
Fredrick Barton Ruud
Albert Martin Ruud*
Gustav Adolph Ruud*
Louis Andrew Ruud, Jr.
Zachary Taylor Ruud
Paula Ruud Kuhlman
Eli Ruud Kuhlman*
Galen Stuart Ruud
Ronald Ruud
Britney Ann Ruud

Kristin Denise Ruud

Dean John Kolnes

Jamie Lynn Kolnes

Loren Lars Kolnes

Elaine Ruud Kolnes*

Kellie Lynn Kolnes

Sarah Anne Kolnes

Karin Elaine Kolnes

About the Author

Esther Ruud Stradling was raised in Waterville, Washington, on the same farm homesteaded in 1883 by her grandfather, Ole Ruud. Much of her childhood was spent beside her father, Oliver, walking over the surrounding hills on their land in the dry Big Bend country located in the central part of the state. Like a sponge, she absorbed the many interesting stories he told of pioneer times—the economic hardships, the personal tragedies, the changing politics, as well as the local gossip.

A retired Oncology R.N., Ms. Stradling currently resides in Cheney, Washington where she raised her family of five children. She continues to pursue her writing interests to preserve family and local history. She reserves ample time to read the works of favorite authors, garden, attend an occasional opera, study Norwegian language, and entertain her grandchildren.

Printed in the United States
55911LVS00004B/321